Effective Legal Remedies in Criminal Justice System. European Perspective

Ius, Lex et Res Publica
Studies in Law, Philosophy and Political Cultures

Edited by Barbara Janusz-Pohl and Anna Jaron

Volume 31

Paweł Wiliński (ed.)

Effective Legal Remedies in Criminal Justice System. European Perspective.

PETER LANG

Lausanne - Berlin - Bruxelles - Chennai - New York - Oxford

Bibliographic Information published by the Deutsche Nationalbibliothek
The Deutsche Nationalbibliothek lists this publication
in the Deutsche Nationalbibliografie; detailed bibliographic
data is available online at http://dnb.d-nb.de.

Library of Congress Cataloging-in-Publication Data
A CIP catalog record for this book has been applied for at the
Library of Congress.

The book was prepared in the framework of the implementation of the Polish National Science Centre research grant No. 2018/29/B/HS5/00185 entitled The right to an effective remedy against the abuse of power by the prosecutor and the court in criminal proceedings. Constitutional and European perspectives.

The cover image courtesy of Benjamin ben Chaim.

ISSN 2191-3250
ISBN 978-3-631-91326-0 (Print)
E-ISBN 978-3-631-91456-4 (E-Book)
E-ISBN 978-3-631-91457-1 (E-PUB)
DOI 10.3726/b21545

Published by Peter Lang GmbH, Berlin, Germany

info@peterlang.com - www.peterlang.com

This publication has been peer reviewed by Prof. Chiara Gabrielli.

Table of contents

Introduction

Effective Legal Remedy (ELR) is a legal concept of universal value. It serves protection of the effectiveness of enacted and applied law. First and foremost, it is designed to protect individual rights and freedoms from violation. It is an instrument with a general formulation and with an enormous potential. Its application in European law is still in the process of discovery. There is also no doubt that further development of the concept will be inevitable. Effective Legal Remedy can play an important role in the deeper integration of the legal systems of the European countries than has been the case so far. This is particularly true in the field of criminal justice.

The book's general aim is to present and discuss current standard of Effective Legal Remedy concept in European Law as it is or may be referred to criminal justice system. The further intention is to provide direct research tools to develop discussion on the quality of implementation of legal remedies into national legislation of European countries, mostly but not only Member States of European Union. The research has therefore both explanatory dimension on how we shall understand concept of remedial law in relation to criminal justice system and the evaluative dimension, in that it presents current jurisprudence of both European courts – European Court of Human Rights (ECtHR) and Court of Justice of the European Union (CJEU).

The book addresses following questions:

1. What is current standard of European concept of Effective Legal Remedies?n
2. Is modern concept of ELR a simple construct of legal remedies in relevant procedures or is a broader concept of a result that should be sometimes achieved even by not identified instrument bringing remedy to the situation?
3. Is concept of ELR in European law a traditional concept or is already something more?
4. Is concept of ELR an useful instrument for integration of national criminal law systems in Europe?

This research should also give some analysis and materials for further study of the question for national legislation on how to implement ELR properly.

The book focuses on the two most important standards of ELR which are common to the European system. These are the guarantees enshrined in Article 13 of the European Convention on Human Rights (ECHR) and Article 47 of the Charter of Universal Rights of European Union (CFR). The work covers the case law of two most important European courts – ECtHR and CJEU. They both establish canons for European criminal justice. The book is based on the premise that the ECHR and the CFR have been creatively interpreted by the Strasbourg Court of Human Rights and the Court of Justice in Luxembourg, respectively.

The research presented does not develop autonomous concept of ELR in any specific national legal system and is not focused on national criminal systems. This is a task to be carried out in successive steps and separately for each country, taking into account its specificities, the assumptions of its legal system and its legal culture. However, the analysis of the implementation of the right to an effective remedy in the European Parliament's directives contained in this work may be a useful tool in this analysis.

These assumptions are in line with the structure of the work. This book is composed of six chapters excluding the Introduction and Conclusion sections. Chapter 1 presents general observations on the nature of the Effective Legal Remedy, including observations on it nature, genesis, the values it upholds and the functions it performs. Its purpose is to provide an introduction to the subject and a concise overview of the essence of this unique measure.

Chapter 2 discusses the standard of Effective Legal Remedy laid down in Article 13 of the ECHR and derived from the case-law of the ECHR. It provides a detailed analysis of the concept and understanding of the effectiveness of a remedy in ECHR case law. It also includes a consideration of the nature of the instrument required to remedy violations of selected Convention guarantees. Particular attention is given to the guarantees contained in Article 2 (Right to live), Article 3 (Prohibition of torture), Article 5 (Right to liberty and security), Article 6 (Right to fair trial) and Article 8 (Right to respect for private and family life).

Chapter 3 sets out the meaning of Article 47 of the CFR and the way in which it has been interpreted in the jurisprudence of the CJEU. It is a twin reflection to the analysis of the essence of a remedy under the European Convention of Human Rights. It reflects both on the nature of the measure itself, its key features, the values it serves and the requirements it imposes on the application in national systems. The chapter also includes considerations comparing the concept of ELR contained in the ECHR and the CFR.

Chapter 4 analysis implementation of the ELR concept in European Parliament Directives. Its principal intention is to present previous attempts to implement the ELR standard into European criminal law. It is thus an endeavour to show the implementation of this particular construction at the level of European direct legislation. Chapter 4 is in some way overview of the European Union criminal law instruments in which the ELR mechanism has been applied. The subjective approach indicating the "right to an effective remedy" appears in several Parliament Directives. Taking the examples of selected Directives, the process of their creation and drafting, we follow here difficulties of introducing European (undisputed) standards into the law in force and the evolution of this process. Five following Directives have been selected for the purpose of analysis and because of their importance for European cooperation in criminal matters: Directive 2012/13/EU on the right to information in criminal proceedings; Directive 2013/48/EU on the right of access to a lawyer; Directive 2016/1919/EU on legal aid for suspects and accused persons; Directive 2016/343/EU on the presumption of innocence; Directive 2016/800/EU on the protection of natural persons with regard to the processing of personal data.

Chapter 5 provides a comparative analysis of the concept of the Effective Legal Remedies in common law. Particular attention is paid to UK and US law. The aim of this exercise is to deepen the analysis of the genesis of the ELR and to find a point of reference for further analysis of the essence of ELR. This perspective also seems to allow for a deeper understanding of the evolution of the ELR concept that is currently taking place in European law.

Chapter 6 comments on the common elements of the ELR and provides a critical analysis of the current state of development of the concept. These remarks are devoted to identification of the essence of the ELR, as well as showing its key features. The main fields of impact of ELR on the position of the individual through prevention, restoration and compensation are also indicated here. Finally, the strengths and weaknesses of the ELR concept as it is understood and used today are pointed out. The chapter concludes with comments on the relevance of the ELR as an instrument that can serve the integration of national systems within the scope of European Union criminal law.

These chapters together form a discussion on main research objectives. Each chapter, however, is a self-contained part of the work and may be useful at different stages of the European discussion on legal remedies. Most of them also contain their own summary and answers for questions indicated at the beginning of the work. For this reason, the conclusion refrains from duplicating the conclusions of each part of the thesis. Rather, it is confined to concise theses, which at least in part presents final conclusions and perspective for further considerations.

This book has been prepared in the framework of the research carried out in the implementation of the Polish National Science Centre research grant No. 2018/29/B/HS5/00185: *The right to an effective remedy against the abuse of power by the prosecutor and the court in criminal proceedings. Constitutional and European Perspectives.* It presents a continuation of previous research results published in monographs in Polish: Wiliński P., *Nadużycie uprawnienia przez prokuratora i sędziego w prawie karnym* (Abuse of power by the prosecutor and judge in criminal law), Wolters Kluwer 2023 and Kiejnich-Kruk K., *Prawo do skutecznego środka naprawczego w postępowaniu dowodowym* (The right to an effective remedy in evidence proceedings), Wolters Kluwer 2022.

I would like to express my appreciations to all Team Members participating in this research. I am also grateful to the Peter Lang publishing house for their kind response to the concept of this book and for all their efforts to publish it in such a short time.

Poznań-Warszawa, October 2023
Paweł Wiliński

Chapter 1 Introducing effective legal remedies

1. The term "Effective Legal Remedy"

We shall start with explaining the dictionary meaning of the term "effective remedie". Its first part is the "remedy", which comes from the Latin word "*remedium*" (Genet. *remedii*) – cure, medicine[1]. According to the Cambridge Dictionary, a remedy is "a successful way of curing an illness or dealing with a problem or difficulty"[2]. To remedy means: (a) to do something to correct or improve something that is wrong, (b) as a noun, a method of curing an illness, a weakness, or a way of dealing with a problem or difficulty. In that sense we can have an effective herbal cure for a headache. In this sense we say that the best remedy for grief is hard work. Love is a great remedy for unhappiness.

Legal remedy is an instrument of law.[3] It is a method, or a way of acting that gives a legal solution to an undesirable situation. In discussions of the law and its effectiveness, the principle of *ubi ius ibi remedium* is often invoked – "where there is a right, there is a remedy."[4] Remedy "generally is a cure for a malady of relief for some form of trouble, in law any of a many actions that might be

1 Latin *remedium* "a cure, remedy, medicine, antidote, that which restores health," from *re-*, here perhaps an intensive prefix (or perhaps literally, "again;"), + *mederi* "to heal" (from PIE root "med-" "take appropriate measures"). Known in XII c. as *remedie*, "means of counteracting sin or evil of any kind; cure for a vice or temptation;" late XIV c., "a cure for a disease or disorder, medicine or process which restores health;" from Anglo-French *remedie*, Old French *remede* "remedy, cure", Online Etymology Dictionary, https://www.etymonline.com/word/remedy.

2 Cambridge Dictionary 2023, on-line, https://dictionary.cambridge.org/dictionary/remedy.

3 Relation between right and remedies see M. Ruffert, Rights and Remedies in European Community Law: A Comparative View, *Common Market Law Review*, vol. 34 (1997), 307–336; W. Van Gerven, Of Rights, Remedies and Procedures, *Common Market Law Review*, vol. 37 (2000), 501–536; T. Eilmansberger, The Relationship between Rights and Remedies in EC Law: In Search of the Missing Link, *Common Market Law Review* (2004), 1199–1246.

4 See e.g., L. J. Laplante, The Law of Remedies and the Clean Hands Doctrine: Exclusionary Reparation Policies in Peru's Political Transition, *23 AM. U. INT'L L. RE*v. 51 (2007), 56–57.

done by a party or ordered by a court or agency to do anything allowed by law or equality and required to protect or to vindicate the interests of a party who successfully brings a claim for relief."[5] We can say that a "legal remedy" is: (a) a method of legally resolving a problem or disagreement; (b) a way of resolving a problem or ordering someone to pay for harm or damage they have caused, using a decision made in a court of law.

The expression "remedy" is often used with the adjective "effective", which seems to be a pleonasm (and makes this addition unnecessary). The word remedy itself, by its very nature, means "a successful way" of dealing with a problem. Solving a situation or curing a harm seems to be, or must be, part of the concept of this remedy. To be a remedy, a method or tool must be "effective". Otherwise, it is not a remedy. Nevertheless, and for a specific reason, we often use the adjective "effective" in the legal concept and in legal acts. This is a way of underlining the importance of the not formal, but the actual and real efforts or effects of certain instruments and methods that are applied as "remedies" or are proclaimed as such.

2. Nature of law and nature of ELR

Before discussing the nature of ELR we begin with some basic recognition of the legal system[6]. Obviously, the law (criminal law) must be effective to have respect and obedience.[7] Respect and obedience come from the belief that the rules it contains are right, and from the belief that everyone will apply them.[8] The law must also be responsive to the needs of society and perpetuate the rules it contains as right, worth preserving and protecting.[9]

---

5 S. M. Sheppard (ed.), *The Wolters Kluwer Bouvier Law Dictionary. Compact Edition*, Wolters Kluwer 2011, pp. 936–937.

6 On questions still open see i.a. J. Q Wilson, R J Herrnstein, *Crime and Human Nature*, Simon & Schuster 1985.

7 See more C. Lauterwein, *The Limits of Criminal Law; A Comparative Analysis of Approaches to Legal Theorizing*, Ashgate 2010; P. Wiliński, *Zarys teorii konfliktu w prawie karnym* (An outline of the Theory of Conflict in Criminal Law), Wolters Kluwer 2020.

8 See H. M. Hart Jr., *The Aims of the Criminal Law*, Law and Contemporary Problems 25 (1958) and discussion T. Lunch (ed.), *In the Name of Justice. Leading Experts Examine the Classic Article "The Aims of the Criminal Law"*, Cato Institute 2009.

9 Plato, *Laws*, 715b, p. 157 "we deny that laws are true laws unless they are enacted in the interest of the common weal of the whole state"; see D. Kelly, *A Short History of Western Legal Theory*, Oxford Univ Press 1992, pp. 432–439.

In principle, there are two contrasting ways in which legal rules are established in society. This is due to the timing of their introduction. The first is the retrospective enactment of legal rules – when rules that are known, accepted, based on their traditional operation, and generally accepted, are perpetuated in law. Such rules are, for example, the respect for property, the prohibition of its infringement, the requirement of respect for individual personal freedom, and the prohibition of its unlawful infringement. This group includes the overwhelming majority of legal rules. The second way of creating legal rules is prospective. In this case, the law is used to create new rules of conduct that are intended to regulate new rules of social life or rules that are developing in a new direction. This is most often the case with new social, legal, and economic phenomena, with new rules of the social order.

The effectiveness of law is a necessary element of law[10]. Designed legal institutions and legislated rules regulate social relations[11]. Above all, they should define the limits and methods of reaching a compromise and resolving conflicting interests.[12] Conflict of interests is a natural feature and is inherent in every legal system. This contradiction occurs in the relationship between individuals as well as between individuals and collectives. Lastly, it can take place in the event of a collision between an individual and a collective, and, in the final analysis, between collectives as well.[13]

However, only one part of interest relations, namely the relations between the interests of individuals and collectivities, is of particular interest to us in this work. Collectives are always more powerful than individuals: states and their institutions, multinational organisations, and companies. But it is the individual who is the foundation, the basic element of society. And it is the individual who forms all collectivities. Individuals are the subject of their own rights and

10 "For when men demand little of law, and enforcement of law is but -enforcement of the ethical minimum necessary for the orderly conduct of society, enforcement of law involves few difficulties" Roscoe Pound, Limits of Effective Legal Action, 3 A.B.A. J. 55 (1917).

11 More J. Bentham, *Introduction to the Principle of Morals and Legislation*, York 1982.

12 Also different perspective G. Beccer, W. Landes (eds.), *Essays in the Economics of Crime and Punishment*, Cambridge 1974.

13 See on criminalization choices J. Feinberg, *Harm to Others: The Moral Limits of the Criminal Law*, Oxford Univ Press 1984; P. Devlin, Morals and the Criminal Law, in: *The Legal Enforcement of Morality*, Oxford Univ. Press 1965; R. A Duff, Towards a Modest Legal Moralism, *Criminal Law and Philosophy* 8 (2012); Ewa Wieczorek, *The Legitimacy of EU Criminal Law*, Hart 2020, pp. 22–33

freedoms.[14] Without the existence and the subjectivity of the individual, there would no longer be any complex and conscious subjects, but only the tools of the collectives. The struggle for the granting and the taking away of the right of the individual to be an autonomous and conscious subject has been and will continue to be valid. For these reasons, in European countries and on many other continents, the protection of the rights and freedoms belonging to the individual is the foundation of the contemporary social order. It is therefore also the foundation of the legal system.[15] An understanding of this regularity leads to the notion of the importance of instruments for the protection of the individual from undue influence by the state and other bodies of collective actors.[16] This is because they have historically had, and continue to have, an interest in limiting individual freedom for its own sake.

The legal system usually contains a well-developed set of rights and freedoms to which the individual has a right to be entitled.[17] These rights are enshrined in supreme laws-international conventions and national constitutions.[18] They are developed and elaborated by subordinate legal acts, i.e. national laws or directives issued by international and supranational organisations, such as the Council of Europe or the European Union.[19]

There is no controversy about enshrining these obvious guarantees at a general level. It is usually done with universal agreement and acceptance[20]. It represents a general understanding of the universal values expressed in these laws and

---

14 About human dignity, identity of a person in law see J. Marschall, *Human Rights Law and Personal Identity*, Routledge 2014, pp. 25–54.

15 More see A. Williams, *EU Human Rights Polices: A Study of Irony*, Oxfor Univ. Press 2004.

16 See B. Thorson, *Individual Rights in EU Law*, Springer 2018.

17 On human rights from global perspective J. Donnelly, *International Human Rights*, Avalon Publishing 2007

18 See A. Hurrell, J. Gaddis, R. Foot, *Order and Justice in International Relations*, Oxford Univ. Press 2003.

19 A. McColgan KC, D. Schiek, G. Moon, J. Gerards, L. Waddington, M. Bell, O. De Schutter, T. Choudhury, *Cases, Materials and Text on National, Supranational and International Non-Discrimination Law Ius Commune Casebooks for the Common Law of Europe*, Bloomsbury 2007; S. Ruggeri, *Human Rights in European Criminal Law. New Developments in European Legislation and Case Law After the Lisbon Treaty*, Springer 2015; on current issues B. Petkova. T. Ojanen, *Fundamental Rights Protection Online. The Future Regulation of Intermediaries*, Elgar 2020.

20 More See D. P. Forsythe, *Human Rights in International Relations*, Cambrigde Univ. Press 2017.

regulations.[21] It is, however, much more important – and much more difficult – to put these rules into practice. As such, their detailed elaboration tends to become much more controversial and contested. They reveal the different perceptions of certain legal instruments, their role and the way they affect society through written law and common law, as well as the conflicting traditions of common law and civil law states. Of course, it is the implementation of these guarantees in practice that is even more difficult.[22] Here the differences are even greater. The authorities of each state acts under different rules of procedure, often a different range of specific powers and procedural duties, a system of control measures, etc.[23] Measures of a twofold nature may serve this purpose, i.e., the implementation of the guarantees.

The first group consists of the primary instruments of the legal system. These should contain only rules that are necessary, appropriate and fair, and which, by virtue of their appropriateness, ensure the effectiveness of the law.[24] This is achieved by the correct draft of the legislation and a well-designed system of its entry into force and enforcement. All instruments in this group are designed with this very premise in mind, that the law is applied in a manner consistent with its content and *not contra legem*. This means that it must always provide for the need to protect individual freedoms and rights.[25] It must only agree to restrict them in exceptional cases and only to the extent necessary.[26] However, this is not always the case for a number of reasons. Law is a social instrument. It is created by consensus and is often the result of a compromise between

21 See W. O. Douglas, R. N. Anshen, *The Anatomy of Liberty. The Rights of Man Without Force*, Literary Licencing 2013.

22 See i.a. A. Lazowski, Stepping into Unchartered Waters No More: The Court of Justice and EU Criminal Law, in: C. Briere, A. Weyembergh (eds.), *The New Balances in EU Criminal Law. Past, Present, Future*, Hart 2020.

23 See i.a. J. R. Spencer, M. Delmas-Marty, *European Criminal Procedures*, Cambridge Univ. Press 2002; Jacqueline E. Ross, S. C. Thaman, *Comparative Criminal Procedure*, Elgar 2016; R. Belfiore, T. Rafaraci, EU *Criminal Justice. Fundamental Rights, Transnational Proceedings and the European Public Prosecutor's Office*, Springer 2018.

24 See Ch. T. Kotuby, Jr., L. A. Sobota, *General Principles of Law and International Due Process. Principles and Norms Applicable in Transnational Disputes*, Oxford Univ. Press 2017.

25 Also R. E. Barnett, *The Structure of Liberty. Justice and the Rule of Law*, Oxford Univ. Press 2000.

26 See B. W. Miller, G. Huscroft, G. Webber, *Proportionality and the Rule of Law. Rights, Justification, Reasoning*, Cambridge University Press 2014.

conflicting interests.[27] It is sometimes ambiguously drafted, frequently amended and ultimately interpreted in many different ways. The procedural authorities in charge of the application of these rules may be subject to abuse of the law for their own benefit. There are many reasons, too numerous to discuss here, why rationally designed laws do not prevent mistakes in their application.[28]

Therefore, additional instruments are also needed – designed to deal with the ineffectiveness of legal provisions defining guarantees of individual freedoms and rights. They are intended to provide an adequate response to the consequences of mistakes and errors, especially those that lead to an unjustified restriction or deprivation of individual freedoms and rights.[29] This gives rise to the second group of regulations. These are rules that are, in a certain sense, of a secondary, protective and remedial nature. They come into play only when a right has not been implemented as intended, i.e., when it has not been correctly applied, and an individual may suffer an unjustified restriction or deprivation of a freedom or a right. There is then a need both for the restoration of what the law should have done and for the repair of the damage which the ineffectiveness of the law has caused.[30] This is when we speak of the existence of ELRs in the legal system as instruments for restoring or compensating for violated freedoms and rights.

The remedy is understood as a proper response to an unlawful decision. Therefore, remedy is most often applied to decisions of public authorities. There are many legal institutions that serve precisely the same purpose as "legal remedies". Their variety is a consequence of the complexity of the legal system. Many of them were developed in parallel in different legal systems, although they serve the same purpose. Thus, among remedies of a corrective nature we have an appeal next to a review, and among compensatory remedies we have reparations next to pecuniary compensation.

---

27 I.a. A. S. Sweet, J. Mathews, *Proportionality Balancing and Constitutional Governance. A Comparative and Global Approach*, Oxford Univ. Press 2019.

28 Univerally H. M. Hart, A. Sacks, *The Legal Process. Basic Problems in the Making and Application of Law*, 1958.

29 See L. M. Leslie, *The Right to Freedom from Arbitrary or Unlawful Deprivation of Liberty*, Lawyers Rights Watch 2023; L. Mancano, *The European Union and Deprivation of Liberty. A Legislative and Judicial Analysis from the Perspective of the Individual*, Bloomsbury 2019.

30 See K. Gutman, The Seence of The Fundamental Right to an Effective Legal Remedy and to a Fair Trial in the Case-Law of the Court of Justice of the European Union: The Best Is Yet to Come, *German Law Journal* 20 (2019).

Some of these instruments are very similar to each other, even though they exist in other national systems (e.g. the appeal model in Poland, Germany or France[31]), while others are very different and specific to a particular legal system.[32] In fact, however, the similarity or dissimilarity of these measures should be determined not so much by the similarity of their wording, but by the role they play and the effect they can have. These are in general instruments of questioning the rulings and decisions of the bodies that apply the law. Such institutions, regardless of how they are formulated in detail, will usually serve the same corrective functions (more Chapter 6). Often, they include also different forms of compensation of a financial nature – i.e. compensation and reparation for damage and harm. They are united by a common goal – the effort to restore the effectiveness of the law, to provide the individual with adequate guarantees.

Broad scope of legal instruments nonetheless their construction has common features serving in fact the same corrective and compensatory purpose. In a broad sense they all can be describe as legal remedies (ELR). Among the basic characteristics of LRs, we will include that they:

(a) are a response to the ineffectiveness (including the incorrect application) of other forms of legal regulation.
(b) are available to individuals and other natural persons in their relations with each other or with governmental or supranational bodies; and
(c) are for the restoration of freedoms or rights which have been infringed.
(d) and, where restitution is not possible, to provide appropriate compensation.
(e) are defined not by the form and manner of acting, but by the effect (restoring the disturbed balance).

3. Genesis of ELR

It is not possible to indicate the origin of each of the measures that fulfil the function of the ELR and lead to the restoration of the right that has been infringed or to compensation for the damage suffered. They are sometimes very elaborate. Some of them are as old as the legal system in which they operate. Appeal,

31 P. Wiliński, *Criminal Procedure*, in: W. Dajczak, T. Nieborak, P. Wiliński (eds.), *Foundations of Law. Polish Perspective*, Wolters Kluwer 2021; M. Bohlander, *Principles of German criminal procedure*, Hart 2004; V. Krey, *German Criminal Procedure Law*, Kohlhammer 2009; C. Elliott, *French Criminal Law*, Routledge 2001.

32 See M. Wasek-Wiaderek, A New Model of Appeal Proceedings in Criminal Cases: Acceleration v. Fairness? A Few Remarks from the Perspective of the Standards of Protecting Human Rights, *Studia Iuridica Lublinensia*, XXX, no. 4 (2021), 187–207.

cassation, revision, complaint and appeal, contestation, complaint, damages, compensation, reopening, extraordinary appeal and dozens of other measures, individual and collective institutions have been known for a long time.[33] Some of them have been in existence since the beginning of the legal system and have always had a corrective function within that system. Numerous publications, in many languages and legal systems, have provided detailed analyses of each one[34].

Just as distant in time is the idea of the need to repair what has been broken by a law that has been badly drafted or has been violated. In fact, at the beginning of any system of criminal law rules is the consideration of the need for a response to the faulty application of the law, for the restoration of the fairness of the process, restoration of violated rights.[35] This is now referred to as the concept of due process, in which everyone should be able to make real use of the procedural rights that are granted to them[36]. However, it has always been clear that rights only exist when exercised.

In this book, however, we are not interested in the genesis of a particular measure, but rather in the genesis of the contemporary construction of Effective Legal Remedies in European law. We are going to treat it as a general and coherent concept of protecting individual freedoms and rights, encompassing all legal instruments according to the criterion of effect. We will include in the ELR any measure, regardless of its origin and form, which leads to a common objective – an effective response to a violation or an undue restriction of the freedom or rights of an individual.

The concept of ELR as it is today is undoubtedly an outgrowth of the common law concept of rights.[37].The notion of "remedies" as a means of responding to

---

33 See i.a. A. Klip, *European Criminal Law: An Integrative Approach*, Intersentia 2021.

34 See i.a. P. L Reichel, *Comparative Criminal Justice Systems: A Topical Approach*, Pearson 2012; M. P. Roth, *Crime and Punishment: A History of the Criminal Justice System*, Wadsworth 2010; H. R. Dammer, J. S. Albanese, *Comparative Criminal Justice Systems*, Pearson 2010; H. R. Dammer, E. Fairchild, *Comparative Criminal Justice Systems*, Wadsworth 2005.

35 On perception of fairness see i.a. T. Tyler, Procedural Justice, in: A. Sadat (ed.), *The Blackwell Companion to Law and Society*, MA Blackwell 2004, pp. 435–452. About trust in justice system see M. Yordanova (ed.), *Crime and Punishment. Studying Justice System for Shaping Criminal Policy*, Center for The Study of Democracy 2011, pp. 7–20.

36 See modern approach in R. E. Kostoris, *Handbook of European Criminal Procedure*, Springer 2018.

37 Wording "Legal remedies" are traditional for common law concept, see B. Kercher, R. Woellner, Effective Consumer Remedies, 2 *LEGAL Service BULL* (1976), 80–83. See also L. Carter, F. Pocar (eds.), *International Criminal Procedure. The Interface of Civil*

the necessary consequences of a breach of the law first appeared in English law, probably already in XII century, with the interpretations of the *Magna Charta*, and was intensively developed in next centuries. It has been also intensively developed also in the American system (see Chapter 5 for more details). Particularly in the 20th century, the concept of effective remedies was intensively developed in the jurisprudence of the US Supreme Court there.

The leading international formulation of the "no right without a remedy" principle comes from the 1928 holding of the Permanent Court of International Justice (PCIJ) in the Chorzów Factory case[38]: "[I]t is a principle of international law, and even a general conception of law, that any breach of an engagement involves an obligation to make reparation." (…) "The essential principle… is that reparation must, as far as possible, wipe out all consequences of the illegal act and reestablish the situation which would, in all probability, have existed if that act had not been committed. It must consist of restitution in kind, or, if this is not possible, payment of a sum corresponding to the value which a restitution in kind would bear."[39]

The existence of effective remedies for faulty application or drafting of the law became a necessary and obvious element in almost all areas of law and refers to the application of many measures: in the context of speedy and expeditious trial[40]; as an instrument in international law[41]; in migrants law[42]; in constitutional law[43]; human rights law[44]; humanitarian law[45]; data protection

---

Law and Common Law Legal Systems, Elgar Publishing 2013, on common law approach G. J. Chin, W. M. Oliver, *Experiencing Criminal Law*, West Academic Publishing 2015.

38 PCIJ, Chorzów Factory Germany v. Poland, 1928 P.C.I.J. (ser. A) No. 17, at 29 (Sept. 13).

39 See laso Sonja B. Starr, *Rethinking Effective Remedies: Remedial Deterrence in International Courts*, *New York Uniw Law Review* 83 (2008), 693; G. Boars, *Public International Law. Contemporary Principles*, Elgar Publishing 2023.

40 A. Teeuwen, *Procedural Rights Supporting Expeditious Trials for Juveniles Effective Remedies and Legal Representation*, Asia–Pacific Journal on Human Rights and the Law 22 (2021), 150–185.

41 Ch. D. Gray, *Judicial Remedies in International Law*, Clarendon Press 1990.

42 S. Ganty, M. Baumgartel, Effective Remedies as Capabilities: Towards a User Perspective on the Human Rights of Migrants in Belgium, 8 *HUM. Rts. & INT'l LEGAL Discourse*, (2014), 215.

43 Thomas R. Philips, *The Constitutional Right to a Remedy*, New Your Univ. Law Review, no. 78, 1309–1345.

44 D. Sheldon, *Remedies in International Human Rights Law*, Oxford Univ. Press 2005.

45 J. P. Grant, J. C. Baker, *Parry &Grant Encyclopedic Dictionary of International Law*, Oxford Univ. Press 2009, p. 515

law[46]; environment protection[47]; administrative law[48]; fighting terrorism[49]; legal remedies for war[50]; victims of UN peacekeeping personnel[51]; civil responsibility for injuries[52]. It is also common in criminal law, specifically in relation to right to a counsel[53], children's rights, right of victims of crime[54], evidence law[55] and many more.

Effective Legal Remedy concept is also commonly linked to the protection of human rights in international law.[56] The same concept has been embodied in human rights treaties combining common law and civil law institutions.[57] In the case of Europe, this was the European Convention on Human Rights[58]. As a result of this development, the right to an effective remedy appears in several fundamental international human rights instruments, such as the Universal Declaration of Human Rights[59] (Article 8) and the International Covenant

---

46 C. T. Ungureanu, *Legal Remedies for Personal Data Protection in European Union*, 6 Logos Universality Mentality Education Novelty Sect.: L. 26 (2018), 26–47.

47 M. A. Rabie, Legal Remedies for Environmental Protection, *COMP. & INT'l L.J. S. AFR*, 5 (1972), 247.

48 Z. Szente, K. Lachmayer, *The Principle of Effective Legal Protection in Administrative Law. A European Perspective*, Routledge 2016.

49 J. Dellapenna, Legal Remedies for Terrorist Acts, *Syracuse J. International Law & Community* 22, no. 13 (1996).

50 Amos, Sheldon. *Political & Leg Remedies for War* (1982).

51 C. E. Sweetser, *Providing Effective Remedies to Victims of Abuse by Peacekeeping Personnel*, N.Y.U. L. REV. 83 (2008), 1643.

52 C. T., Oliwer in. Richard B., Editor Lillich. *International Law of State Responsibility for Injuries to Aliens* (1983).

53 M. M. O'Hear, Bypassing Habeas: The Right to Effective Assistance Requires Earlier Supreme Court Intervention in Cases of Attorney Incompetence, 25 *Fed. Sent'g Rep.* 110, 114 (2012).

54 P. Wilinski, P. Karlik (ed.), *Improving Protection of Victims' Rights: Access to Legal Aid*, Poznań 2014.

55 M. Kusak, *Mutual Admissibility of Evidence in Criminal Matters in the EU. A Study of Telephone Tapping and House Research*, Maklu 2016; Kiejnich-Kruk K., *The Right to an Effective Remedy in Evidence Proceedings* (*Prawo do skutecznego środka naprawczego w postępowaniu dowodowym*), Wolters Kluwer 2022.

56 M. N. Shaw, *International Law*, Cambridge Univ Press 2008, pp. 265–276.

57 Human rights approach to criminal law see S. Zappala, *Human Rights in International Criminal Proceedings*, Oxford Univ Press, 2005.

58 See J. Crawford, *Brownlie's Principles of Public International Law*, Oxford Univ Press 2008, pp. 660–663.

59 United Nations General Assembly, The Universal Declaration of Human Rights, New York: United Nations General Assembly, 1948.

on Civil and Political Rights[60] (Article 2(3)). It is also the basis for some more specific instruments, such as the UN Declaration of Basic Principles of Justice for Victims of Crime and Abuse of Power[61] and the Basic Principles and Guidelines on the Right to a Remedy and Reparation for Victims of Gross Violations of International Human Rights Law and Serious Violations of International Humanitarian Law[62].

The guarantee of the existence of the ELR was enshrined in the provision of Article 13 of the ECHR, although for a long time it did not have an independent meaning and did not see much direct authority in it (see Chapter 2 for more details). The same right to an effective remedy is enshrined in the European Union Charter of Fundamental Rights, Article 47. Again, for a long time this provision did not directly affect the legal system of the European Union (see more in Chapter 3). However, the last two decades have seen a gradual increase in the importance of the concept of the ECHR, which has been written into successive pieces of European Union legislation. (For more details, see Chapter 4 on the regulation of criminal law). Article 47 of the CFR provides a real protection for other rights and freedoms, not only those which are expressed in the Charter, but also those conferred by any act of EU law[63]. Its relevance is now much greater than it might appear at first sight. The role of the ECHR as a concept for protecting individual rights is growing dynamically.

4. Evolution of ELR in European Law

Origins and evolution of ELR are not connected to the criminal law and proceedings but more international public law and private law. Its adoption into criminal law sphere results from two parallel factors:

- general concept of using common law standards and institutions to develop European law;
- general concept of using instruments well working in international and civil law for cooperation in criminal matters.

60 United Nations General Assembly, International Covenant on Civil and Political Rights, Treaty Series 999 (December): 171, 1966.

61 United Nations General Assembly, Declaration of Basic Principles of Justice for Victims of Crime and Abuse of Power: resolution, 1985, A/RES/40/34.

62 United Nations General Assembly, Declaration of Basic Principles of Justice for Victims of Crime and Abuse of Power: resolution, 1985, A/RES/40/34.

63 P. Aalto *et al*, "Article 47,". 1210.

The direct development of the ELR concept and its adaptation to European and continental law is directly linked to the ELR concept incorporated in the European Convention on Human Rights (see Chapter 2)[64]. Article 13 ECHR enshrines the right to an effective remedy as a fundamental individual right.[65] The inclusion of the right to an ELR in Article 13 of the ECHR thus led to the integration of the concept into the European system of thinking on the protection of the rights of the individual.[66] For civil law states, this was of revolutionary importance. Initially, however, they did not really have any idea of the effective use of this power. This is particularly evident in the first few decades of Article 13 of the Convention, when a conservative and cautious approach was taken to its meaning. In fact, it was not given an independent character, but was seen more as a subsidiary power. The right to ELR was therefore most often combined with what it seemed to have most in common, i.e. Article 6 of the Convention and the right to a fair trial[67], or with other guarantees (see Chapter 2). However, there has undoubtedly been an important breakthrough in this respect. Article 13 of the Convention has finally come into its own.

The vagueness of the concept of ELR and the method of assessing national legal systems established by the ECHR in its jurisprudence – based on the criterion of expected effects rather than on the choice of means of achieving these effects – has made it difficult and continues to make it difficult to precisely define its scope and meaning. However, a detailed analysis of the case-law of the Strasbourg Court makes it possible to identify the main features of this measure (See Chapter 6).

A further milestone in developing the ELR concept was to include this guarantee in the Charter of Fundamental Rights of the European Union[68]. In

---

64 See. Van Dijk P., van Hoof F., van Rijn Arjen, Zwaak Leo (eds.): *Theory and Practice of the European Convention of Human Rights*, Intersentia 2018, pp. 1–78, 331–352.

65 See Guide on *Article 13 of the European Convention on Human Rights. Right to Effective Legal Remedy*, Council of Europe 2022, https://www.echr.coe.int/documents/d/echr/guide_art_13_eng.

66 See complex analysis pp. Barkhuseyn T., van Emmerik, Chapter 32 Right to an Effective Remedy, in: Van Dijk P., van Hoof F., van Rijn Arjen, Zwaak Leo (eds.): *Theory and Practice of the European Convention of Human Rights*, Intersentia 2018, pp. 1035–1061.

67 See currnetly H. Morao, R. T. Tavares, da Silva, *Fairness in Criminal Appeal. A Critical and Interdisciplinary Analysis of the ECtHR Case-Law*, Springer 2023.

68 Charter of Fundamental Rights of the European Union, proclaimed by EU in 2000, came into force in Dec. 2009 together with Treaty of Lisbon. See more in G. di Federico (ed.), *The EU Charter of Fundamental Rights. From Declaration to Binding Instrument*, Springer 2011.

this simple way, together with other guarantees, it has become an institution of the European Union.[69] The right to an effective remedy has soon become the leading principle for the interpretation of the provisions of the Treaties on direct actions and the function of national courts to guarantee the full effect of Union law in the Member States.[70] In doing so, it is fascinating to note that there was no doubt about the need to include the right to an ELR in the Charter, despite the imprecision of its wording.[71] The very nature of this right only seems clear when appealing to legal intuition and a system of values worth protecting.[72] But when it comes to the details, this is no longer the case. It is directly enshrined in Article 47 of the Charter, which undoubtedly constitutes one of the fundamental rights of the individual and guarantees his or her subjectivity in the EU.[73]

There is no doubt that the original approach to the ELR from the perspective of the EU has gone through a path of significant development. It has gained significantly in this regard. This can be demonstrated in two different methods. The first is the detailed analysis of the case law of the Court of Justice on Article 47 of the Charter which is presented in the book (Chapter 3). It shows how the Court itself has changed its approach and clarified the meaning of its understanding of the essence of the ECHR. The second is based on a growing understanding of the usefulness of this instrument for integrating the EU's legal systems. It concerns the introduction of this instrument as a universal key for the effective implementation of EU legal acts. The detailed analysis in Chapter 4 of the thesis points to the potential that is, and will continue to be, consciously and unconsciously used to achieve the effect of integrating the Union's legal systems. This applies to criminal law, which, for various reasons, continues to

69 See also T. Rafaraci and R. Belfiore (eds.), *EU Criminal Justice: Fundamental Rights, Transnational Proceedings and the European Public Prosecutor's Office*, Springer 2019.

70 N. Foster, *Foster on EU Law*, Oxford Univ. Press 2011, pp. 160–196.

71 See on the context of relations between EU law and human rights D. Chalmers, G. Davies, G. Monti, *European Union Law*, Cambridge Univ. Press 2010, pp. 233–235; K. Ambos, *European Criminal Law*, Cambride Univ. Press, 2018, pp. 144–145.

72 T. Elholm, R. Colson, The Symbolic Purpose of EU Criminal Law, in: R. Colson, S, Field (eds.), *EU Criminal Justice nad the Challenge of Diversity: Legal Cultures in the Area of Freedom, Security and Justice*, Cambridge Univ. Press 2016.

73 See on legitimacy issues, proportionality of EU law i.a. J. Öberg, *EU Criminal Law, Democratic Legitimacy and Judicial Review of Union Criminal Law Legislation in Wake of the Lisbon Treaty*, Tilburg Law Review, no. 60 (2011); G. Vermeulen, W. De Bondt, C. Ryckman (eds.) *Liability of Legal Persons for Offences in the EU*, Maklu 2012; also A.P. Simester, A. von Hirsch, Crimes, *Harms and Wrongs: on the Principles of Criminalisation*, Oxford Univ. Press 2011.

be extremely resistant to the methods traditionally used to integrate the Union's civil law[74]. This is much due to the fact that, in the field of criminal law, the effective transposition of EU law into national legal systems is the responsibility of the Member States.[75] However, the freedom of the Member States primarily concerns the way in which these issues get regulated, not the result itself.[76] The Member States remain fully responsible for the national instruments and the way in which they are ultimately regulated.[77] They are obliged to ensure the effectiveness of each of these legal instruments.

5. Values of effective legal remedies

Since the law (including criminal law) is to be an instrument of society for the maintenance of order in society[78], it must protect the values that are important to society and its functioning.[79] The law must therefore be a guardian of order, a guardian of respect for property, a guardian of freedom, life, equality and a guardian of security. These values are particularly important. They must be protected at every stage. They are protected in relations between people. It is the duty of the legal system to provide effective instruments for the protection of the rights of individuals, e.g. the enforcement of property rights, respect for privacy, protection of personal rights, etc. This is the first level of protection. However, this is only the first level to get protected.

The second level of protection is the protection of the individual against the faulty actions of the bodies that society has appointed to act properly on

---

74 P. Wiliński, K. Kiejnich-Kruk, Right to an Effective Legal Remedy in Criminal Proceedings in the EU. Implementation and Need for Standards, *Review of European and Comparative Law* 54, no. 3 (2023), 147–167.

75 See V. Mitsilegas, *EU Criminal Law after Lisbon: Rights, Trust and the Transformation of Justice in Europe*. Hart Publishing 2016; J. Öberg, Subsidiarity of EU Procedural Law, *European Criminal Law Review*, no. 19 (2015).

76 See P. de Gert, Division of Competences beetwen National and European Levels with Regard to Justice and Home Affairs, in: *Police and Justice Cooperation in the New European Boarder*, Kluwer Law International 2002.

77 See A. P. Simester, A. von Hirsch, *Crimes, Harms and Wrongs: on the Principles of Criminalisation*, Oxford Univ. Press 2011.

78 More A. P. Simester, *Fundamentals of Criminal Law. Responsibility, Culpability and Wrongdoing*, Oxford Univ. Press 2021, pp. 3–16.

79 See i.a. L.A. Hart, *Punishment and Responsibility: Essays in the Philosophy of Law*, Clarendon Press 1968; G. Robinson, F. McNeil (eds.), *Community Punishment, European Perspective*, Routledge 2016.

its behalf – the actions of the executive, legislative and judicial bodies, the decisions of the state administration. This is because the organs of the state can act incorrectly.[80] Instead of protecting, they can violate the freedoms of the individual, unlawfully depriving him of his liberty, property or freedom of self-determination.

The value of legal remedies is the possibility of a response to unjustified violations of the fundamental rights of individuals. Therefore, when these rights are violated, there must be mechanisms that can be triggered. These mechanisms, in turn, must have the capacity to take effective action. Finally, these mechanisms need to be capable of responding and of achieving the desired results.

The creation of these mechanisms for the monitoring of the proper functioning of the law is a complex process. In most cases, their existence is anchored in a broader conception of the concept of the law as an effective and just instrument of justice. Such constructs are familiar both to the common law legal systems and to the civil law legal systems. Concepts such as the "rule of law" or the "fair trial standard" are most common in European and international legal culture.[81] They are universal in scope.[82] However, they also contain assumptions about the effective restoration of violated individual rights.

We usually consider the "rule of law" to be a sum of different values and elements[83], i.e. the concept of equality before the law, but also the transparency of the law, the independence of the judiciary and accessible legal remedies. The place of the ELR in the concept of the rule of law shows the importance of the construction (See Chapter 5). Without these remedies existing and accessible, the remaining values remain nothing more than general declarations. Not far from the internationally accepted rule of law is the concept of "fair trial"[84]

---

80 See P. Wiliński, *Nadużycie uprawnienia przez prokuratora i sędziego w procesie karnym* (Abuse of power by the prosecutor and judge in criminal law), Warsaw 2023.

81 K. Gutman, The Seence of The Fundamental Right to an Effective Legal Remedy and to a Fair Trial in the Case-Law of the Court of Justice of the European Union: The Best Is Yet to Come, *German Law Journal*, 20 (2019).

82 More Y. McDermott, *Fairness in International Criminal Trials*, Oxford Univ. Press 2016; O. J. Settem, *Applications of the 'Fair Hearing' Norm in ECHR Article 6(1) to Civil Proceedings. With Special Emphasis on the Balance Between Procedural Safeguards and Efficiency*, Springer 2015.

83 See i.a. L. Pech, A Union Founded on the Rule of Law: Meaning and Reality of the Rule of Law as a Constitutional Principle of EU Law, *European Constitutional Law Review*, 6, no. 3 (2010).

84 See J. D. Jackson, S. J. Summers, *Obstacles to Fairness in Criminal Proceedings. Individual Rights and Institutional Forms*, Bloomsbury 2018.

(also known as "due process of law"[85]). This concept is widely recognised and is particularly popular in European law. It is also the same from a criminal law point of view. If we look at the essence of the fair trial standard, we notice that the same values and elements exist as those known from the concept of the rule of Law. It is sometimes interesting to see how the two concepts evolve and relate to each other, but this is not the subject of this research.

6. Functions of ELR

To identify the importance of ELRs for the legal system, and especially for the protection of individual rights, we should ask what functions are performed by this mechanism. This means answering the question of what role these instruments play in the legal system. By identifying the functions of the Remedies, we begin to see how they function and how they matter. It is from this perspective that we can best appreciate what these remedies were created for and what they should serve.

The primary function of ELR is protective. For in this it is expressed first and foremost in the fact that it provides for the protection of individual freedoms against undue interference, against unauthorised action on the part of state authorities.[86] By ordering the restoration of the original state of affairs or compensation for the unauthorised restriction of one of the freedoms or its violation, it actually protects each of these freedoms.

Equally important seems to be the guarantee function of ELRs. This is expressed in the very existence of instruments designed and established for the sole purpose of ensuring the protection of the individual. In doing so, they provide a specific guarantee of security, including the predictability of responding and protecting.[87]

The corrective function of the ELR can be emphasised. In fact, each of these measures, and all of them together, will ultimately correct the erroneous behaviour of the public authorities, including in particular the procedural authorities. The aim of this correction is the elimination of the erroneous decisions taken by these authorities and, above all, the elimination of their consequences[88].

---

85 The essence see Lord Rt.Hon Denning, *The Due Process of Law*, Butterworths 1980.

86 Also J. Almqvist, *Human Rights, Culture, and the Rule of Law*, Hart 2005

87 See i.a. B. Thorsson, *Individual Rights in EU Law*, Springer 2018; L. Pasquali, F. J. P. Vives, C. J. Piernes, *Solidarity and Protection of Individuals in E.U. Law. Addressing New Challenges of the Union*, G. Giappichelli 2017.

88 See E. Weinrib, *Corrective Justice*, Oxford Univ. Press 2012; I. Englard, *Corrective and Distributive Justice. From Aristotle to Modern Times*, Oxford Univ. Press 2009.

The function of prevention is also of great importance. It is to be understood in the sense that the very existence of properly constructed ELRs and the awareness of their existence has an influence on the way the procedural authorities act, discouraging behaviour and decisions which are obviously wrong and which, consequently, will undoubtedly provoke a reaction, the need to revoke the decision or to remedy the effects achieved. Of course, it is difficult to describe the operation of the preventive function by reference to direct evidence of its effectiveness. However, it is reasonable to assume that the authorities are compelled to thoroughly assess the grounds for the legality and proportionality of its action by the mere awareness of the possibility of review of the correctness of its action[89]. Of course, this presupposes, among other things, the existence of a system of effective remedies, i.e. remedies that are adequate and that work, but it is undoubtedly achievable. It is the ELRs which, as part of their preventive function, can constitute the most effective mechanism for preventing violations in a stable and well-designed system of individual protection.

In the very essence of the ELRs there is a function of restitution and a function of compensation. The first is, of course, that the purpose of ELRs is the restoration of what has been unjustly taken away from the individual in the sphere of his or her liberty, insofar as this is possible. However, if restitution is not possible or not to be expected, it is necessary to provide for the possibility of compensating for the damage caused by the infringement or restriction of liberty[90]. We mention these functions at the end, not because they are the least important, but because they are, as it were, the expression of the direct action of the ELR. They are the expression of the substantive content of these mechanisms, an obvious feature of them and, therefore, at the same time their essential function.

Bibliography

Almqvist J., *Human Rights, Culture, and the Rule of Law*, Hart, 2005.

Ambos K., *European Criminal Law*, Cambride Univ. Press, 2018.

Amos S., *Political & Leg Remedies for War*, 1982.

Ashworth A., Zedner L., Tomlin P. (eds.), *Prevention and the Limits of the Criminal Law*, Oxford Univ. Press, 2013.

---

89 See f.e. A. Ashworth, L. Zedner, P. Tomlin (eds.), *Prevention and the Limits of the Criminal Law*, Oxford Univ. Press 2013.

90 See i.a. D. Miers, *Criminal Injuries Compensation. State and Offender Compensation for Violent Crime*, Oxford Univ. Press 2018.

Barkhuseyn T., van Emmerik, Chapetr 32 Right to an Effective Remedy, in: P. Van Dijk, F. van Hoof, van Rijn Arjen, Zwaak Leo (eds.), *Theory and Practice of the European Convention of Human Rights*, Intersentia, 2018.

Barnett R. E., *The Structure of Liberty. Justice and the Rule of Law*, Oxford Univ. Press, 2000.

Beccer G., Landes W. (eds.), *Essays in the Economics of Crime and Punishment*, Cambridge, 1974.

Belfiore R., Rafaraci T., *EU Criminal Justice. Fundamental Rights, Transnational Proceedings and the European Public Prosecutor's Office*, Springer, 2018.

Bentham J., *Introduction to the Principle of Morals and Legislation*, York, 1982.

Boars G., *Public International Law. Contemporary Principles*, Elgar Publishing, 2023.

Bohlander M., *Principles of German Criminal Procedure*, Hart, 2004.

Cambridge Dictionary 2023, on-line, https://dictionary.cambridge.org/dictionary/remedy.

Carter L., Pocar F. (eds.), *International Criminal Procedure. The Interface of Civil Law and Common Law Legal Systems*, Elgar Publishing, 2013.

Chalmers D., Davies G., Monti G., *European Union Law*, Cambridge Univ. Press, 2010.

Chin G. J., Oliver W. M., *Experiencing Criminal Law*, West Academic Publishing, 2015.

Crawford J., *Brownlie's Principles of Public International Law*, Oxford Univ. Press, 2008.

Dammer H. R., Albanese J. S., *Comparative Criminal Justice Systems*, Pearson, 2010.

Dammer H. R., Fairchild E., *Comparative Criminal Justice Systems*, Wadsworth, 2005.

Dellapenna J., Legal Remedies for Terrorist Acts, 22 Syracuse J. *International Law & Community* 13, 1996.

Devlin P., Morals and the Criminal Law, in: *The Legal Enforcement of Morality*, Oxford Univ. Press. 1965.

de Gert P., Division of Competences beetwen National and European Levels with Regard to Justice and Home Affairs, in: *Police and Justice Cooperation in the New European Boarder*, Kluwer Law International, 2002.

di Federico G. (ed.), *The EU Charter of Fundamental Rights. From Declaration to Binding Instrument*, Springer, 2011.

Donnelly J., *International Human Rights*, Avalon Publishing, 2007.

Douglas W. O., Anshen R. N., *The Anatomy of Liberty. The Rights of Man Without Force*, Literary Licencing, 2013.

Duff R. A., Towards a Modest Legal Moralism, *Criminal Law and Philosophy* no. 8, 2012.

Eilmansberger T., The Relationship between Rights and Remedies in EC Law: In search of the Missing Link, *Common Market Law Review*, 2004.

Elliott C., *French Criminal Law*, Routledge, 2001.

Elholm T., Colson R., The Symbolic Purpose of EU Criminal Law, in: R. Colson, S. Field (eds.), *EU Criminal Justice Nad the Challenge of Diversity: Legal Cultures in the Area of Freedom, Security and Justice*, Cambridge Univ. Press, 2016.

Englard I., *Corrective and Distributive Justice. From Aristotle to Modern Times*, Oxford Univ. Press, 2009.

Feinberg J., *Harm to Others: The Moral Limits of the Criminal Law*, Oxford Univ. Press, 1984.

Forsythe D. P., *Human Rights in International Relations*, Cambrigde Univ. Press, 2017.

Foster N., *Foster on EU Law*, Oxford Univ. Press, 2011.

Ganty S., Baumgartel M., Effective Remedies as Capabilities: Towards a User Perspective on the Human Rights of Migrants in Belgium, *Human Rights & International Legal Discourse* 8, 2014, 215.

Van Gerven W., Of Rights, Remedies and Procedures, *Common Market Law Review* 37, 2000.

Grant J. P., Baker J. C., *Parry &Grant Encyclopedic Dictionary of International Law*, Oxford Univ. Press, 2009.

Gray Ch. D., *Judicial Remedies in International Law*, Clarendon Press, 1990.

Guide on *Article 13 of the European Convention on Human Rights. Right to Effective Legal Remedy*, Council of Europe, 2022,https://www.echr.coe.int/documents/d/echr/guide_art_13_eng.

Gutman K., The Seence of The Fundamental Right to an Effective Legal Remedy and to a Fair Trial in the Case-Law of the Court of Justice of the European Union: The Best Is Yet to Come, *German Law Journal* 20, 2019.Hart Jr. H. M., The Aims of the Criminal Law, *Law and Contemporary Problems* 25, 1958.

Hart H. M., Sacks A., *The Legal Process. Basic Problems in the Making and Application of Law*, 1958.

Hart L. A., *Punishment and Responsibility: Essays in the Philosophy of Law*, Clarendon Press, 1968.

Hurrell A., Gaddis J., Foot R., *Order and Justice in International Relations*, Oxford Univ. Press, 2003.

Jackson J. D., Summers S. J., *Obstacles to Fairness in Criminal Proceedings. Individual Rights and Institutional Forms*, Bloomsbury, 2018.

Kelly D., *A Short History of Western Legal Theory*, Oxford Univ. Press, 1992.

Kercher B., Woellner R., Effective Consumer Remedies, *2 LEGAL Service BULL*, 1976.

Kiejnich-Kruk K., *The Right to an Effective Remedy in Evidence Proceedings* (*Prawo do skutecznego środka naprawczego w postępowaniu dowodowym*), Wolters Kluwer, 2022.

Klip A., *European Criminal Law: An Integrative Approach*, Intersentia, 2021.

Kostoris R. E., *Handbook of European Criminal Procedure*, Springer, 2018.

Kotuby, Jr. Ch. T., Sobota L. A., *General Principles of Law and International Due Process. Principles and Norms Applicable in Transnational Disputes*, Oxford Univ. Press, 2017.

Krey V., *German Criminal Procedure Law*, Kohlhammer, 2009.

Kusak M., *Mutual Admissibility of Evidence in Criminal Matters in the EU. A Study of Telephone Tapping and House Research*, Maklu, 2016.

Laplante L. J., The Law of Remedies and the Clean Hands Doctrine: Exclusionary Reparation Policies in Peru's Political Transition, 23 *American University International Law Review* 51, 2007.

Lauterwein C., *The Limits of Criminal Law; A Comparative Analysis of Approaches to Legal Theorizing*, Ashgate, 2010.

Lazowski A., Stepping into Unchartered Waters No More: The Court of Justice and EU Criminal Law, in: C. Briere, A. Weyembergh (eds.), *The New Balances in EU Criminal Law. Past, Present, Future*, Hart, 2020.

Leslie L. M., The Right to Freedom from Arbitrary or Unlawful Deprivation of Liberty, *Lawyers Rights Watch*, 2023.

Lord Rt.Hon Denning, *The Due Process of Law*, Butterworths, 1980.

Lunch T. (ed.), *In the Name of Justice. Leading Experts Examine the Classic Article "The Aims of the Criminal Law"*, Cato Institute, 2009.

Mancano L., *The European Union and Deprivation of Liberty. A Legislative and Judicial Analysis from the Perspective of the Individual*, Bloomsbury, 2019.

Marschall J., *Human Rights Law and Personal Identity*, Routledge, 2014.

McColgan KC A., Schiek D., Moon G., Gerards J., Waddington L., Bell M., De Schutter O., Choudhury T., *Cases, Materials and Text on National, Supranational and International Non-Discrimination Law Ius Commune Casebooks for the Common Law of Europe*, Bloomsbury, 2007.

McDermott Y., *Fairness in International Criminal Trials*, Oxford Univ. Press, 2016.

Miller B. W., Huscroft G., Webber G., *Proportionality and the Rule of Law. Rights, Justification, Reasoning*, Cambridge University Press, 2014.

Miers D., *Criminal Injuries Compensation. State and Offender Compensation for Violent Crime*, Oxford Univ. Press, 2018.

Mitsilegas V., *EU Criminal Law after Lisbon: Rights, Trust and the Transformation of Justice in Europe*. Hart Publishing, 2016.

Morao H., Tavares R. T., da Silva, *Fairness in Criminal Appeal. A Critical and Interdisciplinary Analysis of the ECtHR Case-Law*, Springer, 2023.

Öberg J., Subsidiarity of EU Procedural Law, *European Criminal Law Review*, no. 19, 2015.

Öberg J., EU Criminal Law, Democratic Legitimacy and Judicial Review of Union Criminal Law Legislation in Wake of the Lisbon Treaty, *Tilbrg Law Review*, no. 60, 2011.

O'Hear M. M., Bypassing Habeas: The Right to Effective Assistance Requires Earlier Supreme Court Intervention in Cases of Attorney Incompetence, *Federal Sentencing Reporter* 25, no. 114, 2012, 110.

Oliwer C. T., in. Richard B., Editor Lillich. *International Law of State Responsibility for Injuries to Aliens* (1983).

Online Etymology Dictionary, https://www.etymonline.com/word/remedy.

Pasquali L., Vives F. J. P., Piernes C. J., *Solidarity and Protection of Individuals in E.U. Law. Addressing New Challenges of the Union*, G. Giappichelli, 2017.

Pech L., A Union Founded on the Rule of Law: Meaning and Reality of the Rule of Law as a Constitutional Principle of EU Law, *European Constitutional Law Review* 6, no. 3, 2010.

Petkova B., Ojanen T., *Fundamental Rights Protection Online. The Future Regulation of Intermediaries*, Elgar, 2020.

Philips T. R., The Constitutional Right to a Remedy, *New Your Univ. Law Review*, no. 78, 1309–1345.

Pound R., Limits of Effective Legal Action, *A.B.A. J.*, 3, 1917, 55.

Rabie M. A., Legal Remedies for Environmental Protection, *Comparative and International Law Journal of Southern Africa* 5, 1972, 247.

Rafaraci T., Belfiore R. (eds.), *EU Criminal Justice: Fundamental Rights, Transnational Proceedings and the European Public Prosecutor's Office*, Springer, 2019.

Reichel P. L., *Comparative Criminal Justice Systems: A Topical Approach*, Pearson, 2012.

Robinson G., McNeil F. (eds.), *Community Punishment, European Perspective*, Routledge, 2016.

Ross J. E., Thaman S. C., *Comparative Criminal Procedure*, Elgar, 2016.

Roth M. P., *Crime and Punishment: A History of the Criminal Justice System*, Wadsworth, 2010.

Ruffert M., Rights and Remedies in European Community Law: A Comparative View, *Common Market Law Review* 34, 1997.

Ruggeri S., *Human Rights in European Criminal Law. New Developments in European Legislation and Case Law After the Lisbon Treaty*, Springer, 2015.

Settem O. J., *Applications of the 'Fair Hearing' Norm in ECHR Article 6(1) to Civil Proceedings. With Special Emphasis on the Balance Between Procedural Safeguards and Efficiency*, Springer, 2015.

Shaw M. N., *International Law*, Cambridge Univ. Press, 2008.

Sheldon D., *Remedies in International Human Rights Law*, Oxford Univ. Press, 2005.

Sheppard S. M. (ed.), *The Wolters Kluwer Bouvier Law Dictionary. Compact Edition*, Wolters Kluwer 2011.

Simester A. P., von Hirsch A., *Crimes, Harms and Wrongs: On the Principles of Criminalisation*, Oxford Univ. Press, 2011.

Simester A. P., *Fundamentals of Criminal Law. Responsibility, Culpability and Wrongdoing*, Oxford Univ. Press, 2021.

Spencer J. R., Delmas-Marty M., *European Criminal Procedures*, Cambridge Univ. Press, 2002.

Starr S. B., Rethinking Effective Remedies: Remedial Deterrence in International Courts, *New York Uniw Law Review* 83, 2008.

Sweet A. S., Mathews J., *Proportionality Balancing and Constitutional Governance. A Comparative and Global Approach*, Oxford Univ. Press, 2019.

Sweetser C. E., Providing Effective Remedies to Victims of Abuse by Peacekeeping Personnel, *New York University Law Review* 83, 2008.

Szente Z., Lachmayer K., *The Principle of Effective Legal Protection in Administrative Law. A European Perspective*, Routledge, 2016.

Teeuwen A., Procedural Rights Supporting Expeditious Trials for Juveniles Effective Remedies and Legal Representation, *Asia–Pacific Journal on Human Rights and the Law* 22, 2021.

Thorson B., *Individual Rights in EU Law*, Springer, 2018.

Tyler T., Procedural Justice, in: A. Sadat (ed.), *The Blackwell Companion to Law and Society*, MA Blackwell, 2004.

Ungureanu C. T., Legal Remedies for Personal Data Protection in European Union, *Logos Universality Mentality Education Novelty Sect.: L.* 6, 2018, 26.

Van Dijk P., van Hoof F., van Rijn Arjen Zwaak Leo (eds.), *Theory and Practice of the European Convention of Human Rights*, Intersentia, 2018.

Vermeulen G., De Bondt W., Ryckman C. (eds.), *Liability of Legal Persons for Offences in the EU*, Maklu, 2012.

Wasek-Wiaderek M., A New Model of Appeal Proceedings in Criminal Cases: Acceleration v. Fairness? A Few Remarks from the Perspective of the Standards of Protecting Human Rights, *Studia Iuridica Lublinensia* XXX, no. 4, 2021.

Weinrib E., *Corrective Justice*, Oxford Univ. Press, 2012.

Wieczorek E., *The Legitimacy of EU Criminal Law*, Hart, 2020.

Wilson J. Q., Herrnstein R. J., *Crime and Human Nature*, Simon&Schuster, 1985.

Wiliński P., Karlik P. (ed.), *Improving Protection of Victims' Rights: Access to Legal Aid*, Poznań, 2014.

Wiliński P., *Zarys teorii konfliktu w prawie karnym* (An outline of the Theory of Conflict in Criminal Law), Wolters Kluwer, 2020.

Wiliński P., Criminal Procedure, in: W. Dajczak, T. Nieborak, P. Wiliński (eds.), *Foundations of Law. Polish Perspective*, Wolters Kluwer, 2021.

Wiliński P., *Nadużycie uprawnienia przez prokuratora i sędziego w procesie karnym*, Warsaw, 2023.

Wiliński P., Kiejnich-Kruk K., Right to an Effective Legal Remedy in Criminal Proceedings in the EU. Implementation and Need for Standards, *Review of European and Comparative Law* 54, no. 3, 2023.

Williams A., *EU Human Rights Polices: A Study of Irony*, Oxfor Univ. Press, 2004.

Yordanova M. (ed.), *Crime and Punishment. Studying Justice System for Shaping Criminal Policy*, Center for The Study of Democracy, 2011.

Zappala S., *Human Rights in International Criminal Proceedings*, Oxford Univ. Press, 2005.

Karolina Kiejnich-Kruk

Chapter 2 Effective legal remedies in the European Convention of Human Rights and Jurisprudence of ECHR

1. The concept of an effective legal remedy[91]

The jurisprudence of the European Court of Human Rights on effective remedies is based on an interpretation of Article 13 of the European Convention on Human Rights, which reads: Everyone whose rights and freedoms as set forth in this Convention are violated shall have an effective remedy before a national authority notwithstanding that the violation has been committed by persons acting in an official capacity.

The Court has never indicated a definition of an effective remedy. The concept can nevertheless be derived from several judgments relating to its objectives[92].

---

91 The analysis of the effective remedies in the ECHR and jurisprudence of ECtHR in the context of the evidentiary proceedings is also presented in the monograph: Kiejnich-Kruk K., *Prawo do skutecznego środka naprawczego w postępowaniu dowodowym* (The right to an effective remedy in evidence proceedings), Wolters Kluwer, 2023.

92 ECtHR judgment of 25.06.1997, 20605/92, Halford v. The United Kingdom, HUDOC, p. 64; ECtHR judgment of 16.11.1996, 22414/93, Chahal v. The United Kingdom, HUDOC, p. 145; ECtHR judgment of 10.09.2010, 31333/06, McFarlane v. Ireland, HUDOC, p. 108; ECtHR judgment of 31.07.2003, 50389/99, Doran v. Ireland, HUDOC, p. 55; ECtHR judgment of 28.10.1998, 24760/94, Assenov and Others v. Bulgaria, HUDOC, p. 117; ECtHR judgment of 4.07.2006, 59450/00, Ramirez Sanchez v. France, HUDOC, p. 157; ECtHR Judgment of 27.04.1988, 9659/82, 9658/82, Boyle and Rice v. The United Kingdom, HUDOC, p. 52; ECtHR judgment of 20.03.2008, 15339/02 et al, Budayeva v. Russia, HUDOC, p. 191; ECtHR judgment of 30.10.1991, 3163/87, 13164/87, 13165/87, 13447/87, 13448/87, Vilvarajah and Others v. The United Kingdom, HUDOC, p. 122; ECtHR judgment of 21.09.2000. 35394/97, Khan v. The United Kingdom, HUDOC, p. 44; ECtHR judgment of 28.03.2000, 22535/93, Mahmut Kaya v. Turkey, HUDOC, p. 124; ECtHR judgment of 14.03.2002, 46477/99, Paul and Audrey Edwards v. The United Kingdom, HUDOC, p. 96; ECtHR judgment of 24.04.2003, 24351/94, Aktaş v. Turkey, HUDOC, p. 328; ECtHR judgment of 21.02.1986, 8793/79, James and Others v. The United Kingdom, HUDOC, p. 84; ECtHR judgment of 21.01.2011, 0696/09, M.S.S. v. Belgium and Greece, HUDOC, p. 288; ECtHR judgment of 8.06.2006, 75529/01, Sürmeli v. Germany, HUDOC, p. 98.

A remedy, as understood by the Court, is a measure which enables the competent State authority to confront with an alleged violation of any of the Convention rights and, if it considers that a violation has occurred, to award appropriate compensation. It does not indicate that the effect of the remedy must be to put the applicant in the position in which he or she would have been if the violation not occurred, although such positions are sometimes put forward by applicants[93].

As mentioned above, the general obligation to ensure effective remedies in case of the violation of the Convention, is stated in Article 13. However, the lawmakers decided to envisage the provision constituted specific legal remedy considered *lex specialis* to Art. 13. The provision in question is Article 5(5) of the Convention. As the Court's jurisprudence shows, this provision is *lex specialis* to Article 13 of the Convention[94]. Thus, in the event of detention or arrest in contravention of the guarantees of Article 5 of the Convention and the absence of adequate compensation, whether material or procedural, it is not possible to successfully raise the allegation of a violation of Article 13. Indeed, the appropriate redress should be compensation, and the lack thereof constitutes a violation of Article 5(5) of the Convention.

Other provisions of the Convention or the additional Protocols do not provide for specific remedies that constitute a *lex specialis* to Article 13. However, it is worth pointing out to Articles 2(1), 2(3) and 4(2) of Protocol No. 7 to the Convention for the Protection of Human Rights and Fundamental Freedoms, drawn up on 22 November 1984 in Strasbourg. These provisions provide for the right of appeal in criminal cases, the right to compensation for wrongful conviction and the possibility of reopening proceedings when new facts or gross misconduct come to light. The grounds for triggering these measures are not violations of the Convention, as in the case of remedies under Articles 13 and 5(5), but the possibility of miscarriages of justice. Nevertheless, they should be borne in mind in the context of the forms that remedies in general may take.

To rebuild the concept of the effective remedy, it is therefore necessary to reconstruct:

---

93 "The concept of an 'effective remedy', in the applicants' submission, presupposes that the person concerned should be placed in a position, by means of subsequent information, to defend himself against any inadmissible encroachment upon his guaranteed rights", ECtHR judgment of 6.09.1978, 5029/71, Klass v. Germany, HUDOC, p. 68.

94 Cf. ECtHR judgment of 12.10.2006, 3178/03, Mubilanzila Mayeka and Kaniki Mitunga v. Belgium, HUDOC, p. 110; ECtHR judgment of 15.11.1996, 22414/93, Chahal v. The United Kingdom, HUDOC, p. 126; ECtHR judgment of 15.12.2016, 16483/12, Khlaifia and Others v. Italy, HUDOC, p. 266.

1. requirements for a remedy to be considered effective,
2. notion of arguable claim,
3. possible forms of compensation if a violation is deemed to have occurred.

2. Effectiveness of the remedies

The Court assesses the effectiveness of remedies considering several criteria: the general requirements, the authorities competent to apply remedies, the duration and costs of remedies and the amount of compensation to be paid[95]. These will be discussed below in that order.

First and foremost, the remedy must exist[96]. One of the more frequently indicated requirements is that the remedy must be effective both in law and in practice[97]. It cannot restrict to the illusory protection, formally provided by law. It is also necessary that it can be applied and work in practice. Then, accessibility to the potentially affected person is verified[98]. Remedies must be achievable for everyone. They must also be adequate, proportionate to the breach[99]. As is evident from the case law, the Court does not prejudge exactly which measures meet these requirements. However, it points out that the nature of the potential violation determines the shape of the measure in question[100]. In each case, the chances

95 Piątek W., The Right to an Effective Remedy in European Law: Significance, Content and Interaction, *China-EU Law Journal* 6 (2019): 168–170; Khomenko M., Kostruba A., Kot O., Right to an Effective Remedy of Legal Protection: Practice of the European Court of Human Rights and the Norms of the National Legislation of Ukraine, *Journal of Advanced Research in Law and Economics* 9, no. 7/37 (2018), 2336–2337.

96 ECtHR judgment of 5.01.2010, 22933/02, Frasik v. Poland, HUDOC, p. 104.

97 Cf. ECtHR judgment of 31.07.2003, 50389/99, Doran v. Ireland, HUDOC, p. 69; ECtHR judgment of 21.01.2011, 0696/09, M.S.S. v. Belgium and Greece, HUDOC, p. 288; ECtHR judgment of 26.10.2000, 30210/96, Kudła v. Poland, HUDOC, p. 157; ECtHR judgment of 4.07.2006, 59450/00, Ramirez Sanchez v. France, HUDOC, p. 158; ECtHR judgment of 10.09.2010, 31333/06, McFarlane v. Ireland, HUDOC, p. 109.

98 ECtHR judgment of 21.01.2011, 0696/09, M.S.S. v. Belgium and Greece, HUDOC, p. 318; ECtHR judgment of 10.09.2010. 31333/06, McFarlane v. Ireland, HUDOC, p. 107; ECtHR judgment of 29.03.2006, 62361/00, Riccardi Pizzati v. Italy, HUDOC, p. 38; decision of 11.09.2002, 57220/00, Mifsud v. France, HUDOC, p. 15; ECtHR judgment of 31.07.2003, 50389/99, Doran v. Ireland, HUDOC, p. 56.

99 ECtHR judgment of 31.07.2003, 50389/99, Doran v. Ireland, HUDOC, p. 56.

100 ECtHR judgment of 4.07.2006, 59450/00, Ramirez Sanchez v. France, HUDOC, pp. 158–159; ECtHR judgment of 10.09.2010. 31333/06, McFarlane v. Ireland, HUDOC, p. 109; ECtHR judgment of 16.11.1996, 22414/93, Chahal v. The United

of success and the actual possibility of obtaining appropriate compensation[101] is crucial to the assessment of the effectiveness of the remedy.

Importantly, the Court does not require that the remedies be applied by judicial authorities[102]. Nonetheless, the review must be carried out by an authority characterised by independence, appropriate scope of authority, guarantees, and equipped with adequate powers. In this regard, if the review is carried out by an authority other than a court, the Court assesses these characteristics in a meticulous and in-depth manner[103]. For example, in Silver and Others, the appellate measures were denied the attribute of effectiveness on the grounds that the body hearing them lacked the power to enforce its decisions, to implement its binding decision awarding damages, and lacked independence from other bodies[104]. In many Polish cases, the court held that a flawed judicial appointment procedure amounts to a violation of the right to an independent and impartial court established by law[105].

The Court takes a global approach in some cases, acknowledging that even if a single measure does not meet the requirements of the conditions expressed in Article 13 of the Convention, the totality of the measures available to the

---

Kingdom, HUDOC, pp. 150–151; ECtHR judgment of 21.01.2011, 0696/09, M.S.S. v. Belgium and Greece, HUDOC, p. 293.

101 ECtHR judgment of 10.09.2010, 31333/06, McFarlane v. Ireland, HUDOC, p. 114; ECtHR judgment of 13.09.2018, 58170/13 62322/14 24960/15, Big Brother Watch and Others v. The United Kingdom, HUDOC, p. 247.

102 Gerards J., Glas L., Access to Justice in the European Convention on Human Rights System, *Netherlands Quarterly of Human Rights* 35, no. 1 (2017), 11–30.

103 ECtHR judgment of 21.01.2011, 0696/09, M.S.S. v. Belgium and Greece, HUDOC, pp. 289–290; ECtHR judgment of 26.10.2000, 30210/96, Kudła v. Poland, HUDOC, p. 157; ECtHR judgment of 31.07.2003, 50389/99, Doran v. Ireland, HUDOC, p. 58; ECtHR judgment of 4.07.2006, 59450/00, Ramirez Sanchez v. France, HUDOC, pp. 158–159; ECtHR judgment of 16.11.1996, 22414/93, Chahal v. The United Kingdom, HUDOC, p. 152.

104 ECtHR judgment of 25.03.1983, 5947/72, 6205/73, 7052/75, 7061/75, 7107/75, 7113/75, 7136/75, Silver and Others v. The United Kingdom, HUDOC, pp. 115–116.

105 ECtHR judgment of 3.02.2022, 1469/20, Advance Pharma sp. z o.o. v. Poland, HUDOC, pp. 345–346; 349; ECtHR judgment of 8.11.2021, 49868/19 and 57511/19, Dolińska Ficek and Ozimek v. Poland, HUDOC, pp. 353–357; ECtHR judgment of 7.05.2021, 4907/18, Xero Flor v. Poland, HUDOC, pp. 289–291; ECtHR judgment of 22.07.2021, 43447/19, Reczkowicz v. Poland, HUDOC, pp. 280–282; ECtHR judgment of 6.10.2022, 35599/20, Juszczyszyn v. Poland, HUDOC, pp. 198, 210; cf. Piątek W., The Right to an Effective Remedy in European Law: Significance, Content and Interaction, *China-EU Law Journal* 6 (2019), 166–168.

applicant and their effectiveness must be assessed[106]. However, this is not a well-established line of jurisprudence. At the same time, in some cases, the Court presents a different position – it indicates that if none of the measures presented by the State is effective, the Court does not examine of its own motion the effects of their combined application[107]. It is difficult to indicate the time censuses of the periods in which the Court has leaned towards one of the lines of jurisprudence, but it seems that in most of the judgments issued in the last several years, the global approach has prevailed.

The duration of the resolution procedure and the costs to be borne by the complainant in doing so are also important factors influencing the Court's assessment of the effectiveness of resolution measures. The Court points out that the excessive length of the resolution procedure detracts from its effectiveness and adequacy[108]. According to the case law, the costs associated with filing a complaint about violation, the fear of incurring high costs if the infringement is not established, the taxes charged on the compensation obtained, make the measures inaccessible and consequently ineffective[109]. The Court approves the solution functioning in Poland, namely reimbursement of the complaint fee in case of acknowledged protraction of proceedings[110].

In summary, in assessing the effectiveness of remedies, the Court considers their existence, availability, adequacy, independence and powers of the authorities competent to apply remedies, the duration and cost of the remedial procedure, as well as the amount of compensation, if any, paid. In doing so, it takes a global approach in some cases, considering the effectiveness of the entire set of remedies available to the complainant in the event of an alleged violation of Convention rights.

---

106 ECtHR judgment of 16.11.1996, 22414/93, Chahal v. The United Kingdom, HUDOC, p. 145; ECtHR judgment of 26.03.1987, 9248/81, Leander v. Sweden, HUDOC, p. 30; ECtHR judgment of 28.03.2006. 52495/99, Koss v. Poland, HUDOC, p. 43; ECtHR judgment of 13.12.2012, 22689/07, De Souza Ribeiro v. France, HUDOC, p. 79.

107 ECtHR judgment of 8.06.2006, 75529/01, Sürmeli v. Germany, HUDOC, p. 115; ECtHR judgment of 14.03.2002, 46477/99, Paul and Audrey Edwards v. The United Kingdom, HUDOC, p. 101.

108 ECtHR judgment of 21.01.2011, 0696/09, M.S.S. v. Belgium and Greece, HUDOC, p. 292; ECtHR judgment of 10.09.2010, 31333/06, McFarlane v. Ireland, HUDOC, p. 123; ECtHR judgment of 31.07.2003, 50389/99, Doran v. Ireland, HUDOC, p. 57.

109 ECtHR judgment of 10.09.2010, 31333/06, McFarlane v. Ireland, HUDOC, p. 124; ECtHR judgment of 29.03.2006. 36813/97, Scordino v. Italy (no. 1), HUDOC, p. 201.

110 ECtHR judgment of 29.03.2006. 36813/97, Scordino v. Italy (no. 1), HUDOC, p. 201.

3. The concept of *arguable claim*

Article 13 of the European Convention on Human Rights does not imply an obligation on the State to provide a remedy for every alleged violation of Convention rights[111]. This obligation is limited by the Court to so-called *arguable claims*, i.e., justified complaints[112]. In doing so, it is not necessary that a violation has occurred – it is the State's duty to provide an effective remedial procedure in the event of a person's well-founded allegation that his or her Convention rights have been violated[113]. In other words, it must be possible to examine whether a violation has in fact occurred[114]. The Court has not indicated a definition of the concept of *arguability*, apparently deliberately, stating that it sees no need to define the concept. The justification of complaints should be assessed on a case-by-case basis, considering all the circumstances[115].

4. Possible forms of the remedies

The case law of the European Court of Human Rights distinguishes between two types of remedies: preventive and compensatory ones. This is indicated by the functions which, in the Court's view, these remedies must fulfill – "the remedy required by Article 13 must be 'effective' in practice as well as in law in the sense either of preventing the alleged violation or its continuation, or of providing adequate redress for any violation that has already occurred"[116] . In the Court's view, in the first instance, national systems should apply preventive measures. This is because they have the advantage of being able to prevent future infringements

---

111 ECtHR Judgment of 27.04.1988, 9659/82, 9658/82, Boyle and Rice v. The United Kingdom, HUDOC, p. 52.

112 ECtHR judgment of 10.09.2010, 31333/06, McFarlane v. Ireland, HUDOC, p. 108; ECtHR judgment of 31.07.2003, 50389/99, Doran v. Ireland, HUDOC, p. 55; ECtHR judgment of 28.10.1998, 24760/94, Assenov and Others v. Bulgaria, HUDOC, p. 117; ECtHR judgment of 4.07.2006, 59450/00, Ramirez Sanchez v. France, HUDOC, p. 157; ECtHR judgment of 26.03.1987, 9248/81, Leander v. Sweden, HUDOC, p. 77.

113 ECtHR judgment of 19.01.2017, 63638/14, Posevini v. Bulgaria, HUDOC, p. 83; ECtHR judgment of 6.09.1978, 5029/71, Klass v. Germany, HUDOC, p. 64.

114 ECtHR Judgment of 27.04.1988, 9659/82, 9658/82, Boyle and Rice v. The United Kingdom, HUDOC, p. 53.

115 Judgment of the ECtHR of 27.04.1988, 9659/82, 9658/82, Boyle and Rice v. The United Kingdom, HUDOC, p. 55.

116 ECtHR judgment of 10.01.2012, 42525/07, 60800/08, Ananyev and Others v. Russia, HUDOC, p. 96.

and to respond directly to the infringement by improving the situation of the complainant[117]. Compensatory measures are considered appropriate when the infringement has already occurred, and the complainant does not remain in a situation of vulnerability. In this case, the application of the measure is *a posteriori* and should aim at compensating for past infringements[118]. The Court also welcomes solutions that combine both types of measures, ensuring the cessation of the infringements and the prevention of future infringements, as well as compensation for the damage suffered[119].

Nevertheless, the importance of compensatory measures should not be diminished. The Court has repeatedly emphasised that the application of a compensatory measure alone does not imply that the system of measures is considered ineffective[120]. This assessment will depend in each case on the circumstances of the case, in particular the situation of the applicant. There is a particular case of violations of Articles 2 and 3 of the Convention, in respect of which the Court has expressly indicated that a compensatory measure alone cannot be considered effective[121] . Indeed, the gravity of the violations requires that a meticulous investigation be carried out and that those responsible for the violations be identified and, above all, that the violations be stopped, and future violations prevented[122].

The case law on remedies indicates that when a State opts for a compensation scheme in the case of violations, a wide margin of appreciation should be left to the State as to how to regulate in harmony with the national legal system or how to adapt the amount of compensation to the living conditions in the State. It is also pointed out that national courts are better able to relate the amount of compensation to the realities of the case and the practice of national courts in this regard, even if it will be lower than that awarded by the Court in

---

117 ECtHR judgment of 8.06.2006, 75529/01, Sürmeli v. Germany, HUDOC, p. 100; ECtHR judgment of 29.03.2006. 36813/97, Scordino v. Italy (no. 1), HUDOC, p. 183.

118 ECtHR judgment of 10.09.2010, 31333/06, McFarlane v. Ireland, HUDOC, p. 108.

119 ECtHR judgment of 8.06.2006, 75529/01, Sürmeli v. Germany, HUDOC, p. 100; ECtHR judgment of 29.03.2006. 36813/97, Scordino v. Italy (no. 1), HUDOC, p. 186

120 ECtHR judgment of 29.03.2006. 36813/97, Scordino v. Italy (no. 1), HUDOC, p. 187; Decision of 11.09.2002, 57220/00, Mifsud v. France, HUDOC, p. 17

121 ECtHR judgment of 10.01.2012, 42525/07, 60800/08, Ananyev and Others v. Russia, HUDOC, p. 98; ECtHR judgment of 17.09.2014, 10865/09, 45886/07 and 32431/08, Anca Mocanu and Others v. Romania, HUDOC, p. 227.

122 ECtHR judgment of 10.01.2012, 42525/07, 60800/08, Ananyev and Others v. Russia, HUDOC, p. 119.

similar cases[123]. The State should also not place an undue burden of proof on the applicant to demonstrate his or her non-material harm to obtain compensation. It should only require the submission of evidence that is realistically available to the applicant, i.e., for example, a detailed description of the conditions of detention or treatment by officials[124]. Indeed, as the Court has pointed out, "monetary compensation should be accessible to anyone who has been subjected to inhuman or degrading treatment in breach of Article 3 of the Convention and who has made an application to that effect"[125]. Also important are the length of time taken to remedy and obtain compensation (a maximum of 6 months is indicated[126]) and the amount of compensation or reparation. It must be reasonable in comparison with the amounts awarded by the Court itself[127], subject to the discretion of national courts outlined above.

As already pointed out, compensatory measures should apply primarily in cases where the violation has occurred in the past and is not continuing at the time of the remedy. The Court's emphasis on restoring the situation to conformity with the Convention standards, rather than paying monetary compensation for continuing violations which, despite compensation, persist, is thus evident. It is pointed out, however, that even in cases where the violation continues, in addition to a state response aimed at changing the conditions, compensation is an appropriate remedy for past violations[128]. These measures should therefore coexist in a complementary manner – it is necessary to stop violations immediately and to be able to obtain compensation for violations that have already occurred[129].

123 ECtHR judgment of 29.03.2006. 36813/97, Scordino v. Italy (no. 1), HUDOC, p. 189.

124 ECtHR judgment of 10.01.2012, 42525/07, 60800/08, Ananyev and Others v. Russia, HUDOC, p. 228.

125 ECtHR judgment of 10.01.2012, 42525/07, 60800/08, Ananyev and Others v. Russia, HUDOC, p. 228.

126 ECtHR judgment of 29.03.2006. 36813/97, Scordino v. Italy (no. 1), HUDOC, p. 198.

127 ECtHR judgment of 10.01.2012, 42525/07, 60800/08, Ananyev and Others v. Russia, HUDOC, p. 230; ECtHR judgment of 29.03.2006. 36813/97, Scordino v. Italy (no. 1), HUDOC, p. 202.

128 ECtHR judgment of 10.01.2012, 42525/07, 60800/08, Ananyev and Others v. Russia, HUDOC, p. 221.

129 ECtHR judgment of 8.01.2013, 43517/09, 35315/10, 37818/10, 46882/09, 55400/09, 57875/09, 61535/09, Torreggiani and Others v. Italy, HUDOC, p. 96.

Compensatory measures are not only monetary compensation. Leniency of the judgment is also an important measure[130]. However, for this measure to be considered effective by the Court, the judgment and its reasons must clearly indicate that the judgment has been commuted as compensation for the violations of Convention rights that occurred during the case, and, at the same time, the commutation of the judgment must be clear, significant, and adequate to the violation[131]. The Court has indicated that commutation of sentence can be an effective remedy in cases of protracted proceedings or violations of Article 5(3) of the Convention[132]. Perhaps unsurprisingly, the Court does not exclude it from being considered an effective remedy for violations of Article 3 of the Convention, given adequate justification and adequacy[133]. The controversy in this regard may be triggered by the gravity of the violation. Nevertheless, it should be borne in mind that the Court assesses the circumstances in each case on a case-by-case basis, and the jurisprudence to date allows for confidence in the Court's assessment of the proportionality of the measures and the protection of those affected by the violations.

5. Appropriate remedies for violations of Article 2 of the Convention

Violations of Article 2 of the Convention in the case of law enforcement violations mostly boil down to deaths of persons arrested and detained by law enforcement[134], deaths because of the use of force or violence by officers[135], or law enforcement failures to protect persons and prevent the commission of crimes[136].

---

130 ECtHR judgment of 10.01.2012, 42525/07, 60800/08, Ananyev and Others v. Russia, HUDOC, p. 222; ECtHR judgment of 10.11.2005, 65745/01, Dzelili v. Germany, HUDOC, p. 83.

131 ECtHR judgment of 10.01.2012, 42525/07, 60800/08, Ananyev and Others v. Russia, HUDOC, p. 225; ECtHR judgment of 10.11.2005, 65745/01, Dzelili v. Germany, HUDOC, p. 85.

132 ECtHR judgment of 10.11.2005, 65745/01, Dzelili v. Germany, HUDOC, p. 83.

133 ECtHR judgment of 10.01.2012, 42525/07, 60800/08, Ananyev and Others v. Russia, HUDOC, p. 225.

134 ECtHR judgment of 25.05.1998 in Kurt v. Turkey, 24276/94, HUDOC; ECtHR judgment of 31.07.2012 in Er and Others v. Turkey, 23016/04, HUDOC.

135 ECtHR judgment of 24.04.2003 in Aktaş v. Turkey, 24351/94, HUDOC; ECtHR judgment of 27.09.1995 in McCann and Others v. UK, 18984/91, HUDOC; ECtHR judgment of 4.05.2001 in Hugh Jordan v. UK, 24746/94, HUDOC.

136 ECtHR judgment of 20.03.2008 in Budayeva v. Russia, 15339/02 et al, HUDOC; ECtHR judgment of 14.03.2002 in Paul and Audrey Edwards v. UK, 46477/99, HUDOC.

The most commonly resounding obligation in terms of remedial procedure is the duty to conduct a meticulous and effective investigation. The Court points out that Article 13 of the Convention requires, in addition to the payment of compensation where appropriate,

> a thorough and effective investigation capable of leading to the identification and punishment of those responsible for the deprivation of life and including effective access for the complainant to the investigation procedure[137].

In this regard, the Court draws attention to the right of family members to actively participate in these proceedings, as a form of compensation for their loss[138]. The obligation to conduct effective proceedings is not limited to the pre-trial stage, but also extends to the judicial proceedings[139]. It is also appropriate for the authorities to act ex officio to clarify the circumstances of the case, irrespective of requests from the family or third parties in the case[140] . In assessing the handling of a case, the Court considers several factors and the individual circumstances of the case. The following are key in assessing effectiveness:

1. independence of the investigating authority[141],
2. the speed of law enforcement response and actions taken to clarify the case[142],
3. possibility of detecting the perpetrators[143],
4. the possibility of punishing the perpetrators[144],
5. gathering evidence in the case and carrying out activities in a timely manner[145].

137 ECtHR judgment of 28.03.2000 in Mahmut Kaya p. Turkey, 22535/93, HUDOC, p. 124; ECtHR judgment of 24.04.2003 in Aktaş p. Turkey, 24351/94, HUDOC, p. 329; ECtHR judgment of 13.06.2002 in Anguelova p. Bulgaria, 38361/97, HUDOC, p. 161.

138 ECtHR judgment of of 13.06.2002 in Anguelova p. Bulgaria, 38361/97, HUDOC pp. 161–162.

139 ECtHR judgment of 17.01.2013 in Mosendz v. Ukraine, 52013/08, HUDOC, p. 94.

140 ECtHR judgment of 20.03.2008 in Budayeva v. Russia, 15339/02 et al, HUDOC, p. 192; ECtHR judgment of 24.04.2003 in Aktaş v. Turkey, 24351/94, HUDOC, p. 299.

141 ECtHR judgment of 21.12.2010 in Jasinskis v. Latvia, 45744/08, HUDOC, p. 78; ECtHR judgment of 28.03.2000 in Mahmut Kaya v. Turkey, 22535/93, HUDOC, pp. 96–98; ECtHR judgment of 4.05.2001 in Hugh Jordan v. UK, 24746/94, HUDOC pp. 106–107.

142 ECtHR judgment of 21.12.2010 in Jasinskis v. Latvia, 45744/08, HUDOC, p. 79.

143 ECtHR judgmentof 24.04.2003 in Aktaş v. Turkey, 24351/94, HUDOC, p. 300.

144 ECtHR judgment of 24.04.2003 in Aktaş v. Turkey, 24351/94, HUDOC, p. 300.

145 ECtHR judgment of 24.04.2003 in Aktaş v. Turkey, 24351/94, HUDOC, p. 300.

In terms of identifying and punishing those guilty of violations, the Court in Mosendz set out the distinction that must be made between the criminal responsibility of individuals and the responsibility of the State under international law[146]. It should therefore be made clear that the Court only determines the responsibility of the State in this regard, assessing, inter alia, the investigation and criminal or disciplinary liability as remedies for violations of Article 2 of the Convention.

However, the Court does not limit remedies to the investigation, punishment of the guilty and the active participation of the family in the proceedings. It also points to monetary compensation for the family as a remedy for the death of the next of kin because of the State's violation of Article 2 of the Convention[147]. However, in doing so, he stresses that this compensation should be possible as *part of the range of redress*[148], it therefore appears that it cannot be the only remedy available.

6. Appropriate remedies for violations of Article 3 of the Convention

In the case of violations of Article 3 of the Convention, the Court makes specific requirements for the criminal proceedings against those guilty of violations. These proceedings are to be effective, aimed at uncovering the guilty persons and punishing them[149]. The discontinuation of the proceedings based on the explanations of the suspected officers and the unjustified refusal of the credibility of the victim's testimony certainly does not satisfy the obligation of a conscientious and effective investigation[150]. As the Court points out:

146 ECtHR judgment of 17.01.2013 in Mosendz v. Ukraine, 52013/08, HUDOC, p. 95.

147 ECtHR judgment of 28.03.2000 in Mahmut Kaya p. Turkey, 22535/93, HUDOC, p. 124; ECtHR judgment of 24.04.2003 in Aktaş p. Turkey, 24351/94, HUDOC, p. 329; ECtHR judgment of 13.06.2002 in Anguelova v. Bulgaria, 38361/97, HUDOC, p. 161; ECtHR judgment of 20.03.2008 in Budayeva v. Russia, 15339/02 et al, HUDOC, p. 191.

148 ECtHR judgment of 20.03.2008 in Budayeva v. Russia, 15339/02 et al, HUDOC, p. 191.

149 Cf. ECtHR judgment of 13.12.2012, 39630/09, El Masri v. "The Former Yugoslav Republic of Macedonia", HUDOC, p. 182; ECtHR judgment of 10.05.2001, 29392/95, Z. and Others v. The United Kingdom, HUDOC, p. 109; ECtHR judgment of 13.01.2009, 15562/02, Lewandowski and Lewandowska v. Poland, HUDOC, p. 70; ECtHR judgment of 12.05.2009, 9258/04, Mrozowski v. Poland, HUDOC, pp. 35–39.

150 ECtHR judgment of 23.05.2019, 37023/13, Kanciał v. Poland, HUDOC; ECtHR judgment of 12.05.2009, 9258/04, Mrozowski v. Poland, HUDOC, pp. 35–39.

> in investigating the complainant's allegations of injuries reported at the hands of the police, the Public Prosecutor should show exceptional diligence, and the possibility of seeking damages in the civil courts does not relieve him of his duty to conduct a diligent and effective investigation[151].

It is also pointed out that for remedies to be effective in cases of fear of torture or inhuman or degrading treatment or punishment, a measure automatically suspending the current situation of the complainant is required[152] .

In doing so, it also points to monetary compensation as an appropriate remedy[153]. The above considerations in respect of compensatory measures remain fully valid, the Court pointing out that monetary compensation in cases of violations of Article 3 of the Convention is appropriate both where the violations no longer occur and where the situation in which the complainant finds himself constitutes a permanent violation of that Article[154]. As an example of such a situation, one can point to the conditions of a detainee in prison, where, for example, he is denied medical assistance and is incarcerated in an overcrowded cell together with persons who pose a threat to him. In this regard, it should additionally be pointed out that a mere acknowledgement by the state authorities that a violation has occurred cannot be considered a satisfactory and sufficient remedy. Given the high degree of distress in the case of a violation of Article 3, the Court requires "something more"[155].

A further remedy may be judicial review[156]. It is pointed out here that for it to be effective, the court must be equipped with the power to overturn the decisions made and thus to make a real change in the situation of the applicant[157] . Such a

151 ECtHR judgment of 12.05.2009, 9258/04, Mrozowski v. Poland, HUDOC, p. 41.

152 ECtHR judgment of 21.01.2011, 0696/09, M.S.S. v. Belgium and Greece, HUDOC, p. 293.

153 ECtHR judgment of 24.04.2003. 24351/94, Aktaş v. Turkey, HUDOC, p. 329; ECtHR judgment of 10.01.2012, 42525/07, 60800/08, Ananyev and Others v. Russia, HUDOC, p. 231.

154 ECtHR judgment of 10.01.2012, 42525/07, 60800/08, Ananyev and Others v. Russia, HUDOC, p. 231.

155 ECtHR judgment of 10.01.2012, 42525/07, 60800/08, Ananyev and Others v. Russia, HUDOC, p. 172; ECtHR judgment of 12.05.2009, 9258/04, Mrozowski v. Poland, HUDOC, p. 43.

156 ECtHR judgment of 16.11.1996, 22414/93, Chahal v. The United Kingdom, HUDOC, p. 148; ECtHR judgment of 30.10.1991, 3163/87, 13164/87, 13165/87, 13447/87, 13448/87, Vilvarajah and Others v. The United Kingdom, HUDOC, p. 123.

157 ECtHR judgment of 16.11.1996, 22414/93, Chahal v. The United Kingdom, HUDOC, p. 148; ECtHR judgment of 30.10.1991, 3163/87, 13164/87, 13165/87, 13447/87, 13448/87, Vilvarajah and Others v. The United Kingdom, HUDOC, p. 123.

review will therefore be effective if it allows for the rectification of infringements committed at previous stages of the proceedings or the prevention of the effects of infringements.

Shifting the burden of proof in proceedings before the Court to the State can also be considered a remedy. In situations of violence or excessive use of force by officers, it is for the government to show that, in the circumstances of the case, the measures of direct coercion were adequate, proportionate and not excessive[158]. It is also pointed out that "where an individual is taken into police custody in good health and is found to be injured on release, it is incumbent on the State to provide a plausible explanation of how those injuries were caused, failing which a clear issue arises under Article 3 of the Convention"[159].

Moreover, it should be noted that a person detained or questioned by the authorities is a weaker party, with greater difficulties in proving his/her claims. A person in custody, for example, does not have the possibility to perform an obduracy immediately after the event without the cooperation of the authorities in this respect. This measure is also an expression of the principle that the use of coercion by law enforcement authorities against citizens should be the exception and is only allowed in exceptional situations and to a very limited extent, respecting the standards of proportionality and necessity. Hence, it is right to place the onus on the state to demonstrate that these conditions have been met, rather than expecting the complainant to be able to successfully demonstrate that these conditions have not been met. Demonstrating negative facts is often impossible.

7. Appropriate remedies for violations of Article 5 of the Convention

Violations of Article 5 of the Convention are often linked to violations of Article 2 of the Convention – namely cases of arrests after which detainees disappear without trace[160]. The Court emphasises the importance of an effective investigation

---

158 ECtHR judgment of 23.05.2019, 37023/13, Kanciał v. Poland, HUDOC, p. 73; ECtHR judgment of 4.12.1995, 18896/91, Ribitsch v. Austria, HUDOC, p. 31; ECtHR judgment of 12.05.2009, 9258/04, Mrozowski v. Poland, HUDOC, p. 29

159 ECtHR judgment of 13.01.2009, 15562/02, Lewandowski and Lewandowska v. Poland, HUDOC, p. 58.

160 ECtHR judgment of 25.05.1998 in Kurt v. Turkey, 24276/94, HUDOC; ECtHR judgment of 31.07.2012 in Er and Others v. Turkey, 23016/04, HUDOC; ECtHR judgment of 13.06.2000 in Timurtas v. Turkey, 23531/94, HUDOC.

and the right of the family to participate actively in these proceedings. These proceedings are intended to lead to the disclosure of those guilty of violations and their punishment[161].

However, Article 5 of the Convention is of a special nature in the context of the analysis of effective remedies. Indeed, it provides for two self-contained remedies in the event of arrest or detention.

According to Article 5(4), anyone who has been deprived of his or her liberty by arrest or detention has the right to appeal to a court for the court to determine without delay the lawfulness of the deprivation of liberty and to order his or her release if the deprivation of liberty is unlawful. The importance of judicial review is pointed out. It is submitted that merely placing the issue of detention or arrest under the review of a judicial authority is a sufficient measure to prevent violations and protect the rights of detainees. It is not necessary for the effectiveness of this measure to be acknowledged by a positive outcome for the appellant[162]. Indeed, the remedy is judicial review, not the release of the appellant.

Paragraph 5 of the article in question provides that anyone who has been harmed by arrest or detention in violation of the article is entitled to compensation. Thus, already in the article itself, the drafters of the Convention envisaged a specific measure to compensate for the damage associated with its violation. Compensation is therefore available in the event of a violation of Article 5(1) to (4) of the Convention. It is therefore necessary for national legislation to provide for a mechanism to obtain compensation in the event of infringements, the absence of such regulations will constitute a violation of Article 5(5) of the Convention[163] . The regulation must be effective – the complainant should have a real possibility to claim damages, and the amount of damages must be adequate. For example, the amount of EUR 63 paid as compensation for wrongful deprivation of liberty for three days does not meet this criterion[164].

---

161 ECtHR judgment of 13.06.2000 in Timurtas v. Turkey, 23531/94, HUDOC, p. 113.
162 ECtHR judgment of 15.12.2009 in Leva v. Moldova, 12444/05, HUDOC, p. 74.
163 ECtHR judgment of 6.11.2012 in Stanev v. Bulgaria, 32238/04, HUDOC, p. 184.
164 ECtHR judgment of 17.05.2011 in Ganea v. Moldova, 2474/06, HUDOC, pp. 29–31.

8. Appropriate remedies for violations of Article 6 of the Convention

8.1. Fairness of the proceedings

The fairness of the proceedings is understood in the doctrine and jurisprudence heterogeneously[165] . The right to a fair trial consists of several elements, both explicitly provided for by Article 6 of the Convention and expressed in the case law of the ECHR[166]. The fairness of the trial relates to the whole of Article 6 of the Convention (not limited to paragraph 1 only) and even goes beyond it[167]. Undoubtedly, all stages of criminal proceedings are covered by the scope of this provision[168]. In this section, specific aspects of the right to a fair trial will be discussed that do not relate to the issue of the lengthiness of proceedings or the rights of the defence. Indeed, these issues require separate discussion and are highlighted below.

The issue of gathering the evidence should be considered as central regarding the fair trial model of the proceedings. The acquisition of evidence by authorities is possible in several ways. In this regard, the Court points out that these proceedings must comply with certain standards. About the so-called police provocation, it pointed out that, while this method is not excluded, when assessing its results, the circumstances of the commission of the act must be thoroughly investigated. The public interest cannot justify the admissibility of evidence derived from the officers' provocation constituting *de facto* incitement to commit a crime[169]. It is therefore not the role of law enforcement to test citizens for susceptibility to commit criminal acts. The remedy for a similar abuse is, as the Court has made clear, to exclude such evidence. Based on the German solution, the Court also faced the question of whether a modification of sentence is an appropriate measure in the case of a conviction for an act committed

165 Wiliński P., Pojęcie rzetelnego procesu, in: P. Wiliński (ed.), *Rzetelny proces karny w orzecznictwie sądów polskich i miedzynarodowych*, Warsaw: Wolters Kluwer, 2009, pp. 23–28.

166 Nowak C., Prawo do rzetelnego procesu sądowego w świetle EKPC i orzecznictwa ETPC, in: P. Wiliński (ed.), *Rzetelny proces karny w orzecznictwie sądów polskich i miedzynarodowych*, Warsaw: Wolters Kluwer, 2009, p. 97.

167 Nowak C., Prawo do rzetelnego procesu sądowego w świetle EKPC i orzecznictwa ETPC, p. 97.

168 Nowak C., Prawo do rzetelnego procesu sądowego w świetle EKPC i orzecznictwa ETPC, p. 102.

169 ECtHR judgment of 9.06.1998, 25829/94, Teixeira de Castro v. Portugal, HUDOC, p. 36.

because of police provocation. As pointed out in the Furcht case[170] and reiterated in the Akbay case[171], for a trial to be fair within the meaning of Article 6(1) of the Convention, all evidence obtained because of police incitement must be excluded or a procedure with similar effects must be followed. In the light of this case law, it must be concluded that any measure which does not lead to the exclusion of such evidence or to similar consequences must be regarded as insufficient, failing to satisfy the provision of Article 6(1). The alternative to the exclusion of evidence may be the inadmissibility of the prosecution and the discontinuance of the proceedings, but never the modification of the sentence.

Also inadmissible, in the Court's view, is the use of incriminating evidence from an accused's explanations given during other (administrative) proceedings, in which it was the applicant's duty to give such explanations[172]. Such conduct is contrary to the principle of freedom from self-incrimination and the right to refuse to give evidence in criminal proceedings. In the Saunders case, Article 6(1) was found to have been violated precisely because of the use for sentencing purposes of testimony given by the complainant in proceedings before government authorities, giving of which was mandatory, and the evasion of which was punishable by imprisonment of up to 2 years[173].

The Court has repeatedly stressed that it is not its role to indicate or evaluate the rules of admissibility of evidence, but only to assess the fairness of the proceedings as a whole[174]. However, the Court does happen to indicate when the admission of a certain type of evidence compromises the fairness of the trial. Analysing the case law in this regard[175], the factors affecting the assessment of the fairness of the trial in the context of the admissibility of evidence obtained in violation of Article 3 of the Convention are considered as follows:

1. the intention of the offending authorities,

---

170 ECtHR judgment of 23.10.2014, 54648/09, Furcht v. Germany, HUDOC, pp. 68–69.

171 ECtHR judgment of 15.10.2020, 40495/15, 37273/15, 40913/15, Akbay and Others v. Germany, HUDOC, p. 124.

172 ECtHR judgment of 7.12.1993, 19187/91, Saunders v. The United Kingdom, HUDOC, pp. 69–70 and 75.

173 ECtHR judgment of 7.12.1993, 19187/91, Saunders v. The United Kingdom, HUDOC, pp. 69–70 and 75.

174 ECtHR judgment of 11.07.2006, 54810/00, Jalloh v. Germany, HUDOC, p. 100.

175 ECtHR judgment of 11.07.2006, 54810/00, Jalloh v. Germany, HUDOC, p. 105; ECtHR judgment of 1.06.2010, 22978/05, Gäfgen v. Germany, HUDOC, pp. 185–186; ECtHR judgment of 28.06.2007, 36549/03, Harutyunyan v. Armenia, HUDOC, p. 63.

2. public interest in clarifying the circumstances of the case and punishing those responsible,
3. opportunity to effectively challenge the evidence before the court,
4. the procedural significance of the evidence obtained,
5. the exclusivity of the evidence obtained,
6. competence of national authorities to exclude evidence,
7. violation of the right to defence and freedom from self-incrimination.

The Court also makes distinctions in two areas – firstly, as to the nature of the evidence (personal and material evidence), and secondly, as to the gravity of the violations, i.e. distinguishing between behavior that rises to the level of torture and that considered as inhuman or degrading treatment.

Where treatment is found as torture, both confessions, explanations and material evidence should, in the Court's view, be excluded from the proceedings. In the case of inhuman or degrading treatment, the Court considers it inadmissible to leave explanatory or confessional evidence in the trial. However, it does not take such a categorical position in the case of material evidence. Their admissibility is assessed based on the circumstances of the case, considering the factors indicated above. This problem is related to the issue of indirectly illegal evidence. This is evidence which has been obtained legally, but which would not have been possible to obtain if it had not been for a previously unlawful procedural act[176].

The judgment in the Polish case also seems to be groundbreaking in this respect. In the Ćwik case[177], the fairness of the proceedings before the national courts was questioned due to the admission of evidence from a recording of a private "interrogation" which was conducted on one of the witnesses' using methods prohibited under Article 3 of the Convention. The domestic courts pointed out that the evidentiary prohibitions relate to interrogations conducted by officers and the methods they use, not to private incidents in which state officials are in no way involved. Consequently, the evidence from the recording was not excluded. The Court, by a vote of 5 to 2, found a violation of Article 6(1) of the Convention.

Another issue affecting the fairness of the proceedings, is the disclosure of the materials of the proceedings to the suspect or later the accused[178]. The

176 Jasiński W., Karnoprocesowa dopuszczalność dowodów uzyskanych w wyniku tortur (standardy strasburskie), *Państwo i Prawo* 5 (2011), 47.

177 ECtHR judgment of 5.11.2020, 31454/10, Ćwik v. Poland, HUDOC.

178 ECtHR judgment of 15.09.1997, 28901/95, Rowe and Davis v. The United Kingdom, HUDOC, p. 60.

Court points out that Article 6(1) of the Convention implies an obligation on the authorities to disclose to the defence the materials of the proceedings[179]. Nevertheless, this is not an absolute obligation. Indeed, there are factors, such as public safety, the protection of witnesses or the secrecy of the State's methods of operation, which justify an exception to this obligation. However, as the Court points out, these exceptions are only possible in exceptional situations, and this inequality of the parties must be compensated to the accused by the proper conduct of the judicial authorities acting in the case[180].

It would therefore appear that the appropriate remedy for non-disclosure of the entirety of the materials of the proceedings by the prosecuting authorities is judicial review. It should be recognised that this is a key issue for the essence of the criminal process, as these materials may exculpate the accused who does not have the possibility to gather these materials himself. However, judicial review must meet the requirements of the utmost scrupulousness, impartiality and occur at the appropriate time – certainly the second-instance stage is not appropriate. It seems that it should take place even before the trial proceedings start, to allow the accused to defend himself adequately. Nor should this scrutiny be arbitrary but based on specifically indicated reasons for waiving the obligation to disclose the materials of the proceedings to the parties. It should not be an arbitrary decision by the prosecution not based on any grounds of admissibility for such a determination[181].

Article 6(1) of the Convention provides, inter alia, for the right to a trial by an impartial tribunal. This undoubtedly constitutes an element of a fair trial. The Court points out, as a rule, that in the case of the impartiality of the trial judge, it is necessary to exclude him. Nevertheless, a heterogeneous line of jurisprudence has developed on this issue. In the 1996 Remli judgment, it was held that it is not the Court's role to determine whether acts demonstrating the impartiality of the panel have occurred. The essence of the problem lies in the fact that if a party raises legitimate allegations of impartiality, the remedy should be a thorough examination of the circumstances of the case and the allegations and, if it is considered that the court may in fact be impartial, the exclusion of the judge from the process[182]. In a case involving a Frenchman of Algerian

179 ECtHR judgment of 15.09.1997, 28901/95, Rowe and Davis v. The United Kingdom, HUDOC, p. 60.

180 ECtHR judgment of 15.09.1997, 28901/95, Rowe and Davis v. The United Kingdom, HUDOC, p. 61.

181 ECtHR judgment of 9.10.2008, 62936/00, Moiseyev v. Russia, HUDOC, pp. 213, 216–218, 224.

182 ECtHR judgment of 23.04.1996, 16839/90, Remli v. France, HUDOC, pp. 47–48.

origin alleging that a third party heard a member of the jury admit behind the scenes that he was racist, no remedial procedure was implemented[183]. In the Gregory case, racial bias was also alleged against members of the jury. A note was given to the judge which read: "Jury shows racial bias". The judge showed the note to the prosecution and the defence and warned the jury to judge the case according to the evidence and to set aside any prejudice. He also reminded the jury of its duties and responsibilities. The Court considered that this response was sufficient to conclude that there had been no violation of Article 6(1) of the Convention. It considered it significant that defence counsel had not pressed for the jury's dismissal or asked them in open court whether they were able to proceed and reach a verdict based on the evidence alone[184] . Reference was made to the Remli case, and it was considered that the facts of the two cases presented a different picture – in the Gregory case the court had responded to the allegations of racism and had taken remedial action. In contrast, in Sander, the Court held that merely instructing the jury to divest itself of any racial bias and to adjudicate in a completely impartial manner was not a sufficient remedy in response to an allegation of racism by the jury. In the case, the national court found that at least one member of the bench had uttered jokes and racist comments, to which he had admitted. The allegation was therefore, in the Court's view, far more specific and concrete than in Gregory, and the defence sought the exclusion of the jury members and clearly questioned their impartiality. Hence, unlike in the previous case, it was held that, while the exclusion of a judge need not be the only effective remedy for an allegation of impartiality, it is nevertheless necessary in certain situations[185].

About the protection of the impartiality of the court, the Court also points to the need for systemic regulations to guarantee it. In this regard, examples are given of various procedural arrangements which are unacceptable from the point of view of the fairness of the trial:

- adjudication by a judge who had in the past been a prosecutor in the pre-trial department of the accused – was held to constitute a violation of Article 6(1) of the Convention, irrespective of actual current contacts and information

183 ECHR judgment of 23.04.1996, 16839/90, Remli v. France, HUDOC.

184 ECtHR judgment of 25.02.1997, 22299/93, Gregory v. The United Kingdom, HUDOC, pp. 47–49.

185 ECtHR judgment of 9.05.2000, 34129/96, Sander v. The United Kingdom, HUDOC, pp. 33–34.

exchanged with previous colleagues, as a reasonable doubt of impartiality is sufficient[186],

- adjudication by the judge who made procedural decisions in the case during pre-trial proceedings – it has been pointed out that this situation does not automatically lead to the necessity to exclude the judge and violate the fairness of the trial, as it is necessary to assess the circumstances of the case; nevertheless, when the judge assesses the same facts and makes similar decisions in both stages, it constitutes a violation, due to a kind of pre-trial, as in the case of recognition that there is a high probability of an act justifying the pre-trial detention of the suspect[187],
- judge in the appellate court was involved in the conviction of the co-accused – was found to be a violation of Article 6 of the Convention, which, however, had to be assessed in the context of the circumstances of the case; for it was clearly emphasised in the reasons for the judgment that, in sentencing the co-accused, the court repeatedly referred to the issue of co-conspiracy and the commission of the act jointly and in concert with other persons, hence the fear of impartiality was considered to be fully justified[188],
- even more so, adjudication by the same judge at first and second instance was considered a violation of the principle of judicial impartiality[189] .

8.2. Excessive length of proceedings

The system of remedies for protracted proceedings has been analysed by the Court on several occasions. As indicated, "the means available to the applicant (…) for raising a complaint about the length of the proceedings in his case would have been "effective" in the sense either of preventing the alleged violation or its continuation, or of providing adequate redress for any violation that had already occurred"[190]. In the case of protracted proceedings, both preventive and compensatory measures are possible. More precisely, the Court points out that preventive measures in this case are intended to expedite, to bring proceedings

186 ECtHR judgment of 26.10.1984, 8692/79, Piersack v. Belgium, HUDOC, pp. 31–32.
187 ECtHR judgment of 24.05.1989, 10486/83, Hauschildt v. Denmark, HUDOC, pp. 49–50, 52–53.
188 ECtHR judgment of 7.08.1996, 19874/92, Ferrantelli and Santangelo v. Italy, HUDOC, pp. 59–60.
189 ECtHR judgment of 26.08.1997, 22839/93, De Haan v. Netherlands, HUDOC, p. 51.
190 ECtHR judgment of 26.10.2000, 30210/96, Kudła v. Poland, HUDOC, p. 158; ECtHR judgment of 8.06.2006, 75529/01, Sürmeli v. Germany, HUDOC, p. 99.

to an end, while compensatory measures are intended to provide adequate compensation for any protractedness already experienced[191]. Important in this respect is the position taken in the Eckle case, where the Court confronted the problem of the impact of the actions taken by the accused on the excessive length of the proceedings. As pointed out, the accused cannot be faulted for his use of available means and rights during the proceedings. This position remains valid even if the actions of the accused can objectively be assessed as aimed at prolonging the proceedings, such as repeated requests to exclude judges from the proceedings. Nevertheless, these circumstances are considered when assessing the State's liability for the length of proceedings[192]. Similarly, in the case of Sociedade de Construções Martins & Vieira, Lda, it was pointed out that the accused is not required to cooperate with the judiciary and is fully entitled to use all means at his disposal to act in his interest. However, it was again pointed out that this is not irrelevant to the assessment of the lengthiness of the proceedings[193].

As the Court emphasises, prevention is the best solution. The most effective and appropriate measure is therefore to be the one aimed at speeding up the proceedings and preventing protraction in the future[194] . At the same time, the Court fully endorses the solution of a combination of both measures[195]. Thus, the most appropriate solution is the use of preventive measures aimed at speeding up the proceedings, in case the lengthy proceedings are still incomplete, prevention of future infringements and compensation for the lengthy proceedings completed or for the duration of the length of the uncompleted proceedings so far[196]. For a compensation measure to be considered effective, it is necessary for the government to indicate: the basis of the state's liability for the length of the proceedings, the way compensation will be determined and the amount of compensation that can be expected[197] . The amount may be lower than that awarded by the Court in similar cases, but it must be appropriate to the

191 ECtHR judgment of 31.07.2003, 50389/99, Doran v. Ireland, HUDOC, p. 59.

192 ECtHR judgment of 15.07.1982, 8130/78, Eckle v. Germany, HUDOC, pp. 82–84.

193 ECtHR judgment of 30.10.2014, 56637/10 et al, Sociedade de Construções Martins & Vieira, Lda v. Portugal, HUDOC, p. 48.

194 ECtHR judgment of 29.03.2006. 36813/97, Scordino v. Italy (no. 1), HUDOC, p. 183; ECtHR judgment of 8.06.2006, 75529/01, Sürmeli v. Germany, HUDOC, p. 100.

195 ECtHR judgment of 8.06.2006, 75529/01, Sürmeli v. Germany, HUDOC, p. 100.

196 ECtHR judgment of 29.03.2006. 36813/97, Scordino v. Italy (no. 1), HUDOC, pp. 185, 196 and 206.

197 ECtHR judgment of 31.07.2003, 50389/99, Doran v. Ireland, HUDOC, p. 66.

circumstances and the standard of living in the State[198]. The reparation procedure itself must also be speedy[199].

The Court also accepts the mitigation of the sentence as an effective remedy for lengthy proceedings. It must, however, be adequate to the length of the proceedings, explicit and a result of the lengthiness, which should be clear from the reasoning of the judgment[200]. The ECHR case law also holds that discontinuance of proceedings may be considered an effective remedy in response to protracted proceedings. The Court indicated that, in principle, this is possible in the context of depriving the applicant of victim status, since the discontinuance of the proceedings remedied the damage caused by the violation. However, it can occur that the lengthiness of the proceedings was such that the discontinuance could not effectively remedy the situation caused by it.

One of the most important judgments touching upon the problem of the lengthiness of proceedings is the judgment in the case of Kudła p. Poland[201]. In this judgment, the Court departed from the position that recognition of a violation of Article 6(1) of the Convention in the context of protracted proceedings is *lex specialis* to Article 13 of the Convention[202]. It emphasised the autonomous meaning of Article 13 of the Convention[203].

8.3. Right of defence

Situations of violation of the rights of defence during proceedings are very diverse, hence equally diverse are the reactions of state authorities that may be considered effective. As a rule, it is possible to indicate such conduct of an authority – usually a court – that will lead to safeguarding the interests and rights of the accused and, in the final assessment of the proceedings, allow to assume that the rights of defence, assessed globally, have not been violated.

In the Idalov case, the accused, due to his behavior, was removed from the courtroom. The Court pointed out that this is possible, nevertheless in such a

---

198 ECtHR judgment of 29.03.2006. 36813/97, Scordino v. Italy (no. 1), HUDOC, p. 206.

199 ECtHR judgment of 31.07.2003, 50389/99, Doran v. Ireland, HUDOC, p. 66.

200 ECtHR judgment of 15.07.1982, 8130/78, Eckle v. Germany, HUDOC, p. 87.

201 ECHR judgment of 26.10.2000, 30210/96, Kudła v. Poland, HUDOC.

202 Morawska, E., The Principles of Subsidiarity and Effectiveness: Two Pillars of an Effective Remedy for Excessive Length of Proceedings within the Meaning of Article 13 ECHR, *Polish Yearbook of International Law* 39 (2021), 159–185; Zoroska Kamilovska T., Effective Remedy for Excessive Length of Proceedings: A Macedonian Perspective, *Access to Justice in Eastern Europe* 1, no. 9 (2021), 64–65.

203 ECtHR judgment of 26.10.2000, 30210/96, Kudła v. Poland, HUDOC, pp. 147–149.

situation the right of defence is compromised. To avoid its violation, it is necessary for the court to ensure that the accused knows the possible consequences of his behavior and is aware of the possibility of his expulsion from the courtroom. If evidence is taken in his absence, in the absence of such instructions, the rights of the defence are prejudiced. However, it is possible to rectify it at the appeal stage. This is possible if the model of the appeal procedure includes an examination of both legal and factual issues. In the present case, however, neither the accused nor the defence counsel had the opportunity to confront the witness who had given incriminating testimony at first instance, nor was it possible to question him again and ask questions. Hence, the Court ruled that the second-instance proceedings were not able to rectify the violations committed at first instance. The Court took the view that the appropriate remedy would be to set aside the judgment of the first-instance court and refer it back for a retrial[204].

A rich line of jurisprudence has developed on the issue of the impact of a violation of the right to counsel on the fairness of the proceedings, including remedies capable of remedying violations in this regard[205]. In 1993, in the Imbrioscia case, the Court pointed out that the shape of the right to counsel at the pre-trial stage depends on the circumstances of the case, above all the impact of the actions taken at this stage on the outcome of the court proceedings[206]. The case acknowledged the absence of a violation of Article 6 of the Convention, despite the conduct of many interrogations without the presence of counsel during the pre-trial proceedings. The Court's position has changed in subsequent years. In further rulings, it already clearly indicates that the scope of the right to counsel also includes the pre-trial stage[207], nevertheless, violations in this respect can be remedied by the participation of counsel at the trial stage and the possibility to challenge evidence obtained in the absence of counsel. Furthermore, it is pointed out that the right to counsel may be restricted "for important reasons"[208]. Thus, a global approach prevails, prescribing that the implementation of the right to defence, and consequently the fairness of the trial, should be assessed in the context of the proceedings.

---

204 ECtHR judgment of 5.02.2009 in Idalov v. Russia, 5826/03, HUDOC, pp. 177–180.

205 Cf. also Cora Ł., Minimalne gwarancje prawa do rzetelnego procesu karnego w początkowym etapie ścigania, *Folia Iuridica Universitatis Wratislaviensis* 9, no. 2 (2020), 271– 281; Barcik J., Srogosz T., Prawo dostępu do adwokata w Polsce w świetle dyrektywy 2013/48/U, *Palestra* 7–8 (2015), 245–246.

206 ECtHR judgment of 24.11.1993, 13972/88, Imbrioscia v. Switzerland, HUDOC, p. 38.

207 Cf. ECHR judgment of 2.09.2004, 35841/97, Saraç v. Turkey, HUDOC, p. 4.

208 ECtHR judgment of 2.09.2004, 35841/97, Saraç v. Turkey, HUDOC, p. 4.

The Salduz judgment was undoubtedly a landmark ruling. The Court underlined in the grounds of the judgment the crucial importance of the pre-trial proceedings for the entire trial, the importance of the evidence gathered at this stage, often prejudging the outcome of the case. It also pointed to the situation of the suspect, which, due to the imbalance of parties and the inflation of the law, is worse than at the trial stage. Hence, it is fundamental to ensure the participation of defence counsel in the proceedings from the very first interview[209]. It has been pointed out that the confession of guilt during the interrogation without the participation of the defence counsel was used in the case as a basis for conviction, and neither the participation of the defence counsel at a later stage of the trial, nor the possibility of questioning the evidence gathered, could cure the violations in this respect made at the initial stage of the trial[210]. Attention was drawn to the age of the accused, who was a minor, which undoubtedly placed him in a position of vulnerability[211]. Undoubtedly, this judgment should be regarded as a landmark. For the first time, the Court unequivocally formulated the position that a violation of the right to counsel during pre-trial questioning irreparably undermines the fairness of the trial. It is therefore unacceptable to use the explanations obtained in this way. No other remedy can convalidate the situation of violation. However, attention should be drawn to the specific procedural setting in which the judgment in question was delivered. The applicant was a minor, which was a significant factor for the Court. Therefore, the position taken there should not be overstated, particularly in the context of subsequent judgments, not necessarily in line with the so-called Salduz doctrine, which began with this judgment.

The Panovits judgment continues the line of case law presented. Indeed, it was pointed out that, although it is not the Court's role to pronounce on national rules of admissibility of evidence, the use of evidence from statements obtained during police interrogation in the absence of defence counsel is inadmissible and constitutes a violation of the fairness of the trial[212]. However, the applicant in this case was also a minor. One Polish case raising the same issue is the Adamkiewicz case. The applicant, also a minor, confessed to the murder during questioning in the absence of his defence counsel. Although he withdrew from the confession at a later stage, the confession was used during the proceedings ending in a

209 ECtHR judgment of 27.11.2008, 36391/02, Salduz v. Turkey, HUDOC, p. 54.
210 ECtHR judgment of 27.11.2008, 36391/02, Salduz v. Turkey, HUDOC, pp. 57–58.
211 ECtHR judgment of 27.11.2008, 36391/02, Salduz v. Turkey, HUDOC, p. 60.
212 ECtHR judgment of 27.11.2008, 36391/02, Salduz v. Turkey, HUDOC, pp. 80–86.

conviction. In the Court's view, the use of the explanations thus obtained resulted in an irreparable breach of the fairness of the trial[213].

The judgment that broke the line of jurisprudence initiated by the Salduz judgment can be the Ibrahim and Others judgment[214]. Regarding the one of the applicants, the participation of defence counsel during the hearings was significantly delayed. Consequently, first hearings were conducted in the absence of defence counsel, and the explanations thus obtained were used in the trial. The Court considered that there had been no violation of Article 6 of the Convention in the case. In doing so, it referred to several factors justifying this decision, including the existence of compelling reasons for the temporary restriction on their right to legal assistance in the form of the exceptional situation relating to the threat of a terrorist attack, the desire to protect public safety, the extraordinary situation of detaining 18 persons at the same time and bringing them to a single unit. The Court also pointed to the means available to the applicants: challenging their explanations before the court, submitting evidence, calling witnesses, requesting the exclusion of evidence, as well as the attitude of the court, which instructed the jury on the violations that had occurred, the circumstances of the explanations given in the absence of defence counsel and the rules they should follow in assessing the evidence.

This judgment must be regarded as a step backwards in terms of the effectiveness of the safeguards for the exercise of the rights of defence. It changes the direction in which the Court was going. There is no longer any question of excluding from the proceedings evidence obtained in breach of the fundamental Convention rights of the accused. Undoubtedly, the circumstances of the present case, i.e., the fear of terrorist attacks in Europe, were of great importance. This threat is arguably one of the greatest to public safety in the 21st century. The public and political mood is geared towards resolutely countering terrorism by any or almost any means available. It may appear that the Court did not wish to constrain European states in their counter-terrorism efforts with its judgment. However, it must be recognised that these concerns cannot justify approval of violations of individual rights. Indeed, it is difficult to draw a line between rights that can be relativised in particular circumstances – as was the case here – and inviolable rights. At the same time, it is worth bearing in mind that these rights are enjoyed by persons suspected or accused of committing criminal offences

---

213 ECtHR judgment of 2.03.2010, 54729/00, Adamkiewicz v. Poland, HUDOC, pp. 88–92.

214 ECtHR judgment of 13.09.2016, 50541/08, 50571/08, 50573/08, 40351/09, Ibrahim and Others v. The United Kingdom, HUDOC.

who, at this stage, are covered by the presumption of innocence and may be found innocent because of the proceedings.

Also, the later judgments, devoid of the context of anti-terrorist measures, represent a break with the Salduz doctrine. In Beuze[215], the complainant, who faced charges of attempted murder, was interrogated in police custody without being able to consult his defence counsel beforehand and without the possibility of ensuring his presence, and during the subsequent judicial investigation no defence counsel participated in his interrogations and other investigative activities. Without being sufficiently informed of his right to refuse to testify, the applicant gave detailed explanations in police custody which significantly affected his procedural position and constituted an important piece of evidence. The Court held that there had been a violation of Article 6(1) and (3) of the Convention, not because of violations *per se,* but because the violations committed had not been remedied at the judicial stage. The Beuze judgment in this respect represents a regrettable counter-revolution: it repealed the "as a rule" requirement – already repeated in more than a hundred judgments commonly known as "Salduz jurisprudence" – and radically relativised it to the detriment of procedural guarantees'[216].

In the Simeonovi judgment[217], the applicant claimed that his right to counsel had been restricted at the pre-trial stage, despite his repeated requests. The Bulgarian Government argued that there were no records documenting these demands. The Court pointed out that there was in fact no corroboration of those demands and that it was not possible at this stage to establish whether the applicant had in fact requested the participation of a lawyer at the first stage of the proceedings. The Court considered that the fairness of the trial had not been compromised and chose not to find a violation of Article 6 § 1 of the Convention. It pointed out that the possible violations had been convalidated – first of all, the applicant had confessed to the offences when assisted by a lawyer of his choice and he knew that this confession could be used as evidence against him in support of a possible conviction, his conviction was based not only on these explanations but on a whole body of consistent evidence, moreover, the applicant had made substantial use of his right to counsel, who had assisted him throughout most of the proceedings. The Court points out that the Salduz judgment had already

---

215 ECtHR judgment of 9.11.2018, 71409/10, Beuze v. Belgium, HUDOC.

216 ECtHR judgment of 9.11.2018, 71409/10, Beuze v. Belgium, Dissenting Judgment By Judges Yudkivska, Vučinić, Turković And Hüseynov.

217 ECtHR judgment of 12.05.2017, 21980/04, Simeonovi v. Bulgaria, HUDOC.

indicated that national law could provide for exceptions to the absolute right to counsel, an exception which was made more specific in the Ibrahim and Others judgment. However, while the Salduz judgment indicates that possible exceptions under national law must be assessed in the context of the fairness of the proceedings, and that a derogation from the right to counsel in the absence of statutory grounds always undermines the fairness of the trial, the Ibrahim judgment indicates that, even in the absence of statutory grounds, it is necessary to assess the fairness of the proceedings as a whole, allowing for the possibility of rectifying defects at later stages of the trial. The Beuze and Simeonovi judgments indicate that the Salduz standard is eroding in favour of the standard expressed in the Ibrahim judgment.

The right to waive the use of defence counsel also remains an important issue. The Court points out that this is possible, but that there must nevertheless be an express, voluntary and informed waiver of this right. It will therefore be considered a violation if an authority unjustifiably considers that the accused has waived the right to counsel[218]. It appears that in the case of such a violation, it will be necessary to exclude evidence gathered in the absence of defence counsel[219].

In conclusion , in the case of a violation of the rights of the defence, the Court emphasises the convalidation of violations in the further course of the proceedings – the possibility to challenge evidence, the participation of defence counsel, repetition of actions, appeal proceedings. Only when, due to the gravity of the violation, it cannot be remedied, does the Court point to more stringent measures, such as the exclusion of evidence. This is the case when the rights of the defence have been irretrievably infringed, for then there is also an irreparable breach of the fairness of the trial. These are cases where any other measure is not capable of remedying the situation caused by the breach, such as a confession made by the suspect during the first interrogation without the presence of defence counsel (of a suspect in a particularly sensitive or vulnerable situation).

9. Appropriate remedies for violations of Article 8 of the Convention

Violations of Article 8 of the Convention in the context of remedies in criminal proceedings primarily concern unauthorised searches and wiretapping. Both

218 ECtHR judgment of 3.05.2007, 22744/07, Türk v. Turkey, HUDOC, pp. 52–54.

219 ECtHR judgment of 3.05.2007, 22744/07, Türk v. Turkey, HUDOC, p. 58; ECtHR judgment of 11.12.2018, 9106/09, Rodionov v. Russia, HUDOC, p. 167.

activities are aimed at gathering evidence in the proceedings, hence the analysis in this respect is of utmost importance in this study.

In the case of an unauthorised search of a dwelling, it was pointed out that the remedy of disciplinary proceedings against officers is not sufficient. The emphasis should be on the possibility of challenging the legality of the search and its results in proceedings before the national courts. If there is no possibility in the national order to initiate such a review, and at the same time remedial proceedings, this constitutes a violation of Article 13 of the Convention[220]. Attention is also drawn to special categories, such as the search of a lawyer's office. These are particularly sensitive activities, as they expose the disclosure of sensitive secrets. It is pointed out in this regard that financial compensation or damages cannot be a sufficient remedy either. It is necessary to have the opportunity to initiate proceedings aimed at controlling the actions taken, with the possibility of declaring them invalid[221].

As far as wiretapping is concerned, as the Court points out, the control of covert surveillance measures can be carried out in three phases: when surveillance is ordered, when it is carried out or when it is completed. About the first two phases, the very nature of secret surveillance requires that not only the surveillance itself, but also the control that accompanies it, be carried out without the knowledge of the person concerned. Since the person concerned should be able to lodge an effective remedy and to take part in the resolution procedure, it is important that the regulations in place provide adequate safeguards for the rights of the individual[222]. As a rule, it is desirable that the review be entrusted to a judge, since the judicial system offers guarantees of independence, impartiality, and fairness of the process[223]. However, this is not an absolute requirement. In the case of non-judicial bodies, it is necessary to carefully assess the competence, powers, and procedural guarantees of the body in the context of its effectiveness[224], and above all its independence from the executive[225].

---

220 ECtHR judgment of 19.01.2017, 63638/14, Posevini v. Bulgaria, HUDOC, pp. 83–87.

221 ECtHR judgment of 21.01.2010, 43757/05, Xavier Da Silveira v. France, HUDOC, pp. 48–49.

222 ECtHR judgment of 7.02.2017, 35285/08, İrfan Güzel v. Turkey, HUDOC, pp. 96–98.

223 ECtHR judgment of 7.02.2017, 35285/08, İrfan Güzel v. Turkey, HUDOC, pp. 96–98; ECtHR judgment of 18.05.2010, 26839/05, Kennedy v. The United Kingdom, HUDOC, p. 167.

224 ECtHR judgment of 26.03.1987, 9248/81, Leander v. Sweden, HUDOC, p. 83.

225 ECtHR judgment of 13.09.2018, 58170/13 62322/14 24960/15, Big Brother Watch and Others v. The United Kingdom, HUDOC, p. p. 377.

The Court points out that it is not always possible or required to notify the persons concerned of ongoing surveillance measures. Notifying every person affected by a measure currently being taken could jeopardise the long-term objective that originally motivated the surveillance. It could help to reveal the working methods of the intelligence services, their areas of activity and even the identity of their agents. Nevertheless, the authorities should inform the persons concerned of the activities carried out (in a timely manner), as this is the only way to allow them to be subjected to scrutiny and to lodge a possible remedy[226]. Thus, as the Court has repeatedly emphasised, in the case of covert, surveillance activities, an effective remedy within the meaning of Article 13 must be one that is as effective as possible, within the limited scope inherent in any surveillance system[227].

In doing so, it should be noted that the possibility of appealing to the authority directly supervising the call control management authority will not be considered an effective remedy. This is because this authority does not meet the criterion of independence due to its hierarchical subordination, and therefore this remedy cannot be considered effective[228]. Also, a constitutional complaint is not an effective remedy when several other constitutional complaints in the field of eavesdropping regulation have not had the expected effect[229]. In the Klass case, a global approach was presented, and it was pointed out that a set of the following measures: initiating a review of the legality of police surveillance, bringing a civil action for damages, bringing an action for destruction or return of the data or documents obtained, bringing a constitutional complaint, satisfy the requirements of Article 13 of the Convention in this respect[230].

In the Rotaru case, the complainant alleged that the State kept secret records of data about citizens, including him. As he pointed out, this information was false and probably related to another person with the same name. While it is true that the court awarded damages against the applicant, the Court considered that this was an insufficient measure. It was submitted that, although the complainant's request had been upheld in this respect, the data had been retained in the

226 ECtHR judgment of 4.12.2015, 47143/06, Zakharov v. Russia, HUDOC, pp. 289–290.

227 ECtHR judgment of 7.02.2017, 35285/08, İrfan Güzel v. Turkey, HUDOC, p. 99; ECtHR judgment of 16.11.1996, 22414/93, Chahal v. The United Kingdom, HUDOC, p. 142; ECtHR judgment of 6.09.1978, 5029/71, Klass v. Germany, HUDOC, p. 69; ECtHR judgment of 26.03.1987, 9248/81, Leander v. Sweden, HUDOC, p. 84.

228 ECtHR judgment of 4.12.2015, 47143/06, Zakharov v. Russia, HUDOC, p. 292.

229 ECtHR judgment of 4.12.2015, 47143/06, Zakharov v. Russia, HUDOC, p. 299.

230 ECtHR judgment of 6.09.1978, 5029/71, Klass v. Germany, HUDOC, pp. 69–72.

register, and national law did not specify the scope of information about citizens that the authorities could obtain and retain. The fact that the court had not taken cognisance of the complaint about redress and costs was highlighted. Hence, it could not be considered that effective remedies had been applied[231].

About violations of Article 8, the Court prefers preventive remedies. Measures conducive to further violations, including measures aimed at pure monetary compensation that prevent a change in the procedural situation of the victim of the violation, will not be considered effective. They may exist and are arguably desirable in some cases but must co-exist with preventive measures. The Court seems to consider judicial review of search, interview, or other surveillance activities, coupled with the power of the court to declare the activity illegal, invalid or to exclude the results of the activity conducted, as an appropriate preventive measure in situations of violation of Article 8[232]. The role of national regulations on secret interception, in particular their scope, the period of storage, the length of the operations carried out, the guarantees against abuse and arbitrariness, the proportionality of the operations, the prerequisites for carrying out the operations, cannot be overestimated either[233].

In the Big Brother Watch and Others cases, the debate about the legality of mass surveillance in the online society also remains topical. These cases (joined together) are the result of data revealed by Edward Snowden on mass surveillance carried out by the US authorities, in cooperation with the UK government. The system in place in the UK made it possible (the past tense is appropriate here, as the UK changed its national regulations in the period between the complaint and the judgment):

1. supervision of communication between Internet users, the search for information useful for the interview or the evaluation of material by the intelligence analyst,
2. receiving data from telecommunications operators,

---

231 ECtHR judgment of 4.05.2000, Rotaru v. Romania, 28341/95, HUDOC, p. 36.

232 ECtHR judgment of 7.06.2016, 30083/10, Karabeyoğlu v. Turkey, HUDOC, pp. 130–132.

233 ECtHR judgment of 4.12.2015, 47143/06, Zakharov v. Russia, HUDOC, pp. 302–303; ECtHR judgment of 25.02.1993, 10828/84, Funke v. France, HUDOC, pp. 56–59; ECtHR judgment of 17.07.2007, 48666/99, Kucera v. Slovakia, p. 122; ECtHR judgment of 13.09.2018, 58170/13, 62322/14, 24960/15, Big Brother Watch and Others v. The United Kingdom, HUDOC, p. 315; ECtHR judgment of 21.09.2000, 35394/97, Khan v. The United Kingdom, HUDOC, pp. 26–28.

3. data transfer between the security and intelligence services of different countries[234].

It has been pointed out that the state has some discretion in regulating public security. However, control mechanisms are needed as to the choice of data to be scrutinised and the way in which it is searched to implement surveillance activities. The Court pointed out that the risk of abuse in the case of such extensive surveillance of Internet users is very serious, and that the legislation does not provide sufficient safeguards and protection mechanisms against the infringement of individual privacy rights[235]. It was also pointed out that EU law only allows for data collection when a serious crime is suspected. The absence of any restriction in this respect, as in the case of UK law, will constitute a violation of Article 8 of the Convention[236]. The judgment is considered groundbreaking, not least because it is the first time that the Court has confronted the problem of mass surveillance by the secret services of states. It is important to recognise that the contemporary reality of surveillance activities is very different from the conditions at the time of the Klass, Khan or other judgments, considered fundamental in terms of violations of Article 8 of the Convention. Access to data by the services using the Internet is almost unlimited. Moreover, the threat of terrorism prompts both governments and intelligence services to push further boundaries of individual privacy to obtain information potentially useful for crime prevention. Thus, in its more than 200-page explanatory memorandum to the judgment, the Court highlighted two issues in particular:

1. the need for control mechanisms and means available to everyone to verify and access information on possible surveillance as to their person – thus the existence of effective remedies,
2. the possibility to collect data in the way British intelligence did, only in the case of a threat of the most serious crimes; a catalogue of crimes in this respect therefore seems necessary.

234 ECtHR judgment of 13.09.2018, 58170/13, 62322/14, 24960/15, Big Brother Watch and Others v. The United Kingdom, HUDOC.

235 ECtHR judgment of 13.09.2018, 58170/13, 62322/14, 24960/15, Big Brother Watch and Others v. The United Kingdom, HUDOC, pp. 319–320.

236 ECtHR R judgment of 13.09.2018, 58170/13, 62322/14, 24960/15, Big Brother Watch and Others v. The United Kingdom, HUDOC, pp. 466–467.

10. Conclusions

Regarding the right to an effective remedy, the Court does not provide a simple definition of a remedy. Nor does it indicate a catalogue of possible, desirable or acceptable forms of remedies. In this way, the Court does not limit national legislations in their ability to introduce a variety of systems of remedies and allows to adapt to the changing realities of the modern world, including evolving technologies. The Court defines the concept of remedies through the requirements they must meet and the functions they are intended to perform. In determining the effectiveness of remedies, the Court sets out the factors that are considered in their assessment.

The Court presents two main forms of remedies: preventive (in other words, preventive) and compensatory (also known as compensatory), giving primacy to the former. It thus sets out the right direction for the legislation of states in its assessment, while giving guidance on how to shape legal systems in a desirable way. This does not mean that compensatory measures will be deemed insufficient in every case – as outlined above, depending on the circumstances of the case and the design of national regulations, these measures may satisfy the requirements of Article 13 of the Convention in their entirety. The Court assesses each case, analysing all factors affecting the situation of the applicant. There can be no benchmarks developed by the Court. However, this does not mean that the Court's jurisprudence is inconsistent or unpredictable. On the contrary, the Court is consistent in the development of its jurisprudence and rarely deviates from the principles developed and models of procedure adopted in a particular procedural setting. At the same time, it reacts to changes in the surrounding world, adapting its jurisprudence to its requirements. This makes it possible to present a catalogue of the types of remedies that the Court has found to be effective in the case of the infringements.

These include the following remedies:

1. abandonment of violations and prevention of future violations (e.g. provision of medical care to a detainee[237], termination of protracted proceedings[238], removal of illegally collected data, return of illegally retained documents)[239],
2. exclusion of evidence[240],

237 Cf. ECtHR judgment of 20.01.2009, 28300/06, Musiał v. Poland, HUDOC, pp. 76–77.
238 Cf. ECtHR judgment of 29.03.2006. 36813/97, Scordino v. Italy (no. 1), HUDOC, p. 183.
239 Cf. ECtHR judgment of 4.05.2000, 28341/95, Rotaru v. Romania, HUDOC, p. 36.
240 Cf. ECtHR judgment of 11.07.2006 in Jalloh v. Germany, 54810/00, HUDOC, p. 107.

3. opportunity to challenge the evidence in court proceedings[241],
4. repetition of procedural action[242],
5. mitigation of sentence[243],
6. appeal proceedings[244],
7. judicial review[245],
8. supervision and verification of infringements by ex officio bodies[246],
9. disciplinary sanctions[247],
10. shifting the burden of command[248],
11. discontinuance of proceedings[249],
12. exclusion of the judge[250],
13. redress/monetary compensation[251],
14. constitutional complaint[252].

Bibliography

Literature

Barcik J., Srogosz T., Prawo dostępu do adwokata w Polsce w świetle dyrektywy 2013/48/U, *Palestra*, 2015.

Cora Ł., Minimalne gwarancje prawa do rzetelnego procesu karnego w początkowym etapie ścigania, *Folia Iuridica Universitatis Wratislaviensis* 9, no. 2, 2020.

241 Cf. ECtHR judgment of 12.05.2017, 21980/04, Simeonovi v. Bulgaria, HUDOC, p. 142.

242 Cf. ECtHR judgment of 5.02.2009, 5826/03, Idalov v. Russia, HUDOC, pp. 177–180.

243 Cf. ECtHR judgment of 10.11.2005, 65745/01, Dzelili v. Germany, HUDOC, p. 83.

244 Cf. ECtHR judgment of 16.11.1996, 22414/93, Chahal v. The United Kingdom, HUDOC, p. 148.

245 Cf. ECtHR judgment of 15.09.1997, 28901/95, Rowe and Davis v. The United Kingdom, HUDOC, p. 61.

246 Cf. ECtHR judgment of 24.04.2003, 24351/94, Aktaş v. Turkey, HUDOC, p. 299.

247 Cf. ECtHR judgment of 24.04.2003, 24351/94, Aktaş v. Turkey, HUDOC, p. 329.

248 Cf. ECtHR judgment of 23.05.2019, 37023/13, Kanciał v. Poland, HUDOC, p. 73.

249 Cf. ECtHR judgment of 15.07.1982, 8130/78, Eckle v. Germany, HUDOC, p. 94.

250 Cf. ECtHR judgment of 9.05.2000, 34129/96, Sander v. The United Kingdom, HUDOC, pp. 33–34.

251 Cf. ECtHR judgment of 10.01.2012, 42525/07, 60800/08, Ananyev and Others v. Russia, HUDOC, p. 228.

252 Cf. ECtHR judgment of 6.09.1978, 5029/71, Klass v. Germany, HUDOC, p. 72.

Gerards J., Glas L., Access to justice in the European Convention on Human Rights system, *Netherlands Quarterly of Human Rights* 35, no. 1, 2017.

Jasiński W., Karnoprocesowa dopuszczalność dowodów uzyskanych w wyniku tortur (standardy strasburskie), *Państwo i Prawo* 5, 2011.

Khomenko M., Kostruba A., Kot O., Right to an Effective Remedy of Legal Protection: Practice of the European Court of Human Rights and the Norms of the National Legislation of Ukraine, *Journal of Advanced Research in Law and Economics* 9, no. 7/37, 2018.

Morawska E., The Principles of Subsidiarity and Effectiveness: Two Pillars of an Effective Remedy for Excessive Length of Proceedings within the Meaning of Article 13 ECHR, *Polish Yearbook of International Law* 39, 2021.

Nowak C., Prawo do rzetelnego procesu sądowego w świetle EKPC i orzecznictwa ETPC, in: P. Wiliński (ed.), *Rzetelny proces karny w orzecznictwie sądów polskich i miedzynarodowych*, Warsaw: Wolters Kluwer, 2009.

Piątek W., The Right to an Effective Remedy in European Law: Significance, Content and Interaction, *China-EU Law Journal* 6, 2019.

Wiliński P., Pojęcie rzetelnego procesu, in: P. Wiliński (ed.), *Rzetelny proces karny w orzecznictwie sądów polskich i miedzynarodowych*, Warsaw: Wolters Kluwer, 2009.

Zoroska Kamilovska T., Effective Remedy for Excessive Length of Proceedings: A Macedonian Perspective, *Access to Justice in Eastern Europe* 1, no. 9, 2021.

Judgements

ECtHR judgment of 6.09.1978, 5029/71, Klass v. Germany, HUDOC

ECtHR judgment of 15.07.1982, 8130/78, Eckle v. Germany, HUDOC

ECtHR judgment of 25.03.1983, 5947/72, 6205/73, 7052/75, 7061/75, 7107/75, 7113/75, 7136/75, Silver and Others v. The United Kingdom, HUDOC

ECtHR judgment of 26.10.1984, 8692/79, Piersack v. Belgium, HUDOC

ECtHR judgment of 21.02.1986, 8793/79, James and Others v. The United Kingdom, HUDOC

ECtHR judgment of 26.03.1987, 9248/81, Leander v. Sweden, HUDOC

ECtHR Judgment of 27.04.1988, 9659/82, 9658/82, Boyle and Rice v. The United Kingdom, HUDOC

ECtHR judgment of 24.05.1989, 10486/83, Hauschildt v. Denmark, HUDOC

ECtHR judgment of 30.10.1991, 3163/87, 13164/87, 13165/87, 13447/87, 13448/87, Vilvarajah and Others v. The United Kingdom, HUDOC

ECtHR judgment of 25.02.1993, 10828/84, Funke v. France, HUDOC

ECtHR judgment of 24.11.1993, 13972/88, Imbrioscia v. Switzerland, HUDOC

ECtHR judgment of 7.12.1993, 19187/91, Saunders v. The United Kingdom, HUDOC

ECtHR judgment of 27.09.1995 in McCann and Others v. UK, 18984/91, HUDOC

ECtHR judgment of 4.12.1995, 18896/91, Ribitsch v. Austria, HUDOC

ECtHR judgment of 23.04.1996, 16839/90, Remli v. France, HUDOC

ECtHR judgment of 7.08.1996, 19874/92, Ferrantelli and Santangelo v. Italy, HUDOC

ECtHR judgment of 16.11.1996, 22414/93, Chahal v. The United Kingdom, HUDOC

ECtHR judgment of 25.02.1997, 22299/93, Gregory v. The United Kingdom, HUDOC

ECtHR judgment of 25.06.1997, 20605/92, Halford v. The United Kingdom, HUDOC

ECtHR judgment of 26.08.1997, 22839/93, De Haan v. Netherlands, HUDOC

ECtHR judgment of 15.09.1997, 28901/95, Rowe and Davis v. The United Kingdom, HUDOC

ECtHR judgment of 25.05.1998 in Kurt v. Turkey, 24276/94, HUDOC

ECtHR judgment of 9.06.1998, 25829/94, Teixeira de Castro v. Portugal, HUDOC

ECtHR judgment of 28.10.1998, 24760/94, Assenov and Others v. Bulgaria, HUDOC

ECtHR judgment of 28.03.2000, 22535/93, Mahmut Kaya v. Turkey, HUDOC

ECtHR judgment of 4.05.2000, Rotaru v. Romania, 28341/95, HUDOC

ECtHR judgment of 9.05.2000, 34129/96, Sander v. The United Kingdom, HUDOC

ECtHR judgment of 13.06.2000 in Timurtas v. Turkey, 23531/94, HUDOC

ECtHR judgment of 21.09.2000. 35394/97, Khan v. The United Kingdom, HUDOC

ECtHR judgment of 26.10.2000, 30210/96, Kudła v. Poland, HUDOC

ECtHR judgment of 4.05.2001, Hugh Jordan v. UK, 24746/94, HUDOC

ECtHR judgment of 10.05.2001, 29392/95, Z. and Others v. The United Kingdom, HUDOC

ECtHR judgment of 14.03.2002, 46477/99, Paul and Audrey Edwards v. The United Kingdom, HUDOC

ECtHR judgment of 13.06.2002 in Anguelova p. Bulgaria, 38361/97, HUDOC

ECtHR judgment of 13.06.2002 in Anguelova p. Bulgaria, 38361/97, HUDOC

ECtHR decision of 11.09.2002, 57220/00, Mifsud v. France, HUDOC

ECtHR judgment of 24.04.2003, 24351/94, Aktaş v. Turkey, HUDOC
ECtHR judgment of 31.07.2003, 50389/99, Doran v. Ireland, HUDOC
ECHR judgment of 2.09.2004, 35841/97, Saraç v. Turkey, HUDOC
ECtHR judgment of 10.11.2005, 65745/01, Dzelili v. Germany, HUDOC
ECtHR judgment of 28.03.2006. 52495/99, Koss v. Poland, HUDOC
ECtHR judgment of 29.03.2006, 62361/00, Riccardi Pizzati v. Italy, HUDOC
ECtHR judgment of 29.03.2006. 36813/97, Scordino v. Italy (no. 1), HUDOC
ECtHR judgment of 8.06.2006, 75529/01, Sürmeli v. Germany, HUDOC
ECtHR judgment of 4.07.2006, 59450/00, Ramirez Sanchez v. France, HUDOC
ECtHR judgment of 12.10.2006, 3178/03, Mubilanzila Mayeka and Kaniki Mitunga v. Belgium, HUDOC
ECtHR judgment of 3.05.2007, 22744/07, Türk v. Turkey, HUDOC
ECtHR judgment of 28.06.2007, 36549/03, Harutyunyan v. Armenia, HUDOC
ECtHR judgment of 17.07.2007, 48666/99, Kucera v. Slovakia, HUDOC
ECtHR judgment of 20.03.2008, 15339/02 et al, Budayeva v. Russia, HUDOC
ECtHR judgment of 9.10.2008, 62936/00, Moiseyev v. Russia, HUDOC
ECtHR judgment of 27.11.2008, 36391/02, Salduz v. Turkey, HUDOC
ECtHR judgment of 13.01.2009, 15562/02, Lewandowski and Lewandowska v. Poland, HUDOC
ECHR judgment of 20.01.2009, 28300/06, Musiał v. Poland, HUDOC, p. 76–77.
ECtHR judgment of 5.02.2009 in Idalov v. Russia, 5826/03, HUDOC
ECtHR judgment of 12.05.2009, 9258/04, Mrozowski v. Poland, HUDOC
ECtHR judgment of 15.12.2009 in Leva v. Moldova, 12444/05, HUDOC
ECtHR judgment of 5.01.2010, 22933/02, Frasik v. Poland, HUDOC, p. 104.
ECtHR judgment of 21.01.2010, 43757/05, Xavier Da Silveira v. France, HUDOC
ECtHR judgment of 2.03.2010, 54729/00, Adamkiewicz v. Poland, HUDOC
ECtHR judgment of 18.05.2010, 26839/05, Kennedy v. The United Kingdom, HUDOC ECtHR judgment of 26.03.1987, 9248/81, Leander v. Sweden, HUDOC
ECtHR judgment of 10.09.2010, 31333/06, McFarlane v. Ireland, HUDOC
ECtHR judgment of 21.12.2010 in Jasinskis v. Latvia, 45744/08, HUDOC
ECtHR judgment of 21.01.2011, 0696/09, M.S.S. v. Belgium and Greece, HUDOC
ECtHR judgment of 17.05.2011 in Ganea v. Moldova, 2474/06, HUDOC
ECtHR judgment of 10.01.2012, 42525/07, 60800/08, Ananyev and Others v. Russia, HUDOC

ECtHR judgment of 31.07.2012 in Er and Others v. Turkey, 23016/04, HUDOC

ECtHR judgment of 6.11.2012 in Stanev v. Bulgaria, 32238/04, HUDOC

ECtHR judgment of 13.12.2012, 22689/07, De Souza Ribeiro v. France, HUDOC

ECtHR judgment of 13.12.2012, 39630/09, El Masri v. "The Former Yugoslav Republic of Macedonia", HUDOC

ECtHR judgment of 8.01.2013, 43517/09, 35315/10, 37818/10, 46882/09, 55400/09, 57875/09, 61535/09, Torreggiani and Others v. Italy, HUDOC

ECtHR judgment of 17.01.2013 in Mosendz v. Ukraine, 52013/08, HUDOC

ECtHR judgment of 17.09.2014, 10865/09, 45886/07 and 32431/08, Anca Mocanu and Others v. Romania, HUDOC

ECtHR judgment of 23.10.2014, 54648/09, Furcht v. Germany, HUDOC

ECtHR judgment of 30.10.2014, 56637/10 et al, Sociedade de Construções Martins & Vieira, Lda v. Portugal, HUDOC

ECtHR judgment of 4.12.2015, 47143/06, Zakharov v. Russia, HUDOC

ECtHR judgment of 7.06.2016, 30083/10, Karabeyoğlu v. Turkey, HUDOC

ECtHR judgment of 13.09.2016, 50541/08, 50571/08, 50573/08, 40351/09, Ibrahim and Others v. The United Kingdom, HUDOC

ECtHR judgment of 15.12.2016, 16483/12, Khlaifia and Others v. Italy, HUDOC

ECtHR judgment of 19.01.2017, 63638/14, Posevini v. Bulgaria, HUDOC

ECtHR judgment of 7.02.2017, 35285/08, İrfan Güzel v. Turkey, HUDOC

ECHR judgment of 12.05.2017, 21980/04, Simeonovi v. Bulgaria, HUDOC

ECtHR judgment of 13.09.2018, 58170/13 62322/14 24960/15, Big Brother Watch and Others v. The United Kingdom, HUDOC

ECtHR judgment of 9.11.2018, 71409/10, Beuze v. Belgium, HUDOC

ECtHR judgment of 11.12.2018, 9106/09, Rodionov v. Russia, HUDOC

ECtHR judgment of 23.05.2019, 37023/13, Kanciał v. Poland, HUDOC

ECtHR judgment of 15.10.2020, 40495/15, 37273/15, 40913/15, Akbay and Others v. Germany, HUDOC

ECtHR judgment of 5.11.2020, 31454/10, Ćwik v. Poland, HUDOC

ECHR judgment of 7.05.2021, 4907/18, Xero Flor v. Poland, HUDOC

ECHR judgment of 22.07.2021, 43447/19, Reczkowicz v. Poland, HUDOC

ECHR judgment of 8.11.2021, 49868/19 and 57511/19, Dolińska-Ficek and Ozimek v. Poland, HUDOC

ECHR judgment of 3.02.2022, 1469/20, Advance Pharma sp. z o.o. v. Poland, HUDOC

ECHR judgment of 6.10.2022, 35599/20, Juszczyszyn v. Poland, HUDOC

Zuzanna Grala, Kacper Kobierski

Chapter 3 Effective legal remedies in the Charter of Fundamental Rights and Jurisprudence of CJEU

1. Introduction: Co-habitation of legal standards

Discussing Effective Legal Remedies from EU legal system perspective we must bear in mind specific co-habitation of at least three types of legal standards. These are at first place constitutional traditions of Member States with developed standards of individual rights' protection. They exist together with widely recognised international obligations common to all Council of Europe Member States, arising from European Convention for the Protection of Human Rights and Fundamental Freedoms (ECPHR). Finally, direct perspective and own standards set in The Charter of Fundamental Rights of European Union Member States. In this Chapter the latter will be discussed but we must bear in mind legal standards mentioned above, influencing and developing the Charter. Some comments on nature of the Charter and its relations to the Convention is then also necessary, as far as about consistency between the afforded rights, and secondly to safeguard the autonomy of EU law. In that perspective we can finally provide proper analysis of the essence of ELR in EU law.

2. Nature of the Charter of Fundamental Rights

The Charter of Fundamental Rights of the European Union (Charter) is an innvating legal act setting out the rights and freedoms of EU citizens and creating a system of socio-cultural values for Europeans[253]. The Charter is an expression of the common identity of the EU[254]. From its origins the Charter was aimed to consolidate the understanding of human rights in the Union and to make them more visible[255]. At the time, the weakness of basing the human

253 K. Cymerys, *Aksjologia, idee i zasady ogólne Karty Praw Podstawowych Unii Europejskiej*, Humanum no. 2/2011, p. 385.

254 C. McCrudden, *Future of the EU Charter of Fundamental Rights, Available at SSRN: https://ssrn.com/abstract=299639,* p. 1.

255 See Conclusion of the European Council in Cologne, 3rd and 4th June 1999, Annex IV.

rights protection system on Court of Justice rulings and on Council resolutions was pointed out. The level of European integration was at a much higher level than the level of EU human rights regulation[256]. The Charter was signed and adopted in Nice on 7 December 2000. It should be remembered that at that time the Charter was only a declaration and did not become an EU legal act until the Lisbon Treaty. Thus, with the entry into force of the Lisbon Treaty, the Charter became a legally binding act[257]. From that moment the Charter is a source of primary law in the EU[258].

It is important to stress that creation of the Charter was intended to set out basic rights for the Community as a whole, consolidating the fundamental rights and reinforcing the constitutional nature of the Treaties[259]. This was to facilitate the process of creating future EU laws.

By its very nature, the Charter considers the views and traditions of the various European societies[260]. The importance of the Charter is justified by the fact that respect for human rights is a fundamental principle of the European Union and that the Community itself finds its legitimacy in its existence[261]. It should be noted that the Charter was already intended to be a document setting the framework for the existence of human rights in the EU[262].

The legislators aimed to give the Charter a real and effective character. It is only by ensuring that human rights are uniform and that they are interpreted homogeneously that they will be effectively realized[263]. Thus, it was initially decided to limit the catalogue of rights in favour of their effectiveness. The divergent positions of the members of the Convention resulted in the Charter

256 See G. de Burca, *The Drafting of the European Union Charter of Fundamental Rights,* 6 EUR. L. REV. 799 (2015); J. Menkes, *Karta Praw Podstawowych Unii Europejskiej a konstytucja Europy*, Studia Europejskie 2/2001, p. 33.

257 D. Kornobis-Romanowska, *Poszanowanie praw podstawowych w państwach członkowskich Unii Europejskiej – w stronę zapewnienia spójnego poziomu ochrony praw człowieka w Europie?*, Przegląd Prawa i Administracji C/2, Wrocław 2015, p. 461.

258 J. van Zeben, The Role of the EU Charter of Fundamental Right in Climate Litigation, *German Law Journal*, 22 (2021), 1500; Dz. U. C 326 from 26.10.2012, pp. 391–407.

259 G. Di Federico (ed.), *The EU Charter of Fudamental Rights: From Declaration to Binding Instrument, Ius Gentium: Comparative Perspectives on Law and Justice* 8, p. 11.

260 C. McCrudden, *Future…*, pp. 5–6.

261 C. McCrudden, *Future…*, p. 2.

262 G. Michałowska, *Ochrona praw człowieka w Radzie Europy i Unii Europejskiej*, Warsaw 2007, p. 265.

263 D. Kornobis-Romanowska, *Poszanowanie…*, p. 447.

being a heterogeneous act that contains both declaratory and constitutive provisions[264].

It should be noted that the Charter has significantly deepened the integration of the European Union. During the legislative process, the Convention had to consider the rights and freedoms stemming from the constitutional traditions of the Member States[265]. On the other hand, the Member States must now interpret the rights and freedoms of citizens in the spirit of the Charter.

The Charter contains a broad catalogue of rights of a diverse nature. It contains the fundamental human rights stemming from the constitutions of the individual Member States and the European Convention on Human Rights[266]. The Charter also directly reflects the case law of the Court of Justice of the European Union[267]. It should be pointed out that the Charter is directly applicable to the Member States[268]. This allows for the creation of a uniform system of protection of human rights. The Charter is also intended to guide the drafting of legislation at both European and national levels in the Member States[269]. It should be noted that in the EU legal system, the Charter and the general principles of the Union are on an equal footing[270].

The Charter has an innovative character. In addition to indicating rights and freedoms, the Charter is geared towards their realisation. Includes "new possibilities for exercising them (the rights) and contains regulations to stimulate changes in their understanding and protection"[271]. This allows for the reinterpretation of the Charter's provisions and its broad implementation. The provisions of the Charter give expression to the ideas of humanity, justice, and efficiency. The nature of the Charter allows for the creation of an area of

264 C. McCrudden, *Future…*, p. 16.

265 K. Lenaerts, The Role of the EU Charter in the Member States, in: M. Bobek. J. Adams-Prassl (eds.), *The EU Charter of Fundamental Right in the Member States,* Bloomsbury Publishing 2020, pp. 19–37.

266 D. Triantagyllou, The European Charter of Fundamental Tights and the "Rule of law": Restricting Fundamental Rights by Reference, *Common Market Law Review*, 39 (2002), p. 53–54.

267 G. di Federico, *The EU…*, pp. 55–77.

268 Ł. Kaczmarczyk, *The Charter of Fundamental Rights of the European Union in the Light of the Principle of Unity in Diversity (Part 1),* Nurt SVD 1, 2020, pp. 225–232.

269 D. Triantagyllou, *The European…*, p. 57.

270 K. Lenaerts, J. A. Gutierrez-Fons, The Constitutional Allocation of Powers and General Principles of EU Law, *CML Rev*, no. 47 (2010), p. 1656.

271 M. Nowicki, *Karta Praw Podstawowych Unii Europejskiej: tekst z objaśnieniami Sekretariatu Konwencji*, Cracow 2001.

security, justice, and freedom. The Charter consolidates the rights and freedoms contained in various sources[272].

3. Relationship between the Charter and the European Convention for the Protection of Human Rights and Fundamental Freedoms

According to the Preamble to the Charter of Fundamental Rights of the European Union, the concerned act reaffirms, with due regard for the powers and tasks of the Union and for the principle of subsidiarity, the rights as they result, in particular, from the constitutional traditions and international obligations common to the Member States, the European Convention for the Protection of Human Rights and Fundamental Freedoms, the Social Charters adopted by the Union and by the Council of Europe and the case-law of the Court of Justice of the European Union and of the European Court of Human Rights. Therefore, it is clearly stated that the purpose of adopting the CFR was not to create new rights, but to acknowledge those which were previously derived from various sources.[273]

The most important of these sources appears to be the ECHR interpreted in the light of the case-law of the European Court of Human Rights, which played a major role in the process of formulating the catalogue of fundamental rights.[274]

The impact of the Convention on the shape of the Charter was both direct and indirect. The latter manifested itself in Article 6 (3) of TEU, which states that fundamental rights, as guaranteed by the European Convention for the Protection of Human Rights and Fundamental Freedoms and as they result from the constitutional traditions common to the Member States, shall constitute

---

272 A. Jackiewicz, *Problematyka praw człowieka w świetle Karty Praw Podstawowych w aspekcie integracji Polski z Unią Europejską,* Studia Europejskie 2 (2003), p. 54–55.

273 A. Facchi, N. Riva, European Values in the Charter of Fundamental Rights: An Introduction, *Ratio Juris* 34, no. 1 (March 2021), p. 3.

274 A. Wróbel, Wprowadzenie, in: A. Wróbel (ed.), *Karta Praw Podstawowych Unii Europejskiej. Komentarz,* Warszawa: C. H. Beck 2020, 6; E. H. Morawska, Prawa konstytucyjne człowieka i obywatela w Rzeczypospolitej Polskiej a prawa podstawowe Unii Europejskiej. Analiza porównawcza, *Przegląd Sejmowy,* no. 1 (2009): 47; S. Brittain, The Relationship Between the EU Charter of Fundamental Rights and the European Convention on Human Rights: an Originalist Analysis, *European Constitutional Law Review* 11, no. 3 (December 2015), 495, 500; see also opinion of the Court in Case 2/94, Adhésion de la Communauté à la CEDH, 28 March 1996, p. 33.

general principles of the Union's law. More importantly however, many of the rights and freedoms guaranteed by the Convention have been directly incorporated into the Charter.[275]

The above resulted in the need to regulate the relationship between those two acts. The purpose of the regulation was firstly to ensure the necessary consistency between the afforded rights, and secondly to safeguard the autonomy of EU law and the Court of Justice of the European Union.[276] The relevant provisions were placed in title VII concerning the interpretation and application of the Charter, namely in Article 52 (3) and Article 53.

Article 52(3) states that in so far as the Charter contains rights which correspond to rights guaranteed by the Convention for the Protection of Human Rights and Fundamental Freedoms, the meaning and scope of those rights shall be the same as those laid down by the Convention. Moreover, it contains a caveat that the provision shall not prevent Union law providing more extensive protection.

On the grounds of the considered regulation, we can distinguish the so-called convention rights (in parallel with the treaty and constitutional rights referred to in paragraphs 2 and 4 of Article 52, respectively)[277], which include the rights that correspond to those guaranteed by the ECHR. According to the explanation on Article 52[278] the meaning and the scope of those rights are determined not only by the texts of the Charter and the Convention (as well as its Protocols), but also by the case-law of the European Court of Human Rights and the Court of Justice of the European Union.[279] In view of the above, it may be stated that the regulation in question is in fact an interpretive rule of sorts.[280] Moreover, the reference is of a dynamic nature due to the obligation to take into account the case-law of the ECHR.[281]

However, the most significant conclusion from the interpretation of Article 52 (3) is that the ECHR serves as a determinant of the minimum level of protection

275 A. Wróbel, Wprowadzenie… 6; A. Wróbel, Art. 52, in *Karta Praw…*, p. 1305.

276 See Case C-601/15 PPU, N., 15 February 2016, p. 47, and Case C-18/16, K., 14 September 2017, p. 50 and the case-law cited therein.

277 E. H. Morawska, Prawa konstytucyjne…, p. 45.

278 Explanations relating to the Charter of Fundamental Rights, OJ C 303, 14.12.2007, pp. 17–35.

279 See Case C-467/18, EP, 19 September 2019, p. 42.

280 A. Wróbel, Art. 52, in *Karta Praw…*,, p. 1309.

281 Opinion of Advocate General Trstenjak in Case C-411/10, N.S. v. Secretary of State for the Home Department, 22 September 2011, p. 145.

of those fundamental rights that have their equivalents in the Convention. This follows directly from the wording of the last sentence of the article in question. The stipulation is an expression of the autonomy of EU law, which manifests itself in the potential to provide more extensive protection than the one afforded by the ECHR. Indeed, this possibility has been exercised by the EU legislator as reflected in the explanation to Article 52, which provide a list of "Articles where the meaning is the same as the corresponding Articles of the ECHR, but where the scope is wider".

Also relevant in this regard is Article 53 of the CFR, which states that nothing in this Charter shall be interpreted as restricting or adversely affecting human rights and fundamental freedoms as recognised, in their respective fields of application, by Union law and international law and by international agreements to which the Union or all the Member States are party, including the European Convention for the Protection of Human Rights and Fundamental Freedoms, and by the Member States' constitutions. According to the official explanation, this provision is intended to maintain the level of protection currently afforded within their respective scope by Union law, national law and international law, within which, owing to its importance, mention is made of the ECHR.

Article 53 of the Charter corresponds to Article 53 of the Convention.[282] However, there is a substantial difference in the meaning of those two provisions. Namely, it has been rightly observed based on the case-law of the CJEU that although the ECHR allows states parties to apply more favorable national solutions, the CFR can require countries that are members of the European Union to renounce these more favorable solutions in the interest of effectiveness and consistency of EU law.[283]

In the Melloni case[284], the Court of Justice of the European Union found on the basis of Article 53 of the Charter that, where an EU legal act calls for national implementing measures, national authorities and courts remain free to

282 M. Taborowski, Znaczenie art. 53 Karty Praw Podstawowych Unii Europejskiej dla poziomu ochrony praw podstawowych w krajowym prawie konstytucyjnym, *Państwo i Prawo*, no 1 (2016), p. 43.

283 M. Taborowski, Poziom ochrony praw podstawowych wynikający z Karty Praw Podstawowych UE jako przeszkoda dla przystąpienia Unii Europejskiej do Europejskiej Konwencji Praw Człowieka, *Europejski Przegląd Sądowy*, no. 12 (2015), p. 31; see also M. Visser, "National Constitutional Courts, the Court of Justice and the Protection of Fundamental Rights in a Post-Charter Landscape," *Human Rights Review* 15, no. 1 (March 2014), pp. 46–47.

284 Case C-399/11, Stefano Melloni v. Ministerio Fiscal, 26 February 2013, p. 60.

apply national standards of protection of fundamental rights, provided that the level of protection provided for by the Charter, as interpreted by the Court, and the primacy, unity and effectiveness of EU law are not thereby compromised. In the above circumstances, it is the competence of the CJEU to assess whether a national standard of fundamental rights does not undermine the principles of mutual trust and recognition. Nevertheless, it should be recalled that this applies only to situations in which EU law will apply at all.[285]

4. Effective legal remedies in the Charter of Fundamental Rights and Jurisprudence of CJEU

4.1. The concept of effective legal remedies

The underlying issue that requires resolution at this point is whether on the grounds of the CFR it is at all permissible to speak of the concept of effective legal remedies. Although such a term appears in the literal wording of the Charter, it is inextricably intertwined with the principle of effective judicial protection[286], which is reflected in the right to a fair trial. An effective remedy according to the CFR is therefore first and foremost access to a tribunal in a properly constituted procedure whenever there is an alleged violation of rights and freedoms guaranteed by the law of the Union. This concept is constructed as a procedural mechanism by which it is ensured that the protection granted by EU law is not just an empty statement, but it can be enforced by eligible subjects before the national authorities.[287] This is achieved primarily by guaranteeing judicial review of the acts of the executive. Hence, the provision in question does not confer a right of appeal against a decision issued by a tribunal. The court proceedings required under Article 47 of the CFR may be single instance.[288]

285 M. Taborowski, Znaczenie art. 53...,"p. 43.

286 Case C-93/12, ET Agrokonsulting-04-Wełko Stojanow v. Izpylnitelen direktor na dyrżawen fond "Zemedelie" – Razplasztatelna agencija, 27 June 2013, p. 59.

287 L. Cariolou under the supervision of A. Demetriades, "Article 47 – Right to an Effective Remedy and to a Fair Trial," in: *Commentary of the Charter of Fundamental Rights of the European Union*, EU Network of Independent Experts on Fundamental Rights 2006, 360, https://sites.uclouvain.be/cridho/documents/Download.Rep/NetworkCommentaryFinal.pdf.

288 Case C-180/17, X, Y v. Staatssecretaris van Veiligheid en Justitie, 26 September 2018, p. 30.

The access to an effective remedy is an individual's right composed of a bundle of rights and respective obligations of the Member States.[289] Although the principle of effective judicial protection comprises various elements, in particular, the rights of the defence, the principle of equality of arms, the right of access to a tribunal and the right to be advised, defended and represented,[290] it is sufficient in itself and does not need to be made more specific by further provisions of EU or national law.[291]

Considering the above, the notion under consideration on the grounds of the CFR seems to be first a consequence of an attempt to compress two different ECHR provisions into one, with the result that the right to an effective legal remedy is absorbed by the right to a fair trial. This is since Article 6 (1) of the Convention is generally considered to constitute a *lex specialis* in relation to Article 13 of the ECHR.[292] Thus, by implementing the standards of fair trial into the right to an effective remedy, on the grounds of the Charter the latter has been reduced to a kind of supplement and possibly reinforcement of the former. The purpose of this supplement is primarily to provide effectiveness of the Union acts as required by the general principles of the EU law.[293] Furthermore, on the grounds of the Charter there is virtually no distinction between the procedural remedies in the sense of individual rights of access to a court and the substantive remedies available where the claim is successful.[294] Article 47 approaches those two concepts together and requires a measure that is both fair in procedure as well as effective in awarding redress. However, the features of the necessary measure will be addressed in the later sections of the chapter.

---

289 See Case C-682/15, Berlioz Investment Fund SA v. Directeur de l'administration des contributions directes, 16 May 2017, p. 44.

290 Case C-199/11, Europese Gemeenschap v. Otis and ot., 6 November 2012, p. 48.

291 Case C-414/16, Egenberger v. Evangelisches Werk für Diakonie und Entwicklung eV, 17 April 2018, p. 78.

292 ECtHR judgment of 26.10.2000, 30210/96, Kudła v. Poland, HUDOC, p. 146.

293 See Case C-213/89, The Queen v. Secretary of State for Transport, ex parte Factortame and ot. (Factortame I), 19 June 1990, pp. 19–22.

294 P. Aalto, H. CH Hofmann, L. Holopainen, E. Paunio, L. Pech, D. Sayers, D. Shelton, A. Ward, Article 47 – Right to an Effective Remedy and to a Fair Trial, in: S. Peers, T. Hervey, J. Kenner, A. Ward (eds.), *The EU Charter of Fundamental Rights. A Commentary*, Oxford and Portland, Oregon: Hart Publishing, 2014, p. 1217.

4.2. The nature of the corrective measure – preventive, compensatory

The remedy provided for in Article 47 of the Charter is universal[295]. Under the Charter, the remedy has a dual meaning. The literature distinguishes between both preventive and compensatory character[296]. The wording of Article 47 of the Charter indicates that any violation of a right or freedom guaranteed by Union law entitles a person to seek a remedy before a court under the conditions laid down in the above-mentioned Article. Article 47 of the Charter has an instrumental role in relation to other rights guaranteed by the Union's legal order[297]. It is accepted in the doctrine that, in addition to the explicitly stated guarantees, broader safeguards and guarantees can be implicitly drawn from this provision[298].

The wording of the provision in this way implies a dual function. On the one hand, it has a deterrent function. In the event of a breach of Union law, a remedy will be necessary. This can take different forms, which will be indicated later in the chapter. Thus, the offending person or body will be obliged to remedy its behaviour. In view of the above, Article 47 prevents infringements. The preventive nature of the remedy, in addition to its deterrent function, also prevents erroneous decisions from acquiring legal force or finality. This construction is directly linked to the remedy. Where an infringement has arisen because of an authority's decision, the lodging of a remedy may prevent the infringement from materializing and producing negative consequences for the individual[299]. The preventive character should also be seen in the control of the newly created law. The Charter sets the framework for law-making and provides interpretative direction for fundamental rights. Thus, its respect allows for the prevention of possible violations[300]. The preventive nature of the remedy

---

295 Judgment of the Court, 29 July 2019, C-556/17, Alekszij Torubarov v. Bevándorlási és Menekültügyi Hivatal, p. 56.

296 D. Shelton, Remedies in International Human Right Law, 1999, pp. 255–388.

297 H Hoffmann, 'Article 47' in S Peers, T Hervey, J Kenner and A Ward (eds.), *The EU Charter of Fundamental Rights, A Commentary,* Oxford Hart Publishing 2014, 1211. See for example, case C-682/15 Berlioz Investment Fund, p. 49.

298 A. Kalintriri, Article 47 of the EU Charter of Fundamental Rights in EU Competition Enforcement: A Quantitative and Qualitative Assessment, https://realaw.blog/2023/01/17/article-47-of-the-eu-charter-of-fundamental-rights-in-eu-competition-enforcement-a-quantitative-and-qualitative-assessment-by-andriani-kalintiri/

299 Judgement of the European Court of the Human Right, 26 November 2000, no. 30210/96, Kudła vs. Poland, p. 158.

300 See judgment of the Court, 15 May 1986, C-222/84, Johnston v. Chief Constable of the Royal Ulster Constabulary.

also manifests itself through the possibility of amending existing legislation. The body of doctrine, literature, the activities of non-governmental organizations, all reports, and case law shape the need to amend the law. Noticing a legal loophole, incorrect implementation, or interpretation of the law can lead to violations of Article 47 of the Charter. Thus, it is crucial to prevent violations through correct amendments.

On the other hand, Article 47 of the Charter has a compensatory function. If a violation is found, the victim can ex post to an effective remedy. This entitlement includes the right to a fair and public hearing. This fairness of the remedy is to be ensured by the consideration of the case by an independent and impartial court. The importance of the remedy in the EU legal order is further set out in Article 47 of the Charter. Everyone has a right to a remedy. Asset status must not preclude an effective remedy. In the case of lower financial status, the victim may benefit from legal aid. The content of Article 47 of the Charter fulfils the ideas underlying its creation, namely humanity, justice, and security[301]. At the same time, the wording of Article 47 of the Charter allows for the effective protection of the rights guaranteed by the Charter[302]. Consequently, the remedy under the Charter can be described as effective judicial protection[303]. Article 47 of the Charter requires a Member State to provide a remedy before a court to set aside or amend an unlawful decision[304]. Article 47 of the Charter requires a Member State to provide a remedy before a court to set aside or amend an unlawful decision[305]. According to the case law, "Under Article 47 of the Charter, entitled 'The right to an effective remedy and to a fair trial', everyone whose rights and freedoms guaranteed by the law of the Union have been violated has the right to an effective remedy before a court." The obligation imposed on Member States by Article 19(1)(2) TEU to provide sufficient remedies to ensure effective legal protection in areas covered by Union law corresponds to this right.[306].

---

301 D. Kornobis-Romanowska, Poszanowanie …, p. 458.

302 D. Shelton, Remedies…, pp. 255–388.

303 A. Wróbel (red.), *Karta Praw Podstawowych Unii Europejskiej*, Komentarz, Warsaw 2020, p. 44.

304 T. Bubalović, Pravo na pravni lijek protiv odluka tijela državne vlasti prema domaćem i međunarodnom pravu, Proceedings of the University of Libertas, Zagreb, vol. 3, 2018, p. 270.

305 T. Bubalović, Pravo na pravni lijek protiv odluka tijela državne vlasti prema domaćem i međunarodnom pravu, Proceedings of the University of Libertas, Zagreb, vol. 3, 2018, p. 270;

306 Judgment of the Court, 16 May 2017, C-682/15, Berlioz Investment Fund, p. 44.

The courts, as independent and impartial bodies, are obliged to guarantee the protection of the rights of individuals under Union law and to ensure their effective realization, when a breach is committed by a state authority. According to the jurisprudence, courts can only provide effective protection if they are non-existent. Article 47 of the Charter provides these guarantees[307]. The standard of judicial independence ensured by Article 47 is "indispensable to the proper functioning of the system of judicial cooperation embodied in the preliminary ruling mechanism of Article 267 TFEU". "Article 267 TFEU, which is the cornerstone of the autonomy of the EU legal order, as an expression of mutual trust and a guarantee of the specific nature of the law established by the Treaties"[308]. Shifting the burden of compensation for damage to the courts allows for the real protection of the rights of individuals. The principle of equivalence of the Charter's provisions allows for their uniform or similar interpretation by the Member States[309].

The doctrine points out that a remedy is a response to an unlawful decision. Thus, the compensatory nature of the remedy manifests itself through the elimination of any irregularity or the revocation of the disputed decision. An analysis of the case law of the CJEU makes it possible to conclude that the remedy is most often applied to decisions of public authorities. In view of the above, the content of Article 47 of the Charter is highly relevant. In the face of violations by public authorities, the victim has fewer opportunities to defend his or her rights. Ensuring that the protection of rights is provided for in the whole system of Union law and not only in the provisions of the Charter guarantees its effective existence[310].

The compensatory nature of the remedy is also expressed through the elements that stand out in the text of Article 47 of the Charter. In addition to the remedy, the right to effective judicial protection includes the right to a fair trial and the right to a court of law with appropriate constitutional attributes[311]. This means that a particularisation of the right to a remedy is the right to a fair

---

307 Judgment of the Court, 27 February 2019, C-64/16, *Associação Sindical dos Juízes Portugueses*, pp. 40–41.

308 Judgment of the Court, 6 March 2018, C-284/16, Achmea BV, p. 58.

309 Opinion 1/17 od the Court, 30 April 2019, p. 128.

310 T. Bubalović, Pravo na pravni lijek protiv odluka tijela državne vlasti prema domaćem i međunarodnom pravu, Proceedings of the University of Libertas, Zagreb, vol. 3, 2018, pp. 267–270.

311 M. Krajewski, Akt ustawodawczy o charakterze generalnym a prawo do skutecznej ochrony sądowej, *EPS* , no. 6, (2015), pp. 4–13.

hearing[312]. The right to a remedy thus consists of several further elements. The jurisprudence points to the right of defense, the principle of equality of arms, the right of access to a court, and the right to obtain legal advice, counsel, and representation[313]. The accumulation of the indicated elements allows for the restoration of the previous situation, or the compensation of the justice violated. This definition of the remedy affects its effectiveness. It should be noted that the compensation of violations does not refer to abstract situations, but to individual cases of violations of the rights of a specific individual. Thus, it is crucial to refer to the above-mentioned elements.

The remedy under Article 47 of the Charter is universal in nature. It is accepted in the literature that this right is directly effective[314]. The right to a remedy is regarded as a "meta right" that guarantees the effective protection of other rights[315]. According to Opinion 1/15 of the Court, "The judgment on the compatibility of an agreement with the Treaties may, in this respect, depend, inter alia, not only on provisions concerning the competence, procedure or organisation of the institutions of the European Union, but also on provisions of substantive law. The same applies to the question of the compatibility of the envisaged international agreement with the guarantees contained in the Charter, since the Charter has the same legal status as the Treaties."[316].

It is also worth noting that the application of Article 47 of the Charter is not autonomous. It merely regulates the realisation of judicial protection by ensuring effective implementation of the law. Therefore, it cannot be transferred to the external field[317].

The broad application of Article 47 of the Charter requires that the remedy be tailored to the violation in question. Compensation may be conceived differently

312 M. Górski, Prawo do skutecznego środka prawnego w art. 47 Karty Praw Podstawowych UE – znaczenie i deficyty, *EPS*, no. 8, (2016), pp. 37–44.

313 Judgment of the Court, 26 July 2017, C-348/16, Moussa Sacko vs. Commissione Territoriale per il riconscimento della protezione internazionale di Milano, p. 32.

314 Judgment of the Court, 29 July 2019, C-556/17, Alekszij Torubarov vs. Bevándorlási és Menekültügyi Hivatal, p. 56.

315 K. Gutman, The Essence of the Fundamental Right to an Effective Remedy and to Fair Trial in the Case-Law of the Court of Justice of the European Union: The Best is Yet to Come?*German Law Journal* 29, (2019), 887; M. Górski, Prawo ..., pp. 37–44.

316 Opinion 1/15 of the Court, p. 70.

317 E. Neframi, Article 47 of the Charter in the opinion procedure: some reflections following opinion 1/17, M. Andenas (ed.), Opinion 1/17: Between European and International Perspectives, p. 749.

depending on the nature and form of the violation. The literature indicates that the remedy may be damaged, an order to comply with an obligation, a court order, an obligation to repay, or an order for suspensive measures[318]. However, it should be noted that compensation in addition to damages, injunctive relief, or the imposition of a remedy may also imply a pro-EU interpretation of the rules, disregarding national norms that are incompatible with EU law. The case law points to the competence of the national legislators to introduce new remedies into the legal order of the Member States in accordance with the minimum new remedies' formula[319]. It is incumbent on Member States to create a catalogue of remedies that effectively prevent the violation of rights under Union law[320].

About the remedy of compensation, the imposition of upper limits on the amount would render that remedy ineffective. The infringement would then not be fully compensated[321]. The above underlines the importance of the effectiveness of the Article 47 Charter remedy. On the other hand, the specific function of the measure should be highlighted. Article 47 of the Charter has a limited scope of application. This provision does not constitute a basis for EU legislative intervention. It only provides interpretative guidance to the Union authorities and Member States to ensure correct legislation and implementation of the remedy[322]. However, despite the great importance of Article 47 of the Charter, EU secondary law and the law of the Member States are created based on specific provisions of substantive law, not Article 47 of the Charter. This provision is merely a determinant of law-making[323].

The right to an effective remedy is only assessed secondarily during the implementation of judicial protection. The existence of remedies indicates that a Member State weighs the standards of judicial protection in an appropriate manner. "Article 47 of the Charter acts as a lens through which secondary law is interpreted, balancing it with national procedural rules"[324].

---

318 D. Shelton, Remedies…, pp. 255–388.

319 Judgment of the Court, 3 September 2008, C-402/05 P and C-415/05 P, p. 304.

320 Judgment of the Court, 4 July 2006, C-212/04, Konstantinos Adeneler i in. przeciwko Ellinikos Organismos Galaktos, p. 90.

321 Agencja Praw Podstawowych Unii Europejskiej i Rada Europy, 2016; https://fra.europa.eu/sites/default/files/fra_uploads/fra-ecthr-2016-handbook-on-access-to-justice_pl.pdf.

322 Opinion 1/17 of the Court, p. 129.

323 O. Dubos, The Origins of the Proceduralisation of EU Law: A Grey Area of European Federalism *Review of European Administrative Law* 18 (2015).

324 Judgment of the Court, 7 August 2018, C-300/17, Hochtief AG v. Budapest Főváros Önkormányzata, p. 58; see a case C-619/18, Commission v. Poland.

4.3. Features of the measure

The measure guaranteed in Article 47 of the CFR is to be "effective", however the notion of effectiveness requires further clarification as it does not mean that an appeal must lead in each case to the annulment of the challenged decision. According to the case-law of the CJEU it is enough for the competent authority to have the power to consider all the questions of fact and law that are relevant to the case before it.[325]

To ensure effectiveness of the rights which individuals derive from the direct effect of the Union law it is also necessary for the procedural rules governing such actions before national courts to not be less favorable than those governing similar domestic actions (the principle of equivalence) nor render virtually impossible or excessively difficult the exercise of rights conferred by the law of the EU (the principle of effectiveness).[326] These are the fundamental conditions derived from the principle of sincere cooperation laid down in Article 4(3) of the Treaty on European Union.[327] Measures taken by the Member States must be sufficiently effective to achieve the aim of the legal instruments adopted by the EU institutions and to ensure that the rights conferred upon individuals may be effectively pursued before the courts.[328] The Union law has developed a specific mechanism safeguarding the effectiveness of rights granted in it, which is the obligation of national tribunals to do all that is necessary to set aside national provisions which might prevent the Union law from taking full effect.[329] The Court has also formulated the requirement of the Member States to ensure direct and immediate protection of the interests of those persons who may be

325 Case C-199/11, p. 49.

326 Case C-326/96, Levez v. T. H. Jennings (Harlow Pools) Ltd, 1 December 1998, p. 18 and Case C-120/97, Upjohn Ltd v. The Licensing Authority established by the Medicines Act 1968 and ot., 21 January 1999, p. 32; for more about the relationship between the principle of effectiveness and the principle of effective judicial protection see S. Prechal, R. Widdershoven, Redefining the Relationship between 'Rewe-effectiveness' and Effective Judicial Protection, *Review of European Administrative Law* 4, no. 2 (2011), pp. 38–49.

327 See Case 33/76, Rewe-Zentralfinanz eG and Rewe-Zentral AG v. Landwirtschaftskammer für das Saarland, 16 December 1996, p. 5 and Case C-312/93, Peterbroeck, Van Campenhout & Cie SCS v. Belgian State, 14 December 1995, p. 12.

328 Case 222/84, Johnston v. Chief Constable of the Royal Ulster Constabulary, 15 May 1986, p. 17.

329 P. Aalto *et al.*, Article 47… p. 1212.

affected by any possible infringement of their rights.[330] Conditions and time-limits adopted in national legal systems cannot make it impossible in practice to exercise the rights which the national courts are obliged to protect.[331]

When it comes to the nature of the required substantive protection, as noted in the previous subsection of this chapter, the optimal situation would be for a measure to prevent a violation before it occurs. In this regard, measures granting interim relief are particularly important.[332] The first objective is to avoid and mitigate loss.[333] An action for damages is therefore a remedy of last resort.[334] When it comes to compensatory measures, their effectiveness is also manifested in the amount of awarded redress. The reparation must be commensurate with the loss or damage sustained.[335] Furthermore, the Court does not accept total exclusion of loss of profit as a head of damage for which reparation may be awarded.[336] Redress should be proportional to the gravity of the violations and damages suffered in such a way to allow, whenever possible, restoration of the situation of the victim, which occurred before the infringement.[337] However, even if it is impossible to reverse the effects of the violation, national authorities are obliged to undertake measures, which will prevent similar breaches in the future.[338] That includes a scrupulous investigation into the causes of the infringement as well as ensuring an effective, proportionate and dissuasive penalty for breaches of the EU law.[339]

For an individual to be able to secure the protection of their rights or to file a claim for damages, they must be granted access to a competent tribunal. The access must be factual, not just potential, meaning that the national law should prevent any reprisal measures which could act as deterrents for victims of the

330 Case 13/68, Société par actions Salgoil v. Ministero del commercio con l'estero della Repubblica italiana, 19 December 1968, pp. 462–463.
331 Case 33/76, p. 5.
332 Case C-213/89, p. 21.
333 P. Aalto *et al.*, Article 47…, p. 1235; see opinion of Advocate General Geelhoed in Case C-491/01, The Queen v. Secretary of State for Health, ex parte British American Tobacco (Investments) Ltd and Imperial Tobacco Ltd., 10 September 2002, p. 57.
334 P. Aalto *et al.*, Article 47…, p. 1235.
335 Case C-46/93 and C-48/93, Brasserie du Pêcheur SA v. Federal Republic of Germany and ot., 5 March 1996, p. 82.
336 Case C-46/93 and C-48/93, p. 87.
337 P. Aalto *et al.*, Article 47…, p. 1201.
338 P. Aalto *et al.*, Article 47…, p. 1201.
339 Case C-186/98, Maria Amélia Nunes and Evangelina de Matos, 8 July 1999, p. 10.

infringement, making it virtually impossible to exercise their right to effective judicial protection.[340]

However, on the grounds of the Charter, not only the required substantive remedy has to be effective, but it must also meet further conditions laid down in paragraphs 2 and 3 of Article 47. It follows from these provisions that the procedure for recognizing the measure itself must be structured in such a way as to fulfill the standards of fair trial.[341] These standards are not exhaustively listed in the provision, and thus the concept of a fair process needs to be (and has been) specified in case-law.[342]

First and foremost, the remedy must be heard before a tribunal within the meaning developed in the Court's case-law for the purposes of Article 267 TFEU.[343] The CJEU has formulated a set of criteria for determining whether a body should be considered a national court or tribunal, which include examining whether the body is established by law, whether it is permanent, whether its jurisdiction is compulsory, whether its procedure is *inter partes*, whether it applies rules of law and whether it is independent.[344]

Another necessary component of a fair trial identified by the CJEU (with an undoubted reference to the jurisprudence of the ECtHR) is the principle of equality of arms.[345] This principle entails affording the parties equal (comparable) procedural rights, particularly regarding the ability to present their own arguments and evidence. Such requirement is also linked to the principle of the adversarial nature of the proceedings, which implies that the parties to a case must have the right to examine all the documents or observations submitted to the court for the purpose of influencing its decision, and to comment on them.[346]

---

340 Case C-243/09, Günter Fuß v. Stadt Halle, 14 October 2010, p. 66.

341 See Case C-185/95 P, Baustahlgewebe v. Commission of the European Communities, 17 December 1998, p. 21.

342 D. Zahirović, Is There Something New in the European Union? – Right to a Fair Trial According to the Charter of Fundamental Rights of the European Union, *Anali Pravnog Fakulteta Univerziteta u Zenici* 11, no. 22 (2018), 106.

343 P. Aalto *et al.*, Article 47…, p. 1214, 1251.

344 Case C-54/96, Dorsch Consult Ingenieurgesellschaft mbH v. Bundesbaugesellschaft Berlin mbH., 17 September 1997, p. 23 and the case-law cited therein.

345 Case C-199/11, p. 71 and Case C-169/14, Juan Carlos Sánchez Morcillo i María del Carmen Abril García v. Banco Bilbao Vizcaya Argentaria SA, 17 July 2014, pp. 48–49.

346 Case C-300/11, ZZ v. Secretary of State for the Home Department, 4 June 2013, p. 55; see also Case 17/74, Transocean Marine Paint Association v. Commission, 23 October 1974, p. 15 and Case C-277/11, M. M. v. Minister for Justice, Equality and Law Reform, Ireland, Attorney General, 22 November 2012, pp. 85–88.

The Court has further pointed out that, in order to satisfy the requirements associated with the right to a fair hearing, it is important for the parties to be apprised of, and to be able to debate and be heard on, the matters of fact and of law which will determine the outcome of the proceedings.[347]

Fair trial presupposes transparency of the rationale behind a particular decision.[348] This applies both to administrative proceedings prior to the potential court action, as well as to the court process itself. In both cases, effective protection of an individual's rights requires that the person be informed of the reasons for such a decision.[349]

It has already been noted that effective judicial protection implies an exhaustive examination of the relevant legal and factual circumstances of the case. It is no less permissible to leave it up to the parties to decide the limits of the review by determining the scope of the challenge. In doing so, the court must consider those issues that are relevant in terms of the dispute to be resolved. However, it cannot be required to examine all elements, even those that are irrelevant to the merits of the case under investigation.[350]

Judicial review should also be ensured where Member States are granted a margin of discretion. Indeed, it should be examined whether the limits of this discretion have been exceeded in each case.[351] State discretion is never absolute, especially when it comes to individual rights and freedoms.

Lastly, a fair trial must lead to a ruling within a reasonable time.[352] The notion of "reasonableness" of the length of proceedings is being clarified in the jurisprudence of the CJEU.[353] It has been pointed out that it is impossible to define universal, abstract premises for evaluating different instances. The specific circumstances of a particular case, including its gravity and complexity, as well

347 Case C-472/11, Banif Plus Bank Zrt v. Csaba Csipai, Viktória Csipai, 21 February 2013, p. 30.

348 Case C-372/09 and C-373/09, Josep Peñarroja Fa, 17 March 2011, p. 63 and Case 222/86, Union nationale des entraineurs et cadres' techniques professionnels du football (UNECTEF) v. Georges Heylens, 15 October 1987, p. 15.

349 Case 222/86, p. 15.

350 Case C-122/16 P, British Airways plc v. European Commission, 14 November 2017, p. 105.

351 Case C-287/98, State of the Grand Duchy of Luxembourg v. Berthe Linster, Aloyse Linster and Yvonne Linster, 19 September 2000, p. 37.

352 Case C-185/95 P, p. 21.

353 Case C-403/04 P and C-405/04 P, Sumitomo Metal Industries Ltd and Nippon Steel Corp. v. Commission of the European Communities, 25 January 2007, pp. 116–117.

as the conduct of the parties and authorities, should always be considered.[354] All relevant criteria must be considered, but it is sufficient that one of them justifies the duration of the proceedings.

4.4. What values does it derive from?

The right to an effective legal remedy origins from the rule of law[355], which is one of the foundations of the EU according to Article 2 of the Treaty on European Union.[356]

The rule of law rests on the one hand upon the principle of liability of state and on the other upon the principle of judicial review.[357] As the Court reiterated on numerous occasions, the Treaty of Rome has created its own legal system, which is integrated into the legal systems of the Member States and which their courts are bound to apply. The subjects of that legal system are not only the Member States but also their nationals. Just as it imposes burdens on individuals, Union law is also intended to give rise to rights which become part of their legal patrimony. Those rights arise not only where they are expressly granted by the Treaty but also by virtue of obligations which the Treaty imposes in a clearly defined manner both on individuals and on the Member States and the EU

---

354 Case C-185/95 P, p. 29 and Case C-270/99 P, Z v. European Parliament, 27 November 2001, p. 24.

355 A definition of 'the rule of law' can be found in Article 2(a) of Regulation (EU, Euratom) 2020/2092 of the European Parliament and of the Council of 16 December 2020 on a general regime of conditionality for the protection of the Union budget, OJ L 433I, 22.12.2020, p. 1, which states: *For the purposes of this Regulation, the following definitions apply: 'the rule of law' refers to the Union value enshrined in Article 2 TEU. It includes the principles of legality implying a transparent, accountable, democratic and pluralistic law-making process; legal certainty; prohibition of arbitrariness of the executive powers; effective judicial protection, including access to justice, by independent and impartial courts, also as regards fundamental rights; separation of powers; and non-discrimination and equality before the law. The rule of law shall be understood having regard to the other Union values and principles enshrined in Article 2 TEU.*

356 Case 294/83, 'Les Verts' v. European Parliament, 23 April 1986, p. 23 and Case C-50/00 P, Unión de Pequeños Agricultores v. Council of the European Union, 25 July 2002, p. 38; see also M. Sunnqvist, X. Groussot, L. Maunsbach, Judges Assessing the Independence of Judges. Historical Foundations and Practical Procedures in Facing the Threats against the Rule of Law in Europe, *Journal of Constitutional History / Giornale di Storia Costituzionale*, no. 44 (2022 2nd Quarter), 13–14.

357 Case C-64/16, Associação Sindical dos Juízes Portugueses v. Tribunal de Contas, 27 February 2018, p. 36.

institutions.[358] It is primarily the duty of the national courts to protect the rights granted by the acts of the European Union.[359] Access to justice is an indispensable component of the rule of law.[360] This is why the principle of judicial review, stemming from the constitutional traditions common to the Member States and enshrined in Article 6 and 13 of the European Convention for the Protection of Human Rights, is one of the general principles of the EU law.[361] The same can be said about the right to fair legal process[362] which is reflected in the procedural aspect of the right guaranteed by Article 47 of the CFR. That said, the original source of the above general principles can be found in the objective of respecting human rights and fundamental freedoms.[363]

4.5. Procedural requirements of an effective legal remedy

As indicated above, the right to a remedy may be limited. The case law of the CJEU clearly indicates the criteria for limiting the right to a remedy[364]. However, the primary requirement that each Member State must guarantee is the right to a remedy.

> "It follows that any decision should be capable of being challenged in judicial proceedings enabling its legality to be reviewed in the light of Union law"[365]. On the other hand, the Union rules "do not provide for an obligation to introduce a two-stage judicial procedure. Indeed, all that matters is the existence of a remedy before a single court"[366].

Article 47 of the Charter is primarily intended to guarantee judicial review of acts of the executive. The proceedings may then be single instance. However,

---

358 Case C-6/90 and C-9/90, Francovich and Others v. Italian Republic, 19 November 1991, p. 31 and the case-law cited therein; see also Case C-224/01, Kobler v. Republik Osterreich, 30 September 2003, p. 30 and Case C-46/93 and C-48/93, p. 29.

359 Case C-106/77, Amministrazione delle Finanze dello Stato przeciwko Simmenthal SpA, 9 March 1978, p. 16.

360 A. Facchi, N. Riva, European Values...,p. 5.

361 Case C-506/04, Wilson v. Ordre des avocats du barreau de Luxembourg, 19 September 2006, p. 46 and Case 222/84, p. 18; for the evolution of the principle of effective judicial protection see S. Prechal, R. Widdershoven, Redefining...,p. 34–38.

362 Case C-185/95 P, p. 21.

363 Opinion of the Court in Case 2/94, p. 32.

364 See Judgment of the Court, 2 April 2009, C-394/07, Gambazzi, p. 29.

365 Judgment of the Court, 17 March 2011, C-372/09, C-373/09, Josep Peñarroja Fa., pp. 63.

366 Judgment of the Court, 26 September 2018, C-180/17, XY v. Staatssecretaris van Veiligheid en Justitie, pp. 30.

where effective judicial protection has not been ensured before a court of first instance, it is necessary for the case to be examined by an authority (court) with a greater scope of jurisdiction. It is then necessary to ensure that the proceedings are two-instance.

The aim of the proceedings is to remedy the conduct and to compensate for the damage caused. Thus, the remedial proceedings must be carried out in accordance with all standards. An effective remedy leads to effective judicial protection. This obligation is incumbent on national courts. The case law of the CJEU explicitly points out that "it is for the national courts in particular to ensure the legal protection guaranteed to private parties by the rules of Community law and to ensure that those rules are fully effective"[367]. The extract from the reasoning of the judgment set out above also formulates the meaning of an effective remedy. It is to ensure the full effectiveness of the provisions of Community law.

> In the absence of Union legislation in this field, it is for the domestic legal order of each Member State to designate the courts having jurisdiction and to lay down the rules of procedure in cases involving the protection of the rights of legal persons under Union law, the Member States nevertheless being responsible for ensuring, in each case, that those rights are effectively protected[368].

"In order for this judicial review to be effective, the person concerned must be able to know the reasons for the decision taken in his case, which will enable him to defend himself under the best possible conditions and to choose, in full knowledge of the facts, whether it is expedient for him to take legal action. It follows that the competent national authority is obliged to inform the person concerned of the reasons for its refusal, and this information may either be included in the decision itself or communicated to the person concerned later upon request"[369].

The above constitutes the basic features of the resolution procedure. The absence of a statement of reasons for the decision effectively leads to the impossibility of challenging the disputed decision. Even if technically an appeal is lodged its effectiveness will be negligible. In the absence of a statement of

---

367 Judgment of the Court, 15 April 2008, C-268/06, Impact v. Minister for Agriculture and Food a.o., pp. 42.

368 Judgment of the Court, 18 March 2010, C-317/08, C-318/08, C-319/08 and C-320/08, Rosalba Alassini v. Telecom Italia SpA, Filomena Califano v, Wind SpA, Lucia Anna Giorgia Iacono v Telecom Italia SpA, Multiservice Srl v Telecom Italia SpA, p. 47.

369 Judgment of the Court, 17 March 2011, C-372/09, C-373/09, Josep Peñarroja Fa., p. 63.

reasons for a decision or ruling, it is impossible to know what legal basis and what arguments the authority had in mind when ruling. It should also be pointed out that effective judicial protection is ensured even if "the review of legality by the Union judicature is limited by the forms of order sought by the parties in their pleadings, without that principle in any way requiring that court to extend its review to those elements of the decision which are not relevant to the dispute before it."[370]. In view of the above, it was left to the parties to decide the limits of the review to be exercised.

Effective judicial protection always implies an exhaustive examination of the relevant legal and factual circumstances of the case. Thus, the appellate authority must take all issues into account. It must examine the case within the limits of the appeal. However, a broader examination of the case is warranted during the remedy proceedings. "However, this discretion, which a Member State may exercise when transposing that provision into national law, does not preclude judicial review of the question whether it has been exceeded by the national authorities"[371]. On a positive note, regarding Article 47 of the Charter, the existence in the legislation of the Member States of absolute grounds of appeal, which the authority examines ex officio.

An important issue is the need for judicial protection in discretionary decisions. It is then legitimate to examine whether the limits of this discretion have been exceeded in a particular case. It should be noted that the freedom of a Member State is not and cannot be absolute. In particular, when individual rights and freedoms are at stake. The examination then consists of a proportionality test of the goods.

The object of the court's determination during the resolution procedure as well as its directive is to deal with the case within a reasonable time. The CJEU's case law indicates that this issue must be assessed based on the circumstances specific to each case. "The Court has specified in this context that the list of these criteria is not exhaustive and that the assessment of the question of the reasonableness of the time limit does not require a systematic analysis of the circumstances of the case in relation to each of them if the length of the proceedings appears to be justified by one of these criteria. Also, the complexity of the case may

---

370 Judgment of the Court, 14 November 2011, C-122/16, British Airways v. Commission, p. 105.

371 Judgment of the Court, 19 September 2000, C-287/19, Luxemburg v. Berthe Linster, Aloyse Linster i Yvonne Linster, p. 37.

be considered as justifying prima facie excessively long proceedings"[372]. It is impossible to create universal and abstract premises for the assessment of different cases.

Although the principle of equality of arms is not explicitly expressed, it is implicitly derived from Article 47 of the Charter. It is one of the fundamental elements of the right to a fair (due) trial.

> This principle is an integral part of the effective judicial protection of the rights which individuals derive from Union law, guaranteed by Article 47 of the Charter (…). Indeed, it follows from the Court's settled case-law that the principle of equality of arms, like, inter alia, the principle of the adversarial system, is a consequence of the very concept of a fair trial, which entails the obligation to afford each party a reasonable opportunity to present his case in conditions which do not place him in a clearly less favourable position in relation to the other party[373].

This principle implies equipping the parties with equal (comparable) procedural rights, regarding the possibility of presenting their own arguments and evidence. This requirement is also linked to the principle of the adversarial nature of the proceedings.

Restorative proceedings should meet the criteria of the adversarial principle, which is part of the right to defence, which is explicitly expressed in Article 47 of the Charter. The case law emphasises that "the parties to the proceedings should have the right to acquaint themselves with all documents or observations submitted to the court with a view to influencing its decision and to reply to them"[374].

The remedies provided for in Article 47 of the Charter must meet certain requirements, which the CJEU formulates.

> The Member States are thus bound – inter alia, in accordance with the principle of sincere cooperation expressed in the first subparagraph of Article 4(3) TEU – to ensure the application of and respect for Union law within their territory (…). On that basis, and in accordance with the provision of the second subparagraph of Article 19(1) TEU, Member States shall establish the measures necessary to ensure that individuals respect their right to effective judicial protection in the areas covered by Union law. Thus, it

372 Judgment of the Court, 25 January 2007, C-403/04 and C-405/04, Sumitomo Metal Industries Ltd i Nippon Steel Corp. v. Commission, pp. 116–117.

373 Judgment of the Court, 17 July 2014, C-169/14, Juan Carlos Sánchez Morcillo i María del Carmen Abril García v. Banco Bilbao Vizcaya Argentaria SA, pp. 48–49.

374 Judgment of the Court, 4 June 2013, C-300/11, ZZ v. Secretary of State for the Home Department, p. 58.

> is for the Member States to establish a system of measures and procedures to ensure effective judicial review in these areas[375].

The principle of procedural autonomy of the Member States gives them the freedom to designate courts and to provide appropriate procedures in which individuals can pursue claims based on EU law. The authority that deals with an appeal that seeks to implement a remedy must be characterised by independence and independence. The CJEU gives a broad interpretation of the above concept. However, the key is to ensure the implementation of the principle of effectiveness of the measure. "If a national court were to find such a breach of the principle of effectiveness, it is bound to interpret the national rules on competence as far as possible in such a way as to contribute to the attainment of the objective of guaranteeing effective judicial protection of the rights of the subjects of the law under Community law"[376].

Despite the freedom of choice of procedure and remedy, "Furthermore, although, as the Republic of Poland and Hungary point out, the organisation of the judiciary in the Member States falls within the competence of the latter, the Member States are still obliged, when exercising that competence, to comply with the obligations arising for them under Union law"[377]. The above constitutes a limitation of the principle of national procedural autonomy. It is the role of Member States to ensure the effectiveness of EU law, including the effective protection of fundamental rights. Failure to ensure effective protection of EU law would lead to a loss of the real impact of EU law about individuals. The above is supported by the case law of the CJEU:

> It follows from all the foregoing that the second subparagraph of Article 19(1) TEU imposes an obligation on all Member States to provide for the remedies necessary to ensure effective judicial protection, within the meaning in particular of Article 47 of the Charter of Fundamental Rights, in the areas covered by Union law[378].

To ensure effective judicial protection, it may be necessary to take provisional measures to secure the enforceability of a future judgment.

> It should also be added that the effectiveness of Community law would also be compromised if a rule of national law were to prevent a court hearing a dispute governed by Community law from ordering provisional measures in order to give full effect

375 Judgment of the Court, 27 February 2018, C-64/16, Associação Sindical dos Juízes Portugueses v. Tribunal de Contas, p. 34.

376 Judgment of the Court, 15 April 2008, C-268/06, Impact vs. Ireland, p. 54.

377 Judgment of the Court, 24 June 2019, C-619/18, Commission v. Poland, p. 52.

378 Judgment of the Court, 24 June 2019, C-619/18, Commission v. Poland, p. 54.

> to a future judicial decision on the existence of the Community law rights asserted. Therefore, a court which, in such circumstances, would order provisional measures if not prevented from doing so by a rule of national law is required not to apply that rule.[379].

Under Article 47 of the Charter an effective remedy is intended to provide effective protection. It is irrelevant at what stage it is provided. What is important is that a ruling on an individual's rights at a "certain stage of the proceedings" is subjected to such scrutiny as to enable the complainant to obtain a binding decision from an independent body that protects his or her rights[380].

The authority exercising the right to a remedy should be characterised by independence. This is literally confirmed by the second paragraph of Article 47 of the Charter which lists access to an "independent" tribunal among the requirements linked to the fundamental right to an effective remedy. This requirement of judicial independence, which is an integral part of the judiciary, falls within the essence of the right to effective judicial protection and the fundamental right to a fair trial, which is of fundamental importance as a guarantee for the protection of all rights which legal persons derive from Union law and for the preservation of the values common to the Member States as defined in Article 2 TEU, in particular the value of the rule of law[381].

Thus, the judicial authority must first and foremost meet the criterion of independence. Independence and impartiality are part of the essence of the right to an effective remedy, as the adjudication of a case by an entity subordinate to an authority will not effectively safeguard the rights of the individual against the actions of that authority. This, in turn, is a necessary condition of the rule of law. The jurisprudence emphasises that a body must carry out its "tasks fully autonomously, without subordination within the chain of command, without being subordinated to anyone, free from orders or directions from any source, thus remaining protected from outside interference and pressure which may compromise the independence of judgment of its members and influence their decisions"[382]. This constitutes an external aspect of the body's independence. This criterion is not met by public administrative bodies[383]. It is also important that

379 Judgment of the Court, 19 June 1990, C-213/89, The Queen v. Secretary State for Transport, p. 21.

380 Judgment of the Court, 13 December 2017, C-403/16, Soufiane El Hassani v. Ministry of Foreign Affairs, p. 41.

381 Judgment of the Court, 24 June 2019, C-619/18, Commission v. Poland, pp. 57–58.

382 Judgment of the Court, 24 June 2019, C-619/18, Commission v. Poland, pp. 72–74.

383 Judgment of the Court, 16 May 2017, C-682/15, Berlioz Investment Fund S.A. v. Directeur de l'administration des contributions directes, p. 55.

the body adjudicating in the resolution procedure is a third party to the body that issued the contested decision[384]. The re-examination of a case by the same entity does not therefore constitute an effective defence of rights under Article 47 of the Charter.

The internal aspect of the criterion, on the other hand, is impartiality. This refers to an equal distance from the parties to the dispute and their respective interests in relation to its subject matter.

> This aspect requires the observance of objectivity and the absence of any interest in the specific resolution of the dispute that would go beyond the strict application of a rule of law[385].

The above directly implies procedural rules. The guarantee of impartiality and independence requires the existence of a strict definition of the composition of the body, the appointment of its members, the duration of their term of office, the possibility of exclusion or dismissal. Obviously, the judicial body must be part of a state or supranational organisation[386]. As an aside, it should be noted that the mere possibility of arbitrary removal of judges by, for example, the executive would raise legitimate doubts about the independence of the courts from external influences.

The characteristics of a court are "the statutory legal basis of the body, its permanent nature, the compulsory nature of its jurisdiction, the adversarial nature of the proceedings, the application of the law by the body and its independence"[387]. The demand for a uniform interpretation of the concept of "court" entails the need to consider the criteria developed by CJEU case law in connection with Article 267 TFEU. A contrario, it can be pointed out that the right to effective judicial protection will not be guaranteed when cases are decided by ad hoc bodies set up by the executive, applying unspecified rules for issuing rulings, without the possibility for those concerned to participate in the proceedings. The body considering the right to a remedy "must be empowered

384 Judgment of the Court, 19 September 2006, C-506/04, Graham J. Wilson v. Ordre des avocats du barreau de Luxembourg, p. 49.

385 Judgment of the Court, 24 June 2019, C-619/18, Commission v. Poland, pp. 72–74.

386 Judgment of the Court, C-199/11, 6 November 2012, Europese Gemeenschap v. Otis NV, p. 64.

387 Judgment of the Court, 27 February 2018, C-64/16, Associação Sindical dos Juízes Portugueses v. Tribunal de Contas, p. 68.

to examine all questions of law and fact relevant to the dispute it is deciding"[388]. Only then is it possible to ensure an effective individual right.

The court considering the right to a remedy should be endowed with discretion. According to the case law, the court should have "the right to assess the evidence, to annul the contested decision and to change the amount of the fines."[389].

The above-mentioned criteria and principles clearly underline that the resolution procedure should be characterised by fairness and compliance with the Charter. Given the purpose of such proceedings, this is a necessary condition for them to be fulfilled.

4.6. Limits of the right to effective legal remedy

An effective remedy under Article 47 of the Charter should be compensatory and effective. The doctrine notes the wide range of choices of remedy. Several remedies can be distinguished, which are tailored to the realities of a particular case. Remedies can be divided into substantive as well as procedural[390]. The first category includes compensation, obligation to pay, restitution, or damages. Procedural remedies are the possibility of an appeal, injunction, or order for performance[391].

The CJEU jurisprudence emphasises that fundamental rights, such as respect for the rights of the defence, are not absolute rights but may be subject to restrictions. However, these must correspond to objectives of the general interest pursued by the measure in question and, in view of the purpose pursued, "must not constitute an obvious and disproportionate impairment of the rights guaranteed in this way"[392].

Limitations to the right to an effective remedy are formulated in Article 52(1) of the Charter. Restrictions on the exercise of the rights and freedoms set out in

---

388 Judgment of the Court, C-199/11, 6 November 2012, Europese Gemeenschap v. Otis NV, pp. 49.

389 Judgment of the Court, C-199/11, 6 November 2012, Europese Gemeenschap v. Otis NV, p. 63.

390 A. Wróbel (edit.), *Karta Praw Podstawowych Unii Europejskiej. Komentarz*, article 47, Legalis/online, p. 2.

391 D. Shelton, Remedies…, pp. 255–388; Agencja Praw Podstawowych Unii Europejskiej i Rada Europy, 2016 https://fra.europa.eu/sites/default/files/fra_uploads/fra-ecthr-2016-handbook-on-access-to-justice_pl.pdf.

392 Judgment of the Court, 2 April 2009, C-394, Gambazzi, pp. 29; see also C-317–320/08 Alassini, C-28/05, Dokter, C619/10 Trade Agecny.

the Charter are only possible if they are necessary and genuinely meet objectives of general interest of the EU or of protecting the rights and freedoms of others. At the same time, limitations must be indicated in the law and respect the essence of those rights and freedoms – subject to the principle of proportionality[393].

In view of the above, it should be considered that it is possible, for example, to introduce an obligation to exhaust the remedies provided for in the administrative procedure before bringing a case before a court, if this does not in fact foreclose access to justice and finds a reasonable justification[394].

Firstly, the possibility of limiting access to a remedy must be provided for by law. A limitation clause cannot be established by a state authority acting without legal support. Such a clause must be provided for by generally applicable law. According to CJEU case law, "In any event, the lack of remedy against a decision rejecting an application for aid, such as that at issue in the main proceedings, was provided for by the Seirekomitee and not by law."[395]. The Seirekomitee is a state administrative body. It should always be examined whether the restriction is supported by the law.

The limitation of the right to a remedy must not violate its essence. According to the case law, "the fundamental right to an effective legal remedy would be infringed if a judicial decision were founded on facts and documents which the parties themselves, or one of them, have not had an opportunity to examine and on which they have therefore been unable to state their views"[396].

> By invoking reasons of State security, the court with jurisdiction in the Member State concerned must have at its disposal and apply techniques and rules of procedural law which accommodate, on the one hand, legitimate State security considerations regarding the nature and sources of the information taken into account in the adoption of such a decision and, on the other hand, the need to ensure sufficient compliance with the person's procedural rights, such as the right to be heard and the adversarial principle[397].

---

393 Judgment of the Court, 27 September 2017, C-73/16, Peter Puškár przeciwko Finančné riaditeľstvo Slovenskej republiky, Kriminálny úrad finančnej správy, p. 62.

394 Judgment of the Court, 27 September 2017, C-73/16, Peter Puškár przeciwko Finančné riaditeľstvo Slovenskej republiky, Kriminálny úrad finančnej správy, p. 76.

395 Judgment of the Court, 17 September 2014, C-562/12, Eesti-Lati programii 2007–2013 Seirekomitee, p. 73.

396 Judgment of the Court, 2 December 2009, C-89/08, Commission v. Ireland and Others, pp. 52.

397 Judgment of the Court, 4 June 2013, C-300/11, ZZ v. Secretary for the Home Department, p. 57.

To limit the right to a remedy based on the State security clause, "the Member States are required, first, to provide for effective judicial review both of the existence and validity of the reasons invoked by the national authority with regard to State security and of the legality of the decision taken under Article 27 of Directive 2004/38 and, second, to prescribe techniques and rules"[398]. Thus, "the national court is required to conduct a fair and independent analysis of all the legal issues invoked by the competent national authority and to determine, in accordance with national procedural rules, whether State security precludes such disclosure"[399]. The limitation of the right to effective judicial protection, including a remedy, should be limited only to the extent that is strictly necessary. In the case discussed above, it should be noted that the proportionality of the restriction depends on ensuring that the adversarial principle is respected and that the evidence can be seen. According to the Court, only this allows for an effective defence against the restriction[400].

The CJEU case law is quite critical of restricting access to personal data, both in and out of court proceedings. "The CJEU considered that legislation not providing for any possibility for an individual to pursue legal remedies in order to have access to personal data relating to him, or to obtain the rectification or erasure of such data, did not respect the essence of the right to an effective remedy and to a fair trial, as enshrined in Article 47 of the Charter."[401].

By considering the principle of proportionality is meant an assessment of the consequences in terms of the possibility of obtaining legal protection and the time taken to do so. The criterion is also the appropriate shaping of issues related to the running of the limitation period as well as the costs to be borne by the applicant. The proportionality of a limitation of the right to a remedy will be exceeded if the judicial route of the infringed rights and freedoms is effectively closed[402]. The effective judicial protection guaranteed by Article 47 of the Charter is then impossible. It should be noted that it is only possible to

---

398 Judgment of the Court, 3 September 2008, C-402/05, Kadi and Al Barakaat International Foundation v. Council and Commission, p. 344.

399 Judgment of the Court, 4 June 2013, C-300/11, ZZ v. Secretary for the Home Department, p. 58.

400 Judgment of the Court, 4 June 2013, C-300/11, ZZ v. Secretary for the Home Department, p. 58.

401 Judgment of the Court, 6 October 2015, C-362/14, Schrems; Judgment of the Court, C-314/13, Pefitev, p. 95.

402 Judgment of the Court, 18 March 2010, C-320/08, Alassini and Others v. Telecom Italia SpA, pp. 61–65.

determine the limit of proportionality when analysing all the facts of a particular case. At the same time, the right under Article 47 of the Charter must always be "weighed against the right of others"[403]. The case law of the CJEU imposes an obligation on Member States to adequately transpose Union law and to interpret national law so that it does not conflict with the provisions of the Charter or other fundamental rights[404].

The case law indicates that the protection of the good administration of justice or the protection of public health may constitute limitations on the right to a remedy[405]. However, it should be noted that these limitations must not lead to an infringement of the essence of the right related to the remedy, such as the right of defence. The case law of the CJEU makes it clear that "in the case of judicial review or review by another body, which is a court or tribunal within the meaning of Article 234 EC, in such a way that the proceedings as a whole are compatible with the right to a court. For that purpose, the authority responsible for the review must necessarily have at its disposal the information required to reach a decision with full knowledge of the facts, including confidential information and business secrets."[406].

The rationale for limiting the right to a remedy is also the need to protect other rights and freedoms. It is incumbent on national courts to ensure a balance between conflicting rights and freedoms[407]. As with the principle of proportionality, the assessment is made on a case-by-case basis on the criteria of the individual case. According to the case-law of the CJEU, "In that connection, it is for the national court to ascertain whether the conditions for granting legal aid constitute a limitation on the right of access to the courts which undermines the very core of that right; whether they pursue a legitimate aim; and whether there is a reasonable relationship of proportionality between the means employed and the legitimate aim which it is sought to achieve."[408]. The absence

---

403 Judgment of the Court, 13 July 2006, C-438/04, Mobistar SA v. Institut belge des services postaux et des telecommunicationis, pp. 40.

404 Judgment of the Court, 29 January 2008, C-275/06, Productores de Música de Espana (Promusicae) v. Telefónica de Espana SAU, pp. 70.

405 Judgment of the Court, 2 April 2009, C-394/07, Marco Gambazzi vs. DaimlerChrysler Canada Inc. and CIBC Mellon Trust Company, pp. 30–32.

406 Judgment of the Court, 14 Februaru 2008, C-450/06, Varec SA v. Belgian State, pp. 23.

407 Judgment of the Court, 1 January 2010, C-407/08, Knauf Gips KG vs. European Commission, pp. 91.

408 Judgment of the Court, 22 December 2010, C-279/09, DEB v. Bundesrepublik Deutschalnd, pp. 47.

of a statutory basis for limiting the right to a remedy is a violation of Article 47 of the Charter[409]. It is possible to apply an abuse of rights clause to the right to an effective remedy before a court. However, the case law emphasises that such situations are exceptional and cannot lead to depriving an individual of access to judicial proceedings[410]. The assessment criteria that "the national court must take into account are the reasonable prospects of success, the importance of the case, the effectiveness of the case, the complexity of the matter and the procedure, the effects of the limitation"[411]. Limitation clauses must not deprive the possibility of a remedy such as legal aid[412].

It should be noted that specific elements of the right to a remedy, including the right to a fair trial, may be restricted. Such a limitation should be examined in each case in terms of desirability, adequacy and proportionality[413]. The limitation of the right to a remedy must not prejudice its essence and the essence of the rights guaranteed by it[414].

The limitation of the right to a remedy may also concern the resolution procedure. It is permissible, inter alia, to limit the evidence procedure when it does not render the claim ineffective and admits other means of evidence[415]. However, inadmissibility of a particular means of evidence proving a violation of a right or freedom may lead to a violation of Article 47 of the Charter. Such a limitation of the evidence procedure closes the individual's path to compensation for the violation[416]. About substantive measures, including damages or reparation, it should be noted that it is impossible to impose upper limits on the amount. To

---

409 Judgment of the Court, 9 June 1992, C-97/91, Oleificio Borelli v. Commission, pp. 13–14.

410 Judgment of the Court, 23 March 2000, C-373/97, Dionysios Diamantis v. Elliniko Dimosio i Organismos Oikonomikis Anasygkrotisis Epicheiriseon AE, pp. 44.

411 Judgment of the Court, 22 December 2010, C-279/09, DEB v. Bundesrepublik Deutschalnd, pp. 28.

412 Judgment of the Court, 12 June 2014, C-314/13, Peftiev v. Lithuania.

413 Judgment of the Court, C-348/16, M.G. and N.R. vs. Staatssecretaris vsn Veiligheid en Justitie, pp. 38.

414 Judgment of the Court, 26 July 2017, C-348/16, Moussa Sacko v. Commissione Territoriale per il riconscimento della Protezione internazionale di Milano, pp. 37.

415 Judgment of the Court, 3 February 2000, C-228/98, Charalampos Dounias vs. Ypourgio Oikonomikon, p. 68–72.

416 Judgment of the Court, 27 September 2017, Peter Puskar v. Finančné riaditeľstvo Slovenskej republiky and Kriminálny úrad finančnej správy, C-73/16, pp. 87.

do so would render these measures ineffective[417]. The literature indicates that limitations on the rights and freedoms provided for in the Charter and other acts of Union law should be taken either by a judicial authority or should be subject to judicial review when issued by another authority[418]. A limitation of a Charter right should not go beyond what is necessary and should be strictly limited in time.

5. Comparison of effective legal remedies in the European Convention of Human Rights and the Charter of Fundamental Rights

According to the Explanations relating to the CFR, the content of paragraph 1 of Article 47 of the Charter is based on Article 13 of the ECHR, while paragraph 2 corresponds to Article 6(1) of the ECHR. Whereas the content of paragraph 3 was shaped on the basis of ECtHR case-law.[419] The interpretation of Article 47 of the Charter by the Court of Justice of the European Union cannot, therefore, undermine the level of protection guaranteed by the relevant provisions of the ECHR, as understood in the case-law of the European Court of Human Rights.[420] However, the protection granted by the provision of EU primary law considered here goes beyond the above indicated Convention minimum. Such a conclusion follows from the very fact of associating the right to an effective remedy with the right to a court.[421] Indeed, Article 47 of the Charter explicitly provides that the cognizance of a remedy is a matter for the tribunal, and not merely for the "competent national authority." Courts meet more stringent requirements to ensure full protection of the rights of individuals, especially against violations by

---

417 Agencja Praw Podstawowych Unii Europejskiej i Rada Europy, 2016; https://fra.europa.eu/sites/default/files/fra_uploads/fra-ecthr-2016-handbook-on-access-to-justice_pl.pdf.

418 F. Gołba, Dyrektywa 2012/13/UE w sprawie prawa do informacji w postępowaniu karnym jako instrument europejskiej polityki kryminalnej, Kortowski Przegląd Prawniczy, 3, 2016.

419 N. Półtorak, "Art. 47," in *Karta Praw*, 1203; D. Zahirović, "Is There Something," 105. Under the ECHR, the right to legal aid is expressly provided only for criminal proceedings, while in the CFR it applies to all proceedings concerning violations of rights granted under EU law. Nevertheless, the ECtHR jurisprudence also imposes a requirement to provide effective legal representation in civil cases when its absence could lead to a violation of the right to a fair trial.

420 Case C-180/17, p. 31.

421 P. Aalto *et al.*, Article 47…, p.1197.

public authorities. The jurisprudence of the ECtHR and the CJEU has developed consistent guidelines for determining whether a body qualifies as a court or not. What is important is not the name, but the function it performs, the powers it has and the guarantees it provides.[422]

Moreover, the standard of protection provided in paragraph 2 of Article 47 is higher than that of Article 6(1), since the latter applies only to "civil and criminal cases"[423], whilst the right to a fair trial under Article 47 of the CFR is not limited to a specific type of proceeding or a certain type of court.[424] The only limitation refers to the type of violation, as it must concern rights and freedoms guaranteed by EU law.[425] Generally, where the Charter applies, the rights provided by Article 47 apply as well.[426] At the same time, Article 13 of the ECHR narrows its scope of application to infringements of rights included in the Convention, while the protection of Article 47 of the CFR applies to violations of any rights guaranteed by EU law. Again, it is Article 47 of the CFR that provides more extensive protection, as it is not limited to the rights expressed in the Charter itself but applies to any rights granted in EU law[427], if only in secondary acts.

Neither the CFR nor the ECHR indicates exhaustively the elements that constitute the right to a fair trial. The ECtHR jurisprudence points to, among others: the principle of participation in the proceedings, access to the files, the right to a hearing, equality of arms, the right to a justification of the decision, and the adversarial nature of the proceedings. These requirements have been adopted and developed by the CJEU.[428]

An important difference between the acts under consideration is also revealed in the matter of the subjective scope of the rights granted by them. The subjects of the rights guaranteed by the ECHR are natural persons, which is evident from the

---

422 See European Union Agency for Fundamental Rights and Council of Europe, *Handbook on European law relating to access to justice,* Luxembourg: Publications Office of the European Union, 2016, pp. 30–34, https://fra.europa.eu/sites/default/files/fra_uploads/fra-ecthr-2016-handbook-on-access-to-justice_en.pdf.

423 M. Górski, Prawo do skutecznego środka prawnego w art. 47 Karty Praw Podstawowych UE – znaczenie i deficyty, *Europejski Przegląd Sądowy*, no. 8 (2016), 39–40.

424 P. Aalto *et al.*, "Article 47," 1197, 1210; S. Prechal, R. Widdershoven, "Redefining," 38.

425 F. Godinjak, Article 47. Charter of Fundamental Rights of the European Union in The Light of the C-437/13 Decision of the Court of Justice of the European Union, *Anali Pravnog Fakulteta Univerziteta u Zenici* (2019), 239–240.

426 P. Aalto *et al.*, Article 47…, p.1199.

427 P. Aalto *et al.*, Article 47…, p.1210.

428 See Case C-348/16, Moussa Sacko v. Commissione Territoriale per il riconoscimento della protezione internazionale di Milano, 26 July 2017, p. 32.

very title of this act. Meanwhile, according to the jurisprudence of the CJEU[429], particularly concerning paragraph 3 of Article 47 of the CFR, it follows that the right to legal aid may also be granted to legal persons and even to organizational units without legal personality. Such a conclusion can also be derived from the fact that Article 47 of the CFR is intended to protect (ensure the effectiveness of) all rights and freedoms guaranteed by EU law, and many of those are also granted to organizational units. Therefore, there is no justification for excluding such entities from the guarantee of an effective remedy before the court.

In addition, a point should be made about the limits of states' discretion in choosing the appropriate measure and determining the procedure relating to its recognition. Indeed, national procedural autonomy is subject to significant limitations when implementing the Charter's provisions due to the requirement to comply with the principles of effectiveness and equivalence. The freedom of Member States is only in effect to the extent remaining after they have fulfilled the obligations assumed in the Treaties.[430]

When assessing the effectiveness of measures under both acts, the general approach adopted by the CJEU from the ECtHR case-law applies. This means that the fulfillment of the requirement of effectiveness should not be examined by means of a single institution in isolation but based on the entire system of available legal remedies in total.[431]

At the same time, both systems of protection of fundamental rights establish the admissibility of proportional restrictions on access to court, provided that they do not prevent individuals from exercising the remedies to which they are entitled. The standards developed in this regard in the case-law of the ECtHR should be applied accordingly to the rights granted under the Charter (Article 52(3) of the CFR).[432]

Furthermore, similarly to the ECHR, the CFR does not, in principle, require the introduction of a direct appeal by individuals against laws or legislative acts that violate their rights. This is in part justified by their special democratic mandate. The exception is when the act in question is the last link in the chain of legal

---

429 See Case C-279/09, DEB Deutsche Energiehandels- und Beratungsgesellschaft mbH v. Bundesrepublik Deutschland, 22 December 2010, p. 39.

430 See Case C-619/18, European Commission v. Republic of Poland, 24 June 2019, p. 52.

431 See Case C-175/11, H.I.D., B.A. v. Refugee Applications Commissioner, Refugee Appeals Tribunal, Minister for Justice, Equality and Law Reform, Ireland, Attorney General, 31 January 2013, p. 102.

432 Case C-334/12 RX–II, Oscar Orlando Arango Jaramillo and Others v. European Investment Bank (EIB), 28 February 2013, p. 43.

acts, directly shaping the situation of the individual, and the only possibility of judicial review would be actualized by the violation of the challenged regulation by the individual and thus their exposure to a foreseen sanction.[433]

In conclusion, despite the explicit reference in the Explanations relating to the Charter to the relevant provisions of the ECHR, it should not be forgotten that the right to effective judicial protection granted in Article 47 of the CFR has acquired its own content and distinctiveness. The process of its interpretation should entail not only the international acts, including the ECHR, but also the constitutional traditions common to the Member States as well as the autonomous principles developed in the EU acquis.[434] Indeed, the principle of effective judicial protection is a general principle of EU law, which has been affirmed in the Charter.[435]

6. Summary

Article 47 is said to be perhaps the most important provision of the Charter.[436] The ubiquity of right to ELR should come as no surprise since it is inextricably intertwined with access to justice, which is a procedural means to safeguard the rule of law.[437]

Article 47 of the Charter plays a crucial role in the interpretation of the Charter of Fundamental Rights as a whole. It sets both the standard for judicial proceedings and the concept of a remedy. A proper interpretation of Article 47 of the Charter allows for the proper application of the other provisions of the Charter. The concept of a remedy presupposes the effective implementation of the rights set by EU as well as national legislation. The absence of an exhaustive catalogue of the types of remedy allows for the proper selection of the remedy according to the violation. The existence of Article 47 of the Charter allows the idea that every violation should be remedied. The uniqueness of the remedy

---

433 M. Krajewski, Akt ustawodawczy o charakterze generalnym a prawo do skutecznej ochrony sądowej, *Europejski Przegląd Sądowy*, no. 6 (2015), 10–11; P. Aalto *et al.*, Article 47…, p.1217; Case C-583/11 P, Inuit and Others v. European Parliament and Council of the European Union, 3 October 2013, pp. 104–106.

434 Opinion of Advocate General Cruz Villalón in Case C-69/10, Brahim Samba Diouf v. Ministre du Travail, de l'Emploi et de l'Immigration, 1 March 2011, pp. 38–39.

435 Case C-402/05 P and C-415/05 P, Yassin Abdullah Kadi, Al Barakaat International Foundation, established in Spånga (Sweden) v. Council of the European Union and ot., 3 September 2008, p. 335.

436 P. Aalto *et al.*, Article 47…, p.1209.

437 P. Aalto *et al.*, Article 47…, p.1206.

concept is underlined by the fact that its limitation of the right to effective judicial protection, including a remedy, should be limited only to the extent that is strictly necessary. Additionally, the rationale for limiting the right to a remedy is also the need to protect other rights and freedoms. It is incumbent on national courts to ensure a balance between conflicting rights and freedoms. As with the principle of proportionality, the assessment is made on a case-by-case basis on the criteria of the individual case. In both the literature and the jurisprudence of the CJEU, an effective remedy is equated with a fair legal process.

It should first be pointed out that, in the context of Article 47 of the Charter, the remedy is to be effective. Such a regulation makes it possible to interpret both the nature of the measure, its constituent features and its procedural guidance. An effective remedy may have either a preventive or a compensatory function. In view of the above, it should be stated that it has primarily a compensatory role and aims to rectify the deficiencies. Its effectiveness depends on its adaptation to the factual and legal situation of the case and its accessibility.

Bibliography

Literature

Brittain S., The Relationship Between the EU Charter of Fundamental Rights and the European Convention on Human Rights: an Originalist Analysis, *European Constitutional Law Review* 11, no. 3, December 2015.

Bubalović T., Pravo na pravni lijek protiv odluka tijela državne vlasti prema domaćem i međunarodnom pravu, *Proceedings of the University of Libertas* 3, 2018.

Cariolou L. Under the supervision of A. Demetriades, Article 47 – Right to an effective remedy and to a fair trial, in: Commentary of the Charter of Fundamental Rights of the European Union, EU Network of Independent Experts on Fundamental Rights, 2006.

Cymerys K., Aksjologia, idee i zasady ogólne Karty Praw Podstawowych Unii Europejskie, Humanum no. 2, 2011.

de Burca G., The Drafting of the European Union Charter of Fundamental Rights, *European Law Review* 40, no. 6, 2015.

di Federico G. (ed.), *The EU Charter of Fudamental Rights: From Declaration to Binding Instrument, Ius Gentium: Comparative Perspectives on Law and Justice* 8, Springer, 2010.

Dubos O., The Origins of the Proceduralisation of EU Law: A Grey Area of European Federalism, *Review of European Administrative Law* 8, no. 1, 2015.

European Union Agency for Fundamental Rights and Council of Europe, *Handbook on European Law Relating to Access to Justice,* Publications Office of the European Union, 2016, https://fra.europa.eu/sites/default/files/fra_uploads/fra-ecthr-2016-handbook-on-access-to-justice_en.pdf

Facchi A., Riva N., European Values in the Charter of Fundamental Rights: An Introduction, *Ratio Juris* 34, no. 1, March 2021.

Godinjak F., Article 47. Charter of Fundamental Rights of The European Union in The Light of the C-437/13 Decision of the Court of Justice of the European Union, *Anali Pravnog Fakulteta Univerziteta u Zenici*, 2019.

Gołba F., Dyrektywa 2012/13/UE w sprawie prawa do informacji w postępowaniu karnym jako instrument europejskiej polityki kryminalnej, *Kortowski Przegląd Prawniczy* no. 3, 2016.

Górski M., Prawo do skutecznego środka prawnego w art. 47 Karty Praw Podstawowych UE – znaczenie i deficyty, *Europejski Przegląd Sądowy* no. 8, 2016.

Gutman K., The Essence of the Fundamental Right to an Effective Remedy and to Fair Trial in the Case-Law of the Court of Justice of the European Union: The Best is Yet to Come?, *German Law Journal* 29, 2019.

Jackiewicz A., Problematyka praw człowieka w świetle Karty Praw Podstawowych w aspekcie integracji Polski z Unią Europejską, *Studia Europejskie* 2, 2003.

Kaczmarczyk Ł., The Charter of Fundamental Rights of the European Union in the light of the principle of unity in diversity (Part 1), *Nurt SVD,* no. 1, 2020

Kalintriri A., Article 47 of the EU Charter of Fundamental Rights in EU Competition Enforcement: A Quantitative and Qualitative Assessment, https://realaw.blog/2023/01/17/article-47-of-the-eu-charter-of-fundamental-rights-in-eu-competition-enforcement-a-quantitative-and-qualitative-assessment-by-andriani-kalintiri/

Kornobis-Romanowska D., Poszanowanie praw podstawowych w państwach członkowskich Unii Europejskiej – w stronę zapewnienia spójnego poziomu ochrony praw człowieka w Europie?, *Przegląd Prawa i Administracji C/2*, 2015.

Krajewski M., Akt ustawodawczy o charakterze generalnym a prawo do skutecznej ochrony sądowej, *Europejski Przegląd Sądowy* no. 6, 2015.

Lenaerts K., Gutierrez-Fons J. A., The constitutional allocation of powers and general principles of EU Law, *Common Market Law Review* 47, 2010.

Lenaerts K., The Role of the EU Charter in the Member States, in: M. Bobek, J. Adams-Prassl (eds.), *The EU Charter of Fundamental Rights in the Member States,* Hart, 2020.

McCrudden C., Future of the EU Charter of Fundamental Rights, https://ssrn.com/abstract=299639

Menkes J., Karta Praw Podstawowych Unii Europejskiej a konstytucja Europy, *Studia Europejskie* 2, 2001.

Michałowska G., Ochrona praw człowieka w Radzie Europy i Unii Europejskiej, *Wydawnictwa Akademickie i Profesjonalne*, 2007.

Morawska E. H., Prawa konstytucyjne człowieka i obywatela w Rzeczypospolitej Polskiej a prawa podstawowe Unii Europejskiej. *Analiza porównawcza, Przegląd Sejmowy* no. 1, 2009.

Neframi E., Article 47 of the Charter in the opinion procedure: some reflections following opinion 1/17, *European Papers* 6, no. 1, 2021.

Nowicki M., *Karta Praw Podstawowych Unii Europejskiej: tekst z objaśnieniami Sekretariatu Konwencji*, Zakamycze, 2001.

Peers S., Hervey T., Kenner J., Ward A. (eds.), *The EU Charter of Fundamental Rights*. A Commentary, Hart/Beck, 2014.

Prechal S., Widdershoven R., Redefining the Relationship between 'Rewe-Effectiveness' and Effective Judicial Protection, *Review of European Administrative Law* 4, no. 2, 2011.

Shelton D., *Remedies in International Human Rights Law*, Clarendon Press, 1999.

Sunnqvist M., Groussot X., Maunsbach L., Judges Assessing the Independence of Judges. Historical Foundations and Practical Procedures in Facing the Threats against the Rule of Law in Europe, *Journal of Constitutional History / Giornale di Storia Costituzionale* no. 44, 2022, 2nd Quarter.

Taborowski M., Poziom ochrony praw podstawowych wynikający z Karty Praw Podstawowych UE jako przeszkoda dla przystąpienia Unii Europejskiej do Europejskiej Konwencji Praw Człowieka, *Europejski Przegląd Sądowy* no. 12, 2015.

Taborowski M., Znaczenie art. 53 Karty Praw Podstawowych Unii Europejskiej dla poziomu ochrony praw podstawowych w krajowym prawie konstytucyjnym, *Państwo i Prawo* no 1, 2016.

Triantagyllou D., The European Charter of Fundamental Tights and the "Rule of law": Restricting Fundamental Rights by Reference, *Common Market Law Review* 39, 2002.

van Zeben J., The Role of the EU Charter of Fundamental Right in Climate Litigation, *German Law Journal* 22, 2021.

Visser M., National Constitutional Courts, the Court of Justice and the Protection of Fundamental Rights in a Post-Charter Landscape, *Human Rights Review* 15, no. 1, March 2014.

Wróbel A. (ed.), *Karta Praw Podstawowych Unii Europejskiej*. Komentarz, C.H.Beck, 2020.

Zahirović D., Is There Something New in the European Union? – Right to a Fair Trial According to the Charter of Fundamental Rights of the European Union, *Anali Pravnog Fakulteta Univerziteta u Zenici* 11, no. 22, 2018.

Judgements

Judgements of the Court of Justice of the European Union:

Case 13/68, Société par actions Salgoil v. Ministero del commercio con l'estero della Repubblica italiana, 19 December 1968

Case 17/74, Transocean Marine Paint Association v. Commission, 23 October 1974

Case C-106/77, Amministrazione delle Finanze dello Stato v. Simmenthal SpA, 9 March 1978

Case 294/83, 'Les Verts' v. European Parliament, 23 April 1986

Case 222/84, Johnston v. Chief Constable of the Royal Ulster Constabulary, 15 May 1986

Case 222/86, Union nationale des entraineurs et cadres' techniques professionnels du football (UNECTEF) v. Georges Heylens, 15 October 1987

Case C-213/89, The Queen v. Secretary of State for Transport, ex parte Factortame and ot. (Factortame I), 19 June 1990

Case C-6/90 and C-9/90, Francovich and Others v. Italian Republic, 19 November 1991

Case C-97/91, Oleificio Borelli v. Commission, 9 June 1992

Case C-312/93, Peterbroeck, Van Campenhout & Cie SCS v. Belgian State, 14 December 1995

Case C-46/93 and C-48/93, Brasserie du Pêcheur SA v. Federal Republic of Germany and ot., 5 March 1996

Case 33/76, Rewe-Zentralfinanz eG and Rewe-Zentral AG v. Landwirtschaftskammer für das Saarland, 16 December 1996

Case C-54/96, Dorsch Consult Ingenieurgesellschaft mbH v. Bundesbaugesellschaft Berlin mbH., 17 September 1997

Case C-326/96, Levez v. T. H. Jennings (Harlow Pools) Ltd, 1 December 1998

Case C-185/95 P, Baustahlgewebe v. Commission of the European Communities, 17 December 1998

Case C-120/97, Upjohn Ltd v. The Licensing Authority established by the Medicines Act 1968 and ot., 21 January 1999

Case C-186/98, Maria Amélia Nunes and Evangelina de Matos, 8 July 1999

Case C-228/98, Charalampos Dounias vs. Ypourgio Oikonomikon, 3 February 2000

Case C-373/97, Dionysios Diamantis v. Elliniko Dimosio i Organismos Oikonomikis Anasygkrotisis Epicheiriseon AE, 23 March 2000

Case C-287/98, State of the Grand Duchy of Luxembourg v. Berthe Linster, Aloyse Linster and Yvonne Linster, 19 September 2000

Case C-270/99 P, Z v. European Parliament, 27 November 2001

Case C-50/00 P, Unión de Pequeños Agricultores v. Council of the European Union, 25 July 2002

Case C-224/01, Kobler v. Republik Osterreich, 30 September 2003

Case C-212/04, Konstantinos Adeneler i in. przeciwko Ellinikos Organismos Galaktos, 4 July 2006

Case C-438/04, Mobistar SA v. Institut belge des services postaux et des telecommunicationis, 13 July 2006

Case C-506/04, Wilson v. Ordre des avocats du barreau de Luxembourg, 19 September 2006

Case C-506/04, Graham J. Wilson v. Ordre des avocats du barreau de Luxembourg, 19 September 2006

Case C-403/04 P and C-405/04 P, Sumitomo Metal Industries Ltd and Nippon Steel Corp. v. Commission of the European Communities, 25 January 2007

Case C-275/06, Productores de Música de Espana (Promusicae) v. Telefónica de Espana SAU, 29 January 2008

Case C-450/06, Varec SA v. Belgian State, 14 February 2008

Case C-268/06, Impact v. Minister for Agriculture and Food a.o., 15 April 2008

Case C-402/05 P and C-415/05 P, Yassin Abdullah Kadi, Al Barakaat International Foundation, established in Spånga (Sweden) v. Council of the European Union and ot., 3 September 2008

Case C-394/07, Marco Gambazzi vs. DaimlerChrysler Canada Inc. and CIBC Mellon Trust Company, 2 April 2009

Case C-89/08, Commission v. Ireland and Others, 2 December 2009

Case C-407/08, Knauf Gips KG vs. European Commission, 1 January 2010

Case C-317/08, C-318/08, C-319/08 and C-320/08, Rosalba Alassini v. Telecom Italia SpA, Filomena Califano v, Wind SpA, Lucia Anna Giorgia Iacono v Telecom Italia SpA, Multiservice Srl v Telecom Italia SpA, 18 March 2010

Case C-243/09, Günter Fuß v. Stadt Halle, 14 October 2010

Case C-279/09, DEB Deutsche Energiehandels- und Beratungsgesellschaft mbH v. Bundesrepublik Deutschland, 22 December 2010

Case C-372/09 and C-373/09, Josep Peñarroja Fa, 17 March 2011

Case C-122/16, British Airways v. Commission, 14 November 2011

Case C-199/11, Europese Gemeenschap v. Otis and ot., 6 November 2012

Case C-277/11, M. M. v. Minister for Justice, Equality and Law Reform, Ireland, Attorney General, 22 November 2012

Case C-175/11, H.I.D., B.A. v. Refugee Applications Commissioner, Refugee Appeals Tribunal, Minister for Justice, Equality and Law Reform, Ireland, Attorney General, 31 January 2013

Case C-472/11, Banif Plus Bank Zrt v. Csaba Csipai, Viktória Csipai, 21 February 2013

Case C-399/11, Stefano Melloni v. Ministerio Fiscal, 26 February 2013

Case C-334/12 RX–II, Oscar Orlando Arango Jaramillo and Others v. European Investment Bank (EIB), 28 February 2013

Case C-300/11, ZZ v. Secretary of State for the Home Department, 4 June 2013

Case C-93/12, ET Agrokonsulting-04-Wełko Stojanow v. Izpylnitelen direktor na dyrżawen fond "Zemedelie" – Razplasztatelna agencija, 27 June 2013

Case C-583/11 P, Inuit and Others v. European Parliament and Council of the European Union, 3 October 2013

Case C-314/13, Peftiev v. Lithuania, 12 June 2014

Case C-169/14, Juan Carlos Sánchez Morcillo i María del Carmen Abril García v. Banco Bilbao Vizcaya Argentaria SA, 17 July 2014

Case C-562/12, Eesti-Lati programii 2007–2013 Seirekomitee, 17 September 2014

Case C-362/14, Schrems, 6 October 2015

Case C-601/15 PPU, N., 15 February 2016

Case C-682/15, Berlioz Investment Fund SA v. Directeur de l'administration des contributions directes, 16 May 2017

Case C-348/16, Moussa Sacko v. Commissione Territoriale per il riconoscimento della protezione internazionale di Milano, 26 July 2017

Case C-18/16, K., 14 September 2017

Case C-73/16, Peter Puškár przeciwko Finančné riaditeľstvo Slovenskej republiky, Kriminálny úrad finančnej správy, 27 September 2017

Case C-122/16 P, British Airways plc v. European Commission, 14 November 2017

Case C-403/16, Soufiane El Hassani v. Ministry of Foreign Affairs, 13 December 2017

Case C-64/16, Associação Sindical dos Juízes Portugueses v. Tribunal de Contas, 27 February 2018

Case C-284/16, Achmea BV, 6 March 2018

Case C-414/16, Egenberger v. Evangelisches Werk für Diakonie und Entwicklung eV, 17 April 2018

Case C-300/17, Hochtief AG v. Budapest Főváros Önkormányzata, 7 August 2018

Case C-180/17, X, Y v. Staatssecretaris van Veiligheid en Justitie, 26 September 2018

Case C-619/18, European Commission v. Republic of Poland, 24 June 2019

Case C-556/17, Alekszij Torubarov v. Bevándorlási és Menekültügyi Hivatal, 29 July 2019

Case C-467/18, EP, 19 September 2019

Judgments of the European Court of Human Rights:

Case 30210/96, Kudła v. Poland, 26 October 2000

Others

Opinion of the Court of Justice of the European Union in Case 2/94, Adhésion de la Communauté à la CEDH, 28 March 1996

Opinion of Advocate General Geelhoed in Case C-491/01, The Queen v. Secretary of State for Health, ex parte British American Tobacco (Investments) Ltd and Imperial Tobacco Ltd., 10 September 2002

Opinion of Advocate General Cruz Villalón in Case C-69/10, Brahim Samba Diouf v. Ministre du Travail, de l'Emploi et de l'Immigration, 1 March 2011

Opinion of Advocate General Trstenjak in Case C-411/10, N.S. v. Secretary of State for the Home Department, 22 September 2011

Opinion 1/15 of the Court of Justice of the European Union, 26 July 2017

Opinion 1/17 of the Court of Justice of the European Union, 30 April 2019

Legal Acts

Conclusion of the European Council in Cologne, 3rd and 4th June 1999, Annex IV, https://www.europarl.europa.eu/summits/kol2_en.htm

Explanations relating to the Charter of Fundamental Rights, OJ C 303, 14 December 2007

Regulation (EU, Euratom) 2020/2092 of the European Parliament and of the Council of 16 December 2020 on a general regime of conditionality for the protection of the Union budget, OJ L 433I, 22 December 2020

Zofia Branicka

Chapter 4 Implementation of the right to effective legal remedies in European Parliament Directives

1. Introduction

The case law of the ECHR and the European Court of Justice, presented in Chapters 2 and 3 of this book, provides the current understanding of the ELR. However, it is equally important to have a look at the attempts at implementation of this particular construction at the European level. In this way, we can have a look at the design of ELRs, the areas in which they are being applied and the values for which they are being put in place.

The analysis will focus on the area related to the continuing integration of the European Union in the field of criminal law. It is obvious that it faces a number of difficulties and the pace of its development slowed down considerably at the beginning of the 20th century. However, the process of integration has not been halted[438]. The European Commission i.a drafted in 2004 a proposal for a Council Framework Decision on certain procedural rights in criminal proceedings throughout the European Union[439], unfortunately without success. However, this was the impetus for further legislative efforts to provide individuals with certain procedural rights and adequate protection against violations of these rights.

The concept of approximation of standards for the protection of individual rights through successive directives of the European Council is being developed as a much more effective instrument.[440] In this evolution, effective remedies seem to have been conceived almost from the outset as an instrument of approximation

438 E. Sellier (ed.), *Criminal Procedures and Cross-Border Cooperation in the EU Area of Criminal Justice. Together But Apart?*, Bruxelles, 2020.

439 Proposal for a Council Framework Decision on certain procedural rights in criminal proceedings throughout the European Union, SEC(2004) 491.

440 See i.a. K. Kiejnich, Harmonisation of EU Criminal Law – Issues of Implementing EU Directives, in: A. Kłos (ed.), *European Union and Its Values: Freedom, Solidarity, Democracy*, CeDeWu 2020.

of criminal justice systems, or at least of standards[441]. Thus, a number of legal acts adopted by the European Union provide for the introduction of the right to an effective remedy in the event of a breach of certain procedural guarantees[442]. At this point, it should be clarified that the right to a remedy is enshrined in[443]:

1. Council Framework Decision 2003/577/JHA of 22 July 2003 on the execution in the European Union of orders freezing property or evidence[444]
2. Council Framework Decision 2006/783/JHA of 6 October 2006 on the application of the principle of mutual recognition to confiscation orders[445]
3. Directive 2012/29/EU of the European Parliament and of the Council of 25 October 2012 establishing minimum standards on the rights, support and protection of victims of crime, and replacing Council Framework Decision 2001/220/JHA[446,447]
4. Directive 2012/13/EU of the European Parliament and of the Council of 22 May 2012 on the right to information in criminal proceedings[448]
5. Directive 2013/48/EU of the European Parliament and of the Council of 22 October 2013 on the right of access to a lawyer in criminal proceedings and in European arrest warrant proceedings, and on the right to have a third

441 A. Pivaty, A. Beazley, Y. M. Daly, D. de Vocht, P. ter Vrugt, Strengthening the Protection of the Right to Remain Silent at the Investigative Stage: What Role for the EU Legislator?, *New Journal of European Criminal Law*, 12, no. 3 (2021), pp. 427–448.

442 U. Šadl, The Role of Effet Utile in Preserving the Continuity and Authority of European Union Law: Evidence from the Citation Web of the Pre-accession Case Law of the Court of Justice of the EU, *European Journal of Legal Studies*, no. 1/8 (2015), pp. 18–45.

443 See also P. Wiliński, K. Kiejnich-Kruk, Right to an Effective Legal Remedy in Criminal Proceedings in the EU. Implementation and Need for Standards, *Review of European and Comparative Law*, 54, no. 3, (2023).

444 Council Framework Decision 2003/577/JHA of 22 July 2003 on the execution in the European Union of orders freezing property or evidence, L 196, 02.08.2003, pp. 45–55.

445 Council Framework Decision 2006/783/JHA of 6 October 2006 on the application of the principle of mutual recognition to confiscation orders, L 328, 24.11.2006, p. 59.

446 Directive 2012/29/EU of the European Parliament and of the Council of 25 October 2012 establishing minimum standards on the rights, support and protection of victims of crime, and replacing Council Framework Decision 2001/220/JHA, L 315, 14.11.2012, pp. 57–73.

447 The right to a review of a decision is precisely included in this Directive.

448 Directive 2012/13/EU of the European Parliament and of the Council of 22 May 2012 on the right to information in criminal proceedings, L 142, 01.06.2012, pp. 1–10.

party informed upon deprivation of liberty and to communicate with third persons and with consular authorities while deprived of liberty[449]

6. Directive 2014/41/EU of the European Parliament and of the Council of 3 April 2014 regarding the European Investigation Order in criminal matters[450]
7. Directive 2014/42/EU of the European Parliament and of the Council of 3 April 2014 on the freezing and confiscation of instrumentalities and proceeds of crime in the European Union[451]
8. Directive (EU) 2016/343 of the European Parliament and of the Council of 9 March 2016 on the strengthening of certain aspects of the presumption of innocence and of the right to be present at the trial in criminal proceedings[452]
9. Directive (EU) 2016/680 of the European Parliament and of the Council of 27 April 2016 on the protection of natural persons with regard to the processing of personal data by competent authorities for the purposes of the prevention, investigation, detection or prosecution of criminal offences or the execution of criminal penalties, and on the free movement of such data, and repealing Council Framework Decision 2008/977/JHA[453]

---

449 Directive 2013/48/EU of the European Parliament and of the Council of 22 October 2013 on the right of access to a lawyer in criminal proceedings and in European arrest warrant proceedings, and on the right to have a third party informed upon deprivation of liberty and to communicate with third persons and with consular authorities while deprived of liberty, L 294, 06.11.2013, pp. 1–12.

450 Directive 2014/41/EU of the European Parliament and of the Council of 3 April 2014 regarding the European Investigation Order in criminal matters, L 130, 01.05.2014, pp. 1–36.

451 Directive 2014/42/EU of the European Parliament and of the Council of 3 April 2014 on the freezing and confiscation of instrumentalities and proceeds of crime in the European Union, L 127, 29.04.2014, pp. 39–50.

452 Directive (EU) 2016/343 of the European Parliament and of the Council of 9 March 2016 on the strengthening of certain aspects of the presumption of innocence and of the right to be present at the trial in criminal proceedings, L 65, 11.03.2016, pp. 1–11.

453 Directive (EU) 2016/680 of the European Parliament and of the Council of 27 April 2016 on the protection of natural persons with regard to the processing of personal data by competent authorities for the purposes of the prevention, investigation, detection or prosecution of criminal offences or the execution of criminal penalties, and on the free movement of such data, and repealing Council Framework Decision 2008/977/JHA, L 119, 04.05.2016, pp. 89–131.

10. Directive (EU) 2016/800 of the European Parliament and of the Council of 11 May 2016 on procedural safeguards for children who are suspects or accused persons in criminal proceedings[454]
11. Directive (EU) 2016/1919 of the European Parliament and of the Council of 26 October 2016 on legal aid for suspects and accused persons in criminal proceedings and for requested persons in European arrest warrant proceedings[455]

The regulation of ELR in the above-mentioned European Union acts is in the vast majority of them reduced to a laconic expression: *Member States shall ensure that suspects, accused persons and requested persons have an effective remedy under national law in the event of a breach of their rights under this Directive.*

If following comments we shall focus attention on some of mentioned above Directives, i.e.: 2012/13/EU, 2013/48/EU, 2016/1919/EU, 2016/343/EU and 2016/800/EU. They are adopted as a result of the Resolution of the Council of 30 November 2009 on a Roadmap for strengthening procedural rights of suspected or accused persons in criminal proceedings (hereinafter: Roadmap 2009)[456]. The Roadmap called for the regulation of six legal measures concerning the fundamental procedural rights of suspected or accused persons in criminal proceedings[457] (Measure A: Translation and Interpretation, Measure B: Information on Rights and Information about the Charges, Measure C: Legal Advice and Legal Aid, Measure D: Communication with Relatives, Employers and Consular Authorities, Measure E: Special Safeguards for Suspected or Accused Persons who are Vulnerable, Measure F: A Green Paper on Pre-Trial Detention)[458]. In all of them the right to ELR was designed as instrument of

454 Directive (EU) 2016/800/EU of the European Parliament and of the Council of 11 May 2016 on procedural safeguards for children who are suspects or accused persons in criminal proceedings, L 132, 21.05.2016, pp. 1–20.

455 Directive (EU) 2016/1919 of the European Parliament and of the Council of 26 October 2016 on legal aid for suspects and accused persons in criminal proceedings and for requested persons in European arrest warrant proceedings, L 297, 04.11.2016, pp. 1–8.

456 Resolution of the Council of 30 November 2009 on a Roadmap for strengthening procedural rights of suspected or accused persons in criminal proceedings (Text with EEA relevance), C 295, pp. 1–3.

457 It should be noted that whenever reference is made to rights at any stage of criminal proceedings, only the term "accused" is used.

458 The standards for measures A-D are laid down in directives. The Commission has also published a Green Paper on pre-trial detention "Strengthening mutual trust in the European judicial area – A Green Paper on the application of EU criminal justice legislation in the field of detention", COM(2011) 327 final and Commission

protection of effectiveness of included guaranties. In particular the preamble to the 2009 Roadmap states that the European Union's intention in implementing subsequent legislation is to continue to ensure full implementation of and respect for the standards of the European Convention on Human Rights and Fundamental Freedoms and, where appropriate, to ensure consistent application of existing standards and to raise the level of existing standards[459], including those relating to remedies.

All this is designed to increase mutual trust and give citizens confidence that the European Union and its Member States will protect their rights. Of course, on the basis of Article 82(2) of the Treaty on the Functioning of the European Union[460]

> Adoption of the minimum rules referred to in this paragraph shall not prevent Member States from maintaining or introducing a higher level of protection for individuals.

The content of these directives at first sight do not provide much additional information on the definition of a remedy or its characteristics, as they are directly based on concept known from art. 13 ECHR[461] and art. 47 of the Charter. Yet, it is worth analysing the context of the use of a measure and the negotiation process that took place during the development of the various directives, for this may broaden understanding about the nature of the instrument and may enable to understand the motivations behind the specific form of remedies legislation in force in the countries of the European Union.[462]

Recommendation of 27 November 2013 on procedural safeguards for vulnerable persons suspected or accused in criminal proceedings 2013/C 378/02, OJ C 378/8.

459 The protection of individual procedural rights at EU level has been the subject of extensive discussion, e.g. R. Loof, Shooting from the Hip: Proposed Minimum Rights in Criminal Proceedings throughout the EU, *European Law Journal* 12, no. 3 (2006), 421–430; W. De Bondt, G. Vermeulen, The Procedural Debate. A Bridge Too Far or Still Not Far Enough?, *EUCRIM*, no. 4 (2010), 163–167; L. van Puyenbroeck, G. Vermeulen, Towards Minimum Procedural Guarantees for the Defence in Criminal Proceedings in the EU, *International and Comparative Law Quarterly* 60, no. 4 (2011), 1017–1038.

460 Treaty on the Functioning of the European Union, C 326, 26.10.2012, pp. 79–82.

461 M. A. Nowicki, *Wokół Konwencji Europejskiej. Komentarz do Europejskiej Konwencji Praw Człowieka*, Warsaw, 2013, pp. 947–957, P. Van Dijk, F. van Hoof, A. van Rijn, L. Zwaak, *Theory and Practice of the European Convention of Human Rights*, Cambridge-Antwerp-Portland, Intersentia, 2018, pp. 1–78, 331–352.

462 In should be also emphasised that for practical reasons the subject of further analysis in will be the defendant's right to a remedy in criminal proceedings in the event of a violation of the procedural rights granted to him by the above-mentioned Directives.

2. Right to a remedy in Directive 2012/13/EU

2.1. The right to information about the accusation and the right to information about rights

Obviously the effective exercise of procedural rights by participants in criminal proceedings is only possible if they know and understand their rights beforehand[463]. Therefore, the effective implementation of the right to information is crucially important for the conduct of a fair criminal trial[464]. Efforts to put the above theory into practice in the case of suspects or accused persons and persons subject to a European Arrest Warrant resulted[465], inter alia, in Directive 2012/13/EU. By means of this regulation, the right to information in criminal proceedings is granted to these persons in principle from the time of the charge until the final conclusion of the proceedings (Article 2(1) of Directive 2012/13/EU) and includes:

(a) the right to information about the accusation;
(b) the right to information about rights;
(c) the right of access to the materials of the case.

Directive 2012/13/EU includes provisions to ensure that information is provided in an efficient, diligent and clear manner. In other words, care has been taken to provide not only minimum standards on "what" should be communicated to the suspect in order to fulfil the right to information, but also on "how" this should be done. It has been repeatedly emphasised that the effective implementation of the right to information is closely linked to timing and, in particular, to the obligation to provide information promptly to authorised parties.

According to recital 28 of Directive 2012/13/EU, information on the charge should be provided at the latest before the person is first questioned as a suspect. Moreover, the information should be as detailed as the stage of the criminal proceedings permits, for example, in order to ensure the fairness of the proceedings and to allow for the effective exercise of the rights of the defence. Comprehensive information on the nature of the offence and its legal

463 T. Spronken, G. Vermeulen, D. Vocht, L. van Puyenbroeck, *EU Procedural Rights in Criminal Proceedings*, Maastricht, 2009, p. 10.

464 M. Kolendowska-Matejczuk, M. Mrowicki, *Prawo do informacji o własnych prawach w postępowaniu karnym jako jeden z wymiarów edukacji praw człowieka*, Krakowskie Studia Międzynarodowe, 2019/4, pp. 102–113.

465 A. Efrat, Assessing mutual trust among EU members: Evidence from European Arrest Warrant, *Journal of European Public Policy*, no. 26 (2019), p. 656 and next.

classification must be provided to the accused at the latest when the case is transferred to the judicial stage (Article 6(3) of Directive 2012/13/EU). In turn, according to Article 6(4) of Directive 2012/13, the right to information about the accusation also applies to the obligation to inform the suspected person of material changes in the charge.

Similarly, the right to information on rights should also be implemented without delay (Recital 11 and Article 3(1) of Directive 2012/13/EU) and include at least information on the right of access to a lawyer, any entitlement to free legal advice and the conditions for obtaining such advice, the right to be informed of the accusation, the right to interpretation and translation; the right to remain silent (Article 3(1) of Directive 2012/13/EU), i.e. the absolute foundations of a fair criminal trial.

According to recital 20 of Directive 2012/13/EU, the procedural authority is not, in principle, obliged to repeat the instructions unless specific circumstances justify it. However, the Directive emphasises "the effectiveness of the information given and obliges Member States to provide such information in writing or orally in simple and accessible language, taking into account any specific needs of suspected or accused persons who require special treatment"[466]. Recital 38 of Directive 2012/13/EU even indicates that measures to ensure the comprehensibility of instructions, and thus the effective implementation of the right to information in this respect, can also be achieved by non-legislative means.

Directive 2012/13/EU sets out additional requirements for the cautioning of pre-trial detainees, i.e. persons who are subject to a coercive measure of deprivation of liberty prior to the establishment of guilt. The warning of a pre-trial detainee must always be given in writing[467]. Furthermore, in accordance with Article 3(2) of Directive 2012/13/EU, in addition to the information on procedural rights referred to above, the Letter of Rights on arrest should also contain information on the right of access to the materials of the case, the right

466 T. Marguery, European Union Fundamental Rights and Member States Action in EU Criminal Law, *Maastricht Journal of European and Comparative Law*, no. 2 (2013), 283; P. Starzyński, *7.1.2.4.* Akty wprowadzające i zalecenia Komisji Europejskiej, in: P. Hofmański, C. Kulesza (eds.) *System Prawa Karnego Procesowego Tom 6. Strony i inni uczestnicy postępowania karnego*, Warsaw, 2016, http://lex-1amu-1edu-1pl-1015e98yb07ab.han.amu.edu.pl/#/monograph/369404601/312930/hofmanski-piotr-red-kulesza-cezary-red-system-prawa-karnego-procesowego-tom-vi-strony-i-inni...?keyword=dyrektywa%202012~2F13%20prawo%20do%20informacji%20&unitId=passage_1573 (access: 2023-07-30 15:04).

467 See recital 22 and Article 4(1) of Directive 2012/13/EU.

to have consular authorities and one person informed, the right of access to urgent medical assistance; and the maximum number of hours or days suspects or accused persons may be deprived of liberty before being brought before a judicial authority. The Letter of Rights shall also contain basic information about any possibility, under national law, of challenging the lawfulness of the arrest; obtaining a review of the detention; or making a request for provisional release.

2.2. The right of access to the materials of the case

Finally, in the light of Directive 2012/13/EU, the right to information in criminal proceedings refers to the right to have access, in principle free of charge, to evidence gathered in the course of criminal proceedings[468] (with the exception of the possibility of charging for copies of documents)[469]. Access to all evidence must take place at the latest when the case is transferred to the judicial stage (Article 7(3) of Directive 2012/13/EU). Exceptions to this rule may only be made for reasons of the protection of an overriding public interest or the protection of the life or fundamental rights of third parties[470]. The evidence may then be limited accordingly. This possible additional restriction does not apply to a pre-trial detainee. Directive 2012/13/EU has introduced a specific regime whereby he has an absolute right of access to pre-trial detention material[471].

2.3. The right to a remedy

In the course of drafting Directive 2012/13/EU, the need for provisions applicable to situations of violation of the right to information in criminal proceedings was recognised. "This is due to the fact that rights to information under Arts 5 and 6 ECHR does not go far enough and applications to the European Court of Human Rights may take years to be decided and only lead to an ex post remedy of limited effectiveness"[472]. In the draft presented by the European Commission on 20 July 2010, the issue of the right to an effective remedy is directly addressed in Article 8(2) as follows:

---

468 See recital 31 and Article 7 of Directive 2012/13/EU.

469 See recital 34 and Article 7(5) of Directive 2012/13/EU.

470 See recital 32 and Article 7(4) of Directive 2012/13/EU.

471 See recital 30 and Article 7(1) of Directive 2012/13/EU.

472 Proposal for a Directive of the European Parliament and of the Council on the right to information in criminal proceedings, COM (2010) 392 final.

Member States shall ensure that a suspected or accused person has an effective remedy in instances where he does not receive this information. [indicated in the Directive][473].

I is however difficult to find in the working documents any broader comments on the introduction of this provision, explaining, for example, what cases the phrase "where he does not receive this information" might cover. There is above all no explanation of the nature and characteristics of the remedy. There is nothing in the European Council's press releases on the negotiations on the final version of Directive 2012/13/EU to indicate that a discussion on the right to an effective remedy has taken place[474]. No discussion on that was revealed during negotiation process even if the scope of the mandate for ELR was defined extremely broadly.

The problem of this being too broadly regulated formula of ELR was noted in the opinion of the Legal Affairs Committee of 27 January 2011[475], which supported amendments to clarify the issue:

Amendment 19: Article 7 paragraph 2 b (new) Member States shall ensure that an effective remedy is available before an impartial tribunal to challenge the decision not to allow access to certain documents contained in the evidentiary materials of the case[476].

Amendment 22: Article 8 – paragraph 1 (new)

1. Member States shall ensure that a suspected or accused person has the right to challenge, in accordance with procedures in national law, the possible failure or refusal of the competent authorities to provide the information required in accordance with the provisions of this Directive.

Amendment 23: Article 8 – paragraph 1

473 Commission Staff working document summary of the impact assessment accompanying the Proposal for a Directive of the European Parliament and of the Council on the right to information in criminal proceedings, COM (2010) 392 final.

474 See Press Release 3034th Council meeting Justice and Home Affairs, Luxembourg, 7–8 October 2010, 14423/10; Press Release 3043rd Council meeting Justice and Home Affairs Brussels, 8 and 9 November 2010, 15848/10; Press Release 3051st Council meeting Justice and Home Affairs Brussels, 2–3 December 2010, 16918/10.

475 Opinion of the Committee on Legal Affairs for the Committee on Civil Liberties, Justice and Home Affairs on the proposal for a directive of the European Parliament and of the Council on the right to information in criminal proceedings (COM(2010)0392 – C7 0189/2010 – 2010/0215(COD)), 27.01.2011.

476 Opinion of the Committee on Legal Affairs for the Committee on Civil Liberties, Justice and Home Affairs on the proposal for a directive of the European Parliament and of the Council on the right to information in criminal proceedings (COM(2010)0392 – C7 0189/2010 – 2010/0215(COD)), 27.01.2011.

> 1. Member States shall ensure that a procedure is in place to ascertain whether a suspected or accused person has received all information relevant to him in accordance with this Directive.

The reason for the change was to clarify the content and meaning of remedies. This solution still left much to be desired, but on the other hand solved some of the problems. Amendments made it clear that a remedy should be available in the event of failure or refusal by the competent authorities to provide the information required in accordance with the provisions of this Directive, and that States are free to choose the remedy. The question of a decision not to allow access to certain documents contained in the evidentiary materials of the case is described in more detail. In such a case, Member States shall ensure that an effective remedy is available before an impartial tribunal and is available to challenge the decision not to allow access. The Committee on Civil Liberties, Justice and Home Affairs has included the amendments in a new draft legislative resolution of the European Parliament accompanying its report of 25 November 2011. The justification was as follows:

> *In order to ensure that the right to information is effectively granted, the proposal provides that a procedure is in place to assess whether the suspected or accused person has received the information and that an effective remedy is in place in case he/she has not*[477].

Finally, the issue of the right to an effective remedy is addressed in two articles of Directive 2012/13/EU. Article 7(4) of Directive 2012/13/EU grants the right to an effective remedy in the event of a breach of the right of access to the file:

> By way of derogation from paragraphs 2 and 3, provided that this does not prejudice the right to a fair trial, access to certain materials may be refused if such access may lead to a serious threat to the life or the fundamental rights of another person or if such refusal is strictly necessary to safeguard an important public interest, such as in cases where access could prejudice an ongoing investigation or seriously harm the national security of the Member State in which the criminal proceedings are instituted. Member States shall ensure that, in accordance with procedures in national law, a decision to refuse access to certain materials in accordance with this paragraph is taken by a judicial authority or is at least subject to judicial review.

In turn, Article 8(2) of Directive 2012/13 regulates the right to a remedy in the event of a breach of the other rights granted by the Directive under review:

---

477 Report on the proposal for a directive of the European Parliament and of the Council on the right to information in criminal proceedings (COM(2010)0392 – C7-0189/2010 – 2010/0215(COD)), A7-0408/2011, 25.11.2011.

> "Member States shall ensure that suspects or accused persons or their lawyers have the right to challenge, in accordance with procedures in national law, the possible failure or refusal of the competent authorities to provide information in accordance with this Directive."

For a correct interpretation of these provisions, reference should also be made to recital 36 of Directive 2012/13/EU:

> Suspects or accused persons or their lawyers should have the right to challenge, in accordance with national law, the possible failure or refusal of the competent authorities to provide information or to disclose certain materials of the case in accordance with this Directive. That right does not entail the obligation for Member States to provide for a specific appeal procedure, a separate mechanism, or a complaint procedure in which such failure or refusal may be challenged.

2.4. Conclusion

In view of the above, it must be concluded that the regulation of the right to an effective remedy has nevertheless remained very laconic. The working documents show that the drafting of Directive 2012/13/EU took into account the valuable acquis of the European Court of Human Rights. Staying in the realm of values, it is also worth mentioning that Article 10 explicitly provides that "nothing in this Directive shall be construed as limiting or derogating from any of the rights or procedural safeguards that are ensured under the Charter, the ECHR, other relevant provisions of international law or the law of any Member State which provides a higher level of protection".

Unfortunately, there is no clarification of the definition of a remedy and no description of its characteristics in Directive 2012/13/EU. Even the provision on its effectiveness was removed during the drafting of the regulation. Instead, the reluctance of Member States to describe remedies in more detail became apparent during the discussion phase.

It can only be inferred from the Directive that there should be remedies for breaches of the right to information in criminal proceedings, which:

- apply, like the other rights laid down in the Directive, from the time persons are made aware by the competent authorities of a Member State that they are suspected or accused of having committed a criminal offence until the conclusion of the proceedings, which is understood to mean the final determination of the question whether the suspect or accused person has committed the criminal offence, including, where applicable, sentencing and the resolution of any appeal[478].

478 In some Member States an authority other than a court having jurisdiction in criminal matters has competence for imposing sanctions in relation to relatively minor offences.

- concern suspected or accused persons or their lawyers
- are of a supervisory nature,
- in the event of a failure or refusal of the competent authorities to provide information or to disclose certain materials of the case in accordance with Directive 2012/13/EU.

At the same time, Member States should use national mechanisms for this purpose. They are not obliged to introduce new solutions for this purpose (recital 36 of Directive 2012/13/EU). The only additional proviso appears in the case of remedies for access to the file: decision to refuse access to certain materials in accordance with this paragraph is taken by a judicial authority or is at least subject to judicial review. It is here that we learn the characteristics of the authority exercising the right of appeal.

3. The right to a remedy in Directive 2013/48/EU and Directive 2016/1919/EU

3.1. The right of access to a lawyer in criminal proceedings

The right to information on procedural rights, including the right to access to a lawyer in criminal proceedings as one of the foundations of the right of defence, was granted by Directive 2012/13/EU, already discussed above.[479] Directives 2013/48/EU and 2016/1919/EU, on the other hand, aimed to create minimum standards making it a reality for suspects, accused and persons subject to proceedings for a European Arrest Warrant to take any action seeking to protect their interests, either alone or with the assistance of their defence lawyers.

On the basis of the provisions of Article 2 of Directive 2013/48, persons have the right to be assisted by a legal counsel from the moment they are informed by

---

That may be the case, for example, in relation to traffic offences which are committed on a large scale and which might be established following a traffic control. In such situations, it would be unreasonable to require that the competent authority ensure all the rights under this Directive. Where the law of a Member State provides for the imposition of a sanction regarding minor offences by such an authority and there is either a right of appeal or the possibility for the case to be otherwise referred to a court having jurisdiction in criminal matters, this Directive should therefore apply only to the proceedings before that court following such an appeal or referral (recital 17 of Directive 2012/13/EU).

479 See also P. Wiliński, K. Kiejnich-Kruk, Right to an Effective Legal Remedy in Criminal Proceedings in the EU. Implementation and Need for Standards, *Review of European and Comparative Law,* 54, no. 3 (2023), pp. 151, 155–159.

the judicial authorities of their status as suspects until the final conclusion of the criminal proceedings.[480] In all cases, it should not be theoretical, but should enable the real and effective exercise of the right of defence (Article 3 of Directive 2013/48). The accused may, however, waive this right[481].

As indicated in Article 3(2) of Directive 2013/48/EU, the right to the participation of a defence counsel in criminal proceedings shall be granted without undue delay, starting from the earliest of the following dates:

(a) before they are questioned by the police or by another law enforcement or judicial authority;
(b) upon the carrying out by investigating or other competent authorities of an investigative or other evidence-gathering act in accordance with point (c) of paragraph 3;
(c) without undue delay after deprivation of liberty;
(d) where they have been summoned to appear before a court having jurisdiction in criminal matters, in due time before they appear before that court[482].

However, temporary derogations from this right are allowed in exceptional situations[483]. These must comply with the general conditions set out in Article 8 of Directive 2013/48/EU, including proportionality, necessity, precision of the law or indication of the reasonableness of the restriction in the procedural decision. The right to be assisted by a defence counsel may only be restricted in strictly defined cases, e.g. where the geographical remoteness of the suspect makes it impossible to ensure this right (Article 3(5) of Directive 2013/48/EU). During the period of such derogation, the trial authority should not question the suspect or carry out other procedural acts[484]. At the pre-trial stage, the right of defence counsel to participate may be restricted if it is necessary to prevent a threat to the life, liberty or physical integrity of any person[485], or if it is necessary to take procedural steps to the extent necessary[486]. Based on the provisions of Article 3(3) of Directive 2013/48/EU, the right to the participation of counsel comprises three rights:

---

480 See i.a. A. Soo, (Effective) Remedies for a Violation of the Right to Counsel during Criminal Proceedings in the European Union: An Empirical Study, *Utrecht Law Review* 14, no. 1 (2018), pp. 18–60.

481 See recital 39–41 and Article 9 of Directive 2013/48/EU.

482 See recital 39 of Directive 2013/48/EU.

483 See recital 38 and Article 8 of Directive 2013/48/EU.

484 See recital 30 of Directive 2013/48/EU.

485 See recital 31 and Article 3(6a) of Directive 2013/48/EU.

486 See recital 32 and Article 3(6b) of Directive 2013/48/EU.

(a) the right to meet in private and communicate with the lawyer representing them;
(b) the right for their lawyer to be present and participate effectively when questioned;
(c) the right to have lawyer to attend in certain the investigative or evidence-gathering acts.

The right to communicate with the defence counsel should exist at any stage of the criminal proceedings, including before the first questioning of the accused by the trial authority[487]. According to Article 4, sentence 2, of Directive 2013/48/EU, communication should be understood as meetings, correspondence, telephone calls and other authorised forms of communication. The confidentiality of these contacts is crucial for the effective exercise of the accused's right to communicate with his defence counsel[488]. Therefore, Member States are obliged to respect this principle without any derogation, except for limitations related to operational or procedural control[489].

The right to the presence and effective participation of the defence counsel in the questioning of the accused also applies at any stage of the criminal proceedings[490]. The defence counsel may, inter alia, ask questions, request explanations and make statements. The right to the participation of the defence counsel in procedural activities is granted in situations where the presence of the accused in these activities is mandatory or permitted[491]. The Directive identifies certain procedural acts in which the defence counsel should be able to participate, i.e. presentation for identification, confrontation and trial experimentation.

According to Article 3(4) of Directive 2013/48/EU, the accused should be informed of his/her right to the participation of a defence counsel[492]. If a person has been deprived of his or her liberty, the procedural authorities should take measures to enable him or her to effectively exercise the right to the participation of a defence counsel[493]. In some cases, this may involve the right to legal aid ex officio.

Directive 2013/48/EU does not regulate minimum standards for the right to legal aid ex officio and leaves this issue to national law (Article 11 of Directive

---

487 See recitals 22–23 and Article 3(3a) of Directive 2013/48/EU.
488 See recital 33 and Article 4 of Directive 2013/48/EU.
489 See recital 34 of Directive 2013/48/EU.
490 See recital 25 of Directive 2013/48/EU.
491 See recital 26 and Article 3 (3c) of Directive 2013/48/EU.
492 See recital 27 of Directive 2013/48/EU.
493 See recital 28 and Article 3(4) of Directive 2013/48/EU.

2013/48/EU). However, it should not be forgotten that minimum standards for the right to legal aid ex officio were established in Directive 2016/1919/EU. According to Article 4(6) of Directive 2016/1919/EU, the appointment of a public defender is only possible within the framework of criminal proceedings already in progress. The granting of legal aid ex officio should take place without undue delay, at the latest before the hearing by the procedural authority or the performance of the procedural act[494]. Ex officio legal aid means the financing by an EU Member State, in whole or in part, of the assistance of a defence counsel in order to enable the accused to exercise his right to have a defence[495]. Based on the provisions in Article 4(1) of Directive 2016/1919/EU, the right to the appointment of a public defender is granted to an accused who does not have the means to pay for the assistance of a defence counsel when the interests of justice so require. In order to determine whether the accused is entitled to the appointment of a public defender, an assessment of the financial situation, an assessment of reasonableness or both may be used[496]. In the assessment of the financial situation, factors such as, for example, the economic and personal situation of the accused, his income and the cost of legal assistance shall be taken into account. The assessment of reasonableness takes into account the gravity of the criminal act, the complexity of the case, the severity of the threatened punishment and the interests of justice (Article 4(3) of Directive 2016/1919/EU).

In the light of Directive 2016/1919/EU, the right to the appointment of a public defender should always be granted in situations where the accused is deprived of his or her liberty or is brought before a court for a pre-trial detention measure. It should be noted that deprivation of liberty within the meaning of Directive 2016/1919/EU is detention and pre-trial detention.

Pursuant to Article 6 of Directive 2016/1919/EU, the procedural authority shall issue a procedural decision on the appointment of a public defender and immediately notify the accused of its contents.

3.2. Other rights of the accused in Directive 2013/48/EU

One of the measures identified in the Roadmap is Measure D on the right to communicate with relatives, employers and consular authorities. The European Union decided to address this issue in Directive 2013/48/EU. The defendant is granted the right to inform a third party of his detention and the right to

494 See recital 19 and Article 4(5) of Directive 2016/1919/EU.
495 See recital 8 and Article 3 of Directive 2016/1919/EU.
496 See recital 17 and Article 4(2) of Directive 2016/1919/EU.

communicate with third parties while deprived of liberty. If the person deprived of his or her liberty is a foreigner, he or she also has the right to inform and communicate with a consular authority. It must be concluded that the deprivation of liberty within the meaning of Directive 2013/48/EU is pre-trial detention and remand in custody. The right to inform a third party of a deprivation of liberty is governed by Article 5(1) of Directive 2013/48/EU. Immediate notification of at least one third party shall take place at the request of the suspect. It is the person deprived of liberty who indicates who should be informed. This could be, for example, a relative or an employer. According to Article 5(3) of Directive 2013/48/EU, the right to notify a third person of the deprivation of liberty may be temporarily restricted – under the general conditions of Article 8 of Directive 2013/48/EU – in two cases:

1. where there is a need to prevent adverse consequences for the life, liberty or physical integrity of a person (Article 5(3)(a));
2. where there is a risk that the criminal proceedings will be seriously prejudiced (Article 5(3)(b)).

However, if the need to limit this power concerns a specific third person, the judicial authority should consider whether it could not inform another person. According to Article 6(1) of Directive 2013/48/EU, a suspected person deprived of his or her liberty has the right to communicate promptly with one or more third persons of his or her choice. However, this right may be restricted for reasons of overriding interest or operational necessity. In addition, the provision in Article 7(1) of Directive 2013/48/EU guarantees an accused person deprived of his or her liberty who is a foreigner the right to notify and communicate with consular authorities. This includes meeting with the consular authority, conversation, correspondence and the organisation of legal representation (Article 7(2) of Directive 2013/48/EU). Finally, it should be noted that Article 9 of Directive 2013/48/EU allows the suspected person to waive the rights granted to him or her (as is the case with the right of defence).

3.3. The right to an effective remedy in Directive 2013/48/EU

In the draft adopted by the European Commission on 8 June 2011[497], the right to an effective remedy is enshrined in Article 13:

497 Proposal for a Directive of the European Parliament and of the Council on the right of access to a lawyer in criminal proceedings and on the right to communicate upon arrest, COM/2011/0326 final – COD 2011/0154.

1. Member States shall ensure that a person to whom Article 2 refers has an effective remedy in instances where his right of access to a lawyer has been breached.
2. The remedy shall have the effect of placing the suspect or accused person in the same position in which he would have found himself had the breach not occurred.
3. Member States shall ensure that statements made by the suspect or accused person or evidence obtained in breach of his right to a lawyer or in cases where a derogation to this right was authorised in accordance with Article 8, may not be used at any stage of the procedure as evidence against him, unless the use of such evidence would not prejudice the rights of the defence.

The purpose of this implementation was stated as follows:

> This Article reflects ECHR jurisprudence that the most appropriate form of redress for breaching the ECHR right to a fair trial is to ensure that a suspect or accused person is put, as far as possible, in the position in which he would have been had his rights not been so breached (*Salduz v Turkey*, judgment of 27 November 2008, application no. 36391/02, § 72). The ECHR has ruled that even where compelling reasons may exceptionally justify denial of access to a lawyer, such restriction – whatever its justification – must not unduly prejudice the rights of the accused under Article 6 of the ECHR and such rights will in principle be irretrievably prejudiced when incriminating statements made during police interrogation without access to a lawyer are used for a conviction. Therefore, this Article bans, in principle, the use of evidence obtained where access to a lawyer was denied save in those exceptional cases where the use of such evidence will not prejudice the rights of the defence.[498]

This purpose was subsequently supplemented in the Preamble, as follows:

(25) The principle of effectiveness of EU law should require that Member States put in place adequate, effective remedies in the event of a breach to a right conferred upon individuals by Union law;

(26) The European Court of Human Rights has consistently held that any adverse consequences deriving from a breach of the right to a lawyer must be undone by placing the person in the same position they would have found themselves had the breach not occurred. This may require retrial or equivalent measures if a final conviction was made in breach of the right to a lawyer;

498 Proposal for a Directive of the European Parliament and of the Council on the right of access to a lawyer in criminal proceedings and on the right to communicate upon arrest, COM/2011/0326 final – COD 2011/0154.

(27) Since the European Court of Human Rights has established that irretrievable damage to the rights of the defence results from the use of an incriminating statement made by the suspect or accused person without access to a lawyer, Member States should be required in principle to prohibit the use of any statements given in breach of the right of access to a lawyer as evidence against the suspect or accused person unless the use of such evidence would not prejudice the rights of the defence. This should be without prejudice to the use of statements for other purposes permitted under national law, such as the need to execute urgent investigative acts or to avoid the perpetration of other offences or serious adverse consequences for any person.[499]

It follows from the proposal made that the right to an effective remedy was to be available only in the event of a breach of the right to counsel. Remedies should be remedial in nature, and thus their purpose should be to restore the lawful state of affairs. The proposed provision also chose to prohibit the use of evidence obtained in violation of the right to participation of defence counsel. However, this was met with opposition from the majority of EU Member States[500]. It was pointed out that such regulation excessively interferes with national systems and limits the discretion of EU Member State judges. Admittedly, The European Economic and Social Committee, in its opinion of 7 December 2011, made no reference to the regulation of remedial measures.[501] However, the European Parliament introduced several amendments to the Commission's proposal. In amendments to the preamble, paragraph 26 was deleted and paragraphs 25 and 27 were rewritten as follows:

(25) In accordance with the principle of effectiveness of Union law, Member States should put in place adequate and effective remedies to protect the rights conferred upon individuals by this Directive.

---

499 Proposal for a Directive of the European Parliament and of the Council on the right of access to a lawyer in criminal proceedings and on the right to communicate upon arrest, COM/2011/0326 final – COD/2011/0154.

500 See Press release of the 3121st Council meeting Justice and Home Affairs, 27 and 28 October 2011, mo. 16042/11, Report from the Council on the "Proposal for a Directive of the European Parliament and of the Council on the right of access to a lawyer in criminal proceedings and on the right to communicate upon arrest", 6 December 2011, no. 18215/11.

501 Opinion of the European Economic and Social Committee on the "Proposal for a Directive of the European Parliament and of the Council on the right of access to a lawyer in criminal proceedings and on the right to communicate upon arrest", COM/ 2011/326 final – COD/2011/0154.

(27) Member States should ensure that in the assessment of statements made by a suspect or accused person or of evidence obtained in breach of his right to a lawyer or in cases where a derogation to this right was authorised in accordance with this Directive, the rights of the defence and the fairness of the proceedings should be respected; in this context, regard should be had at the case-law of the European Court of Human Rights, which has established that the rights of the defence will in principle be irretrievably prejudiced when incriminating statements made during police interrogation without access to a lawyer are used for a conviction. This should be without prejudice to the use of statements for other purposes permitted under national law, such as the need to execute urgent investigative acts to avoid the perpetration of other offences or serious adverse consequences for any person or related to an urgent need to prevent a substantial jeopardy to criminal proceedings where access to a lawyer or delaying the investigation would irretrievably prejudice the on-going investigations regarding a serious crime. Further, this should be without prejudice to national rules or systems regarding admissibility of evidence and should not prevent Member States from maintaining a system whereby all existing evidence can be adduced before a court or a judge, without there being any separate or prior assessment as to admissibility of such evidence.[502]

Consequently, different wording for Art. 13 was eventually proposed:

1. Member States shall ensure that suspects or accused persons in criminal proceedings as well as requested persons in European Arrest Warrant proceedings have an effective remedy under national law in instances where their rights under this Directive have been breached.
   (…)
2. Without prejudice to national rules and systems on the admissibility of evidence, Member States shall ensure that, in criminal proceedings, in the assessment of statements made by a suspect or accused person or of evidence obtained in breach of his right to a lawyer or in cases where a derogation to this right was authorised in accordance with Article 3(6), the rights of the defence and the fairness of the proceedings are respected.[503]

---

502 Report from the Council on the "Proposal for a Directive of the European Parliament and of the Council on the right of access to a lawyer in criminal proceedings and on the right to communicate upon arrest", 6 December 2011, no. 18215/11.

503 Report from the Council on the "Proposal for a Directive of the European Parliament and of the Council on the right of access to a lawyer in criminal proceedings and on the right to communicate upon arrest", 6 December 2011, no. 18215/11.

In this way, a compromise was sought despite the different positions of the EU Member States[504]. Discussions on the provisions of the Directive, including the issue of redress, continued until 22 October 2013, when the final version of Directive 2013/48/EU was adopted[505]. In the end, the right to an effective remedy was included in Article 12(1) of Directive 2013/48/EU:

> Member States shall ensure that suspects or accused persons in criminal proceedings, as well as requested persons in European arrest warrant proceedings, have an effective remedy under national law in the event of a breach of the rights under this Directive.

Recital 49 of Directive 2013/48/EU indicates:

> In accordance with the principle of effectiveness of Union law, Member States should put in place adequate and effective remedies to protect the rights that are conferred upon individuals by this Directive.

Consequently, they give rise to two powers:

(a) the right to an effective remedy in the case of a breach of the rights provided for in the Directive; and
(b) the right to a judicial review of evidence obtained in breach of the right of access to a lawyer or in cases where a derogation from that right has been allowed in accordance with the Directive, in compliance with the standards of the right to defense and the right to a fair trial.

However, these provisions do not oblige Member States to exclude evidence. More importantly, they do not provide any explanation of the concept of an effective remedy, its aims or its expected results[506].

Following the implementation of the amendments, the reluctance of the Member States to interfere with EU law in domestic systems for the admissibility of evidence in criminal proceedings can also be clearly seen.[507] The Legal Affairs Committee also took the view during the legislative phase that "this

---

504 See Press release of the 3172st Council meeting Justice and Home Affairs, 7 and 8 June 2012, no. 10760/12.

505 See e.g. European Commission press release of 28 May 2013, MEMO/13/468; speech by Viviane Reding, ice-President of the European Commission, at the press conference of 6 June 2013; European Commission press release of 19 June 2013, MEMO/13/589.

506 A. Soo, (Effective) Remedies for a Violation of the Right to Counsel during Criminal Proceedings in the European Union: An Empirical Study, *Utrecht L. Rev.*, 14 (2018), pp. 53–54.

507 K. Kiejnich-Kruk, *Prawo do skutecznego środka naprawczego w postępowaniu dowodowym*, Warsaw, 2023, p. 89.

Directive should not seek to impose a choice between a legalistic approach to the admissibility of evidence and a more flexible approach in which courts have the right to evaluate evidence based on how it was obtained",[508] suggesting the change to the fragment of Art. 13(3) of the Directive proposed by the Commission.

The proposal for Directive 2013/48/EU contained bold draft regulations in the field of effective remedies, specifying them significantly. This specification was supposed to give detail in two areas:

1. the draft contained a reference to one of the definitions of an effective remedy functioning in the European space, emphasizing the restoration of the situation as it was before the infringement. This could have been of great importance for the issue of effective remedies in EU law. Up to now, neither this definition nor even a clear standard has been formulated in the EU criminal law system.
2. a specific remedy was indicated: evidence obtained in breach of the right to a lawyer or in situations where a derogation from this right was allowed was inadmissible unless its use would not infringe the right of the defense.

During the legislative procedure, the obligation of Member States to implement regulations to exclude evidence from a criminal procedure was abandoned. It was made clear that the requirement for an effective remedy does not interfere with the national system for the admissibility of evidence.

As a result, the text of the Directive that was adopted reflects the conservative position of the Member States. It is vague and does not lead to the actual introduction of a right to an effective remedy in the event of an infringement of the Directive. The Directive grants the accused the right to an effective remedy, but it is impossible to understand from the content of the Directive what such a remedy might be, and what would be its functions, objectives and results. We must assess this solution negatively.

The Commission's proposal here was further-reaching and clearer, and it set higher standards for the rights of the defense by specifying the right to an effective remedy. However, as the legislative work on the draft has shown, the Member States were not ready for its adoption or to accept an undertaking referring to the exclusion of evidence and the definition of an effective remedy.

---

508 Report from the Council on the "Proposal for a Directive of the European Parliament and of the Council on the right of access to a lawyer in criminal proceedings and on the right to communicate upon arrest", 6 December 2011, no. 18215/11.

3.4. The right to an effective remedy in Directive 2016/1919/EU

The draft presented by the European Commission on 27 November 2013[509] did not provide for a right to an effective remedy in the event of a breach of the right to ex officio legal aid. Only later was a proposal made to regulate this issue[510]. Eventually, the right to an effective remedy in this respect was granted in Article 8 of Directive 2016/1919/EU:

> Member States shall ensure that suspects, accused persons and requested persons have an effective remedy under national law in the event of a breach of their rights under this Directive.

For a correct interpretation of this provision, reference should also be made to recital 27 of the directive under consideration:

> In order to monitor and evaluate the effectiveness of this Directive, there is a need for collection of relevant data, from available data, with regard to the implementation of the rights set out in this Directive. Such data include, where possible, the number of requests for legal aid in criminal proceedings, as well as in European arrest warrant proceedings where the Member State concerned acts as an issuing or executing Member State, the number of cases where legal aid was granted, and the number of cases where a request for legal aid was refused. Data on the costs of providing legal aid to suspects or accused persons and to requested persons should also be collected in so far as possible.

The EU legislator has therefore identified situations in which the defendant should be entitled to an effective remedy. However, it is in vain to find any indication in Directive 2016/1919/EU as to what the nature of the remedy should be in the event of a breach of the right to legal aid of the court's own motion. Guidance must therefore be sought in the working documents drawn up during the legislative process. An analysis of these documents leads to the conclusion that the remedy for a breach of the right to legal aid of the court's own motion should be of a controlling nature. A person who claims that his right has been infringed should be able to bring an action before the competent procedural authority, which will examine whether his right has in fact been infringed.

---

509 Proposal for a Directive of the European Parliament and of the Council on provisional legal aid for suspects or accused persons deprived of liberty and legal aid in European arrest warrant proceedings, 27 November 2013, COM/2013/824/final.

510 Report of 18 May 2015 on the Proposal for a Directive of the European Parliament and of the Council on provisional legal aid for suspects or accused persons deprived of liberty and legal aid in European arrest warrant proceedings, mo. A8-0165/2015.

4. The right to an effective remedy in Directive 2016/343/EU

4.1. Aspect of the presumption of innocence

It is one of the most important principles of criminal procedure and lies at the heart of the right to a fair trial that a defendant in a criminal case must be presumed innocent until proven guilty according to law.[511] Accordingly, in 2006 the European Commission presented a Green Paper on the presumption of innocence[512], which aimed to examine and describe the definition of the presumption of innocence in each Member State. Following its publication, the European Council called on the European Commission to assess whether the presumption of innocence needed to be regulated at EU law level[513]. As a consequence of the discussions and actions undertaken, Directive 2016/343/EU was adopted on 9 March 2016, which established the principle of the presumption of innocence (Article 3 of Directive 2016/343/EU). Further provisions regulate the obligations incumbent on procedural authorities and the rights of the accused arising from this principle. Pursuant to Article 4(1) of Directive 2016/343/EU, public authorities and, above all, procedural authorities may not, in public statements and procedural decisions, portray the suspect or the accused as guilty. This regulation does not, however, prevent information about criminal proceedings from being made public where this is necessary for reasons relating to the pre-trial proceedings or the public interest[514].

Nor should suspects or accused persons be presented to the public as guilty by the use of physical restraints, such as handcuffs, unless the circumstances of the case so require[515]. The principle of the presumption of innocence also follows from the rule that the burden of proof is on the prosecution and that any doubt as to guilt is to be resolved in favour of the accused (Article 6 of Directive 2016/343/EU). In addition, Directive 2016/343/EU grants the accused the right not to incriminate himself (Article 7(1)) and the right not to incriminate himself (Article 7(2)). These are instruments designed to protect the accused against

511 See P. Wiliński, K. Kiejnich-Kruk, Right to an Effective Legal Remedy in Criminal Proceedings in the EU. Implementation and Need for Standards, *Review of European and Comparative Law* 54, no. 3 (2023), pp. 159–163.

512 Commission Green Paper of 26 April 2006 on the presumption of innocence COM/2006/174/final.

513 See recital 7 of Directive 2016/343/EU.

514 See recital 16 and 18 and Article 4(2) of Directive 2016/343/EU.

515 See recital 20 and Article 5 of Directive 2016/343/EU.

self-incrimination[516]. According to Article 7(5) of Directive 2016/343/EU, their exercise must not have adverse procedural consequences for the accused.

4.2. The right to be present at the trial

Article 8(1) of the same Directive also grants the accused the right to be present at the trial. This right exists in cases where the accused is found guilty or not guilty[517], and thus applies to the trial and the sentencing. However, it is not absolute[518]. A decision on the guilt or innocence of the accused may be taken at the trial, notwithstanding his absence, if at least one of the conditions set out in Article 8(2) of Directive 2016/343/EU is met:

(a) the suspected person has been duly informed of the date of the trial and of the consequences of his or her failure to appear;
(b) the suspected person is represented by legal counsel

or where the whereabouts of the suspected person could not be established despite the efforts of the judicial authorities (Article 9(4) of Directive 2016/343/EU). However, in such a situation, it is necessary that the suspect is also informed of the remedies available to him or her at the time when the content of the decision is notified. In accordance with Article 9(5) of Directive 2016/343, the right to be present at the trial does not exclude the possibility of temporarily excluding the accused person from the trial if this is necessary to ensure the proper conduct of the criminal proceedings. In such cases, however, the exercise of the right of defence must be guaranteed.

4.3. The right to an effective remedy

The need for a remedy to be regulated in Directive 2016/343 has been argued in the Explanatory Memorandum as follows:

> The ECtHR has consistently held that the most appropriate form of redress for a violation of the right to a fair trial in Article 6(2) ECHR would be to ensure that suspects or accused persons, as far as possible, are put in the position in which they would have been had their rights not been disregarded (See Teteriny v. Russia (judgment

516 See recital 24 and 25 of Directive 2016/343/EU.

517 See Commission Staff working document impact assessment accompanying the document Proposal for measures on the strengthening of certain aspects of the presumption of innocence and of the right to be present at trial in criminal proceedings, COM/2013/821/final.

518 See recital 35 of Directive 2016/343/EU.

> of 30.6.2005, application 11931/03, paragraph 56), Jeličić v. Bosnia and Herzegovina (judgment of 31.10.2006, application 41183/02, paragraph 53), and Mehmet and Suna Yiğit v. Turkey (judgment of 17.7.2007, application 52658/99, paragraph 47), Salduz v Turkey, paragraph 72)[519].

and furthermore

> Article 9 establishes that a remedy (as established by the ECtHR) in cases where the right to be present at trial has not been observed is an obligation to provide for a re-trial. (Colozza v. Italy)[520].

The general regulation of the right to an effective remedy in the event of a breach of the rights granted by Directive 2016/343/EU is finally included in Article 10(1):

> 1. Member States shall ensure that suspects and accused persons have an effective remedy if their rights under this Directive are breached.

This laconic formulation is further developed in recitals 44–46 of Directive 2016/343/EU:

The principle of effectiveness of Union law requires that Member States put in place adequate and effective remedies in the event of a breach of a right conferred upon individuals by Union law. An effective remedy, which is available in the event of a breach of any of the rights laid down in this Directive, should, as far as possible, have the effect of placing the suspects or accused persons in the same position in which they would have found themselves had the breach not occurred, with a view to protecting the right to a fair trial and the rights of the defence.

When assessing statements made by suspects or accused persons or evidence obtained in breach of the right to remain silent or the right not to incriminate oneself, courts and judges should respect the rights of the defence and the fairness of the proceedings. In that context, regard should be had to the case-law of the European Court of Human Rights, according to which the admission of statements obtained as a result of torture or of other ill-treatment in breach of Article 3 ECHR as evidence to establish the relevant facts in criminal

---

519 Proposal for a Directive of the European Parliament and of the Council on the strengthening of certain aspects of the presumption of innocence and of the right to be present at trial in criminal proceedings, COM/2013/0821 final – COD/2013/0407, p. 9–10.

520 Proposal for a Directive of the European Parliament and of the Council on the strengthening of certain aspects of the presumption of innocence and of the right to be present at trial in criminal proceedings, COM/2013/0821 final – COD/2013/0407, p. 8.

proceedings would render the proceedings as a whole unfair. Under the UN Convention against Torture and Other Cruel, Inhuman or Degrading Treatment or Punishment, statements established to have been made as a result of torture cannot be used as evidence in any proceedings, except against a person accused of torture as evidence that the statement was made.

This way the Directive upholds the fundamental rights and principles recognised by the Charter and by the ECHR, including the right to an effective remedy and the right to a fair trial, the presumption of innocence and the rights of the defence. Regard should be had, in particular, to Article 6 of the Treaty on European Union (TEU), according to which the Union recognises the rights, freedoms and principles set out in the Charter, and according to which fundamental rights, as guaranteed by the ECHR and as they result from the constitutional traditions common to the Member States, are to constitute general principles of Union law.

It should also be noted that Article 4(2) of Directive 2016/343/EU indicates that the right to an effective remedy should also be available when the trial authority has violated the prohibition to speak publicly about the guilt of the accused:

> 2. Member States shall ensure that appropriate measures are available in the event of a breach of the obligation laid down in paragraph 1 of this Article not to refer to suspects or accused persons as being guilty, in accordance with this Directive and, in particular, with Article 10.

In contrast, Article 9 of Directive 2016/343/EU regulates a specific remedy for violations of the right to be present at the trial in criminal proceedings:

> Member States shall ensure that, where suspects or accused persons were not present at their trial and the conditions laid down in Article 8(2) were not met, they have the right to a new trial, or to another legal remedy, which allows a fresh determination of the merits of the case, including examination of new evidence, and which may lead to the original decision being reversed. In that regard, Member States shall ensure that those suspects and accused persons have the right to be present, to participate effectively, in accordance with procedures under national law, and to exercise the rights of the defence.

The earlier proposal to regulate this provision was stronger:

> Article 9 establishes that a remedy (as established by the ECtHR) in cases where the right to be present at trial has not been observed is an obligation to provide for a re-trial[521]

---

521 Proposal for a Directive of the European Parliament and of the Council on the strengthening of certain aspects of the presumption of innocence and of the right to be present at trial in criminal proceedings, COM/2013/0821 final – COD/2013/0407.

At this point, it is worth mentioning Article 10(2) of Directive 2016/343/EU:

> 2. Without prejudice to national rules and systems on the admissibility of evidence, Member States shall ensure that, in the assessment of statements made by suspects or accused persons or of evidence obtained in breach of the right to remain silent or the right not to incriminate oneself, the rights of the defence and the fairness of the proceedings are respected.

The proposed regulation reflects a compromise between EU Member States. In the draft directive presented on 27 November 2013, recital 26 of the Commission's proposal states the following: "The principle of effectiveness of Union law requires Member States to provide for adequate and effective remedies in the event of a breach of a right conferred on individuals by Union law. An effective remedy available in the event of a breach of any of the principles set out in this Directive should have the effect, where possible, of placing suspects or accused persons in the same position in which they would have found themselves had the breach not occurred"[522].

There was also a specific remedy for violations of the right to silence – a prohibition on the use of the accused's statements as evidence[523]:

> Any inferences drawn from the fact that suspects or accused persons make use of these rights should be excluded. Without this, the right would be merely illusory if the suspects or accused had to fear that their non-cooperation or their silence will be used against them later in the criminal proceedings. This is the sole way to ensure the effective exercise of these rights by suspects or accused persons without a fear that such exercise can be used against them at a later stage. Therefore, the Directive also provides a specific and immediate remedy that any use of evidence obtained in breach of these rights is not allowed, save in those very exceptional cases where the use of such evidence will not prejudice the overall fairness of the proceedings.[524]

---

522 Proposal for a Directive of the European Parliament and of the Council on the strengthening of certain aspects of the presumption of innocence and of the right to be present at trial in criminal proceedings, COM/2013/0821 final – COD/2013/0407, p. 14.

523 See Opinion of the European Economic and Social Committee on the Proposal for a Directive of the European Parliament and of the Council on the strengthening of certain aspects of the presumption of innocence and of the right to be present at trial in criminal proceedings, COM/2013/821, final.

524 Proposal for a Directive of the European Parliament and of the Council on the strengthening of certain aspects of the presumption of innocence and of the right to be present at trial in criminal proceedings, COM/2013/0821 final – COD/2013/0407.

However, this form of regulation was not agreed to by EU Member States[525]. This was left to the EU Member States, indicating only that the admissibility of evidence must take into account the rights of the defence and a fair trial. Recital 45 of Directive 2016/343/EU emphasises, however, that the evidentiary ban should always apply where the violation was related to torture or inhuman treatment. However, this is only a suggestion by the EU legislator.

4.1. Conclusion

The drafters of the Directive unequivocally endorse the acquis of the European Court of Human Rights, but at the same time set lower standards for Member States in terms of protecting the rights of defendants and suspects. This is particularly relevant in the context of Article 13 of the Directive, which states that nothing in the Directive shall be construed as limiting or diminishing the rights and procedural safeguards afforded under the Charter, the ECHR or other relevant provisions of international law, or the law of any Member State that provides a higher level of protection. In summary, it follows from the provisions of Directive 2016/343 that the right to an effective remedy exists in cases of violation of:

(a) the prohibition of public statements on the guilt of the accused before the final conclusion of the proceedings;
(b) the right not to make a statement and not to incriminate oneself;
(c) the right to be present at the trial.

The remedy should be remedial in nature, but again it is up to EU Member States to choose specific solutions in national law. In other words, an effective remedy for violations of certain aspects of the presumption of innocence and the right to be present at the trial in criminal proceedings should be remedial in nature.

---

525 See Proposal for a Directive of the European Parliament and of the Council on the strengthening of certain aspects of the presumption of innocence and of the right to be present at trial in criminal proceedings – General approach, 4 December 2014, no. 16531/14.

5. The right to an effective remedy in Directive 2016/800/EU

5.1. Procedural rights of child defendants in criminal proceedings

The Roadmap for strengthening procedural rights of suspected or accused persons in criminal proceedings also included Measure E, which was described as follows:

> In order to safeguard the fairness of the proceedings, it is important that special attention is shown to suspected or accused persons who cannot understand or follow the content or the meaning of the proceedings, owing, for example, to their age, mental or physical condition.

To date, EU Member States have not agreed on who are vulnerable persons and what this treatment should consist of. At the stage of work on the implementation of Measure E, EU countries were in no doubt only that the list of such persons should include children[526]. The European Convention for the Protection of Human Rights and Fundamental Freedoms does not explicitly provide for the regulation of children's rights in criminal proceedings[527]. However, it follows from the case law of the ECtHR that the guarantees of Article 6 ECHR also apply to children[528]. When a child is an accused in criminal proceedings, it is necessary to take into account the child's age, maturity and intellectual and emotional capacities in order to ensure his or her effective participation in the process. Consequently, measures have also been taken to strengthen the procedural rights of a child accused in criminal proceedings[529].

More specifically, Directive 2016/800/EU lays down minimum standards on certain procedural rights of children who are suspects or accused persons in criminal proceedings and children who are the subject of a European arrest warrant (Article 1 of Directive 2016/800/EU). According to Article 3(1) of

---

526 See Communication from the European Criminal Bar Association (ECBA) of 15 May 2013, http://ecba.org/extdocserv/20130515_ECBAonMeasureE.pdf (access: 06.03.2019).

527 I. Radic, Right of the Child to Information according to the Directive 2016/800/EU on Procedural Safeguards for Children Who Are Suspects or Accused Persons in Criminal Proceedings, *EU and Comparative Law Issues and Challenges Series*, no. 2 (2018), p. 475.

528 The EU Agency for Fundamental Rights (FRA), *Handbook on the European Law Relating to the Rights of the Child*, Luxemburg, 2015, p. 199.

529 S. E. Rap, D. Zlotnik, The Right to Legal and Other Appropriate Assistance for Child Suspects and Accused, *European Journal of Crime, Criminal Law and Criminal Justice*, 26 (2018), p. 113.

Directive 2016/800/EU, a child is a person below the age of 18. In the light of Article 2(3) of Directive 2016/800/EU, the provisions of the Directive should also apply to persons who were children at the time of the proceedings and who have subsequently reached the age of 18, if the circumstances of the case so justify[530]. Member States may decide that the provisions of the Directive do not apply when a person reaches the age of 21. It should also be noted that the provisions of the Directive under consideration relate only to criminal proceedings. They are not intended to apply to other types of proceedings, including those specifically aimed at children. According to Article 2(1) of Directive 2016/800/EU, the rights granted to the child are to be enjoyed by the child until the final conclusion of the criminal proceedings. The Directive does not explicitly specify the starting point, but indicates that it is the moment when the child becomes a person suspected of having committed a criminal offence.

Directive 2016/800/EU differs from other directives on the procedural rights of the accused in criminal proceedings in that it regulates procedural rights of a different nature:

1. the right to information on procedural rights,
2. the right to legal assistance,
3. the right to an individual assessment,
4. the right to privacy,
5. the right to be accompanied by a parent or guardian,
6. the right to be present at the trial,
7. the right to limitation of detention and alternative measures,
8. the right to a medical examination in the event of deprivation of liberty,
9. the right to special treatment when deprived of liberty.

What is also unusual is that it often refers to the provisions of the earlier directives, sometimes only adding additional guarantees. For example, the child should be informed about the general aspects of the conduct of proceedings, the rights granted under Directives 2012/13/EU and 2016/343/EU. The child has the right to be assisted by a defence counsel (Article 6 of Directive 2016/800/EU), and Member States are obliged to adequately regulate the right to be represented by a defence counsel (Article 18 of Directive 2016/800/EU). It should be noted that Directive 2013/48/EU and Directive 2016/1919/EU already set minimum standards in this respect. Directive 2016/800/EU, in contrast to the previously discussed EU regulations, regulates a wide range of rights in criminal

530 See recitals 10–12 of Directive 2016/800/EU.

proceedings for a single subject. Consequently, potential remedies should also be regulated in such a way as to cover a very wide range of potential violations.

The above clearly shows that Directive 2016/800/EU, unlike the previously discussed EU regulations, regulates a wide range of rights in criminal proceedings for a single subject. Consequently, potential remedies should also be regulated in such a way as to cover a very wide range of potential violations.

5.2. The right to an effective remedy

Surprisingly, the right of a child defendant to an effective remedy for violation of his or her procedural rights was not initially included[531]. However, this was amended in a later version of the draft directive[532] and approved by the European Parliament[533]. The right to an effective remedy for the rights granted in Directive 2016/800/EU is finally regulated in Article 19:

> Member States shall ensure that children who are suspects or accused persons in criminal proceedings and children who are requested persons have an effective remedy under national law in the event of a breach of their rights under this Directive.
> Despite the laconic wording of this provision, there is no indication in the preamble of any motives guiding the legislative work on the right to an effective remedy. In principle, the EU legislature left no indication as to the nature of the remedies in relation to particular procedural rights. Only Article 16(2) of Directive 2016/800/EU regulates the remedy for violation of the right to be present at the trial:
> Member States shall ensure that children who were not present at their trial have the right to a new trial or to another legal remedy, in accordance with, and under the conditions set out in, Directive (EU) 2016/343/EU.

Moreover, EU Member States are free to decide on the nature of remedies for violations of specific procedural rights of the child. However, EU Member States should take into account the existing solutions adopted in the various Directives

531 See Proposal for a Directive of the European Parliament and of the Council on procedural safeguards for children suspected or accused in criminal proceedings, 27 November 2013, COM/2013/0822 final - COD/2013/0408.

532 See working version of Directive of the European Parliament and of the Council on procedural safeguards for children suspected or accused in criminal proceedings given by the Council representative by letter of 16 December 2015 to approve the position of the European Parliament, no. 15272/15.

533 European Parliament legislative resolution of 9 March 2016 on the proposal for a directive of the European Parliament and of the Council on procedural safeguards for children suspected or accused in criminal proceedings, COM/2013/0822 – C7-0428/2013 – COD/2013/0408.

on the procedural rights of the accused and the functions to be fulfilled by a particular procedural right.

As already mentioned, the EU legislator referred to the previously discussed directives when granting particular rights to the child. This makes it at least possible to interpret the enigmatic regulation on remedies. For example, the right to procedural information, as well as the child's right to have the parent informed of the child's rights, found support in the provisions of Directive 2012/13/EU. Consequently, remedies for violations of the child's right to information in criminal proceedings of a controlling nature are automatically guaranteed. On the other hand, the minimum standards on the right of children to counsel are based on the provisions of Directives 2013/48 and 2016/19. By analogy, therefore, remedies for violations of the right to be assisted by counsel should be remedial in nature and remedies for violations of the right to be appointed counsel should be controlling in nature. The right to an individual assessment has not yet been the subject of EU regulation. Bearing in mind the purpose of this entitlement, it should be stated that – in the event of a violation of this right – the child should be entitled to measures that will lead to such an individual assessment. Consequently, a violation of this entitlement should entail the granting of remedies of a remedial nature to the child. In summary, Directive 2016/800/EU not only provides no additional rationale for interpreting the concept of an effective remedy, but makes one refer to the previous laconic indications in earlier directives.

6. Directive on the right to an effective remedy – Roadmap 2020

Above mentioned directives have introduced many international standards into European criminal procedure, adopting also concept of legal remedies as derived mostly from case law of the ECHR and Court of Justice of the European Union[534]. A continuation of this evolutionary process is the need for further instruments[535]. Much should be discussed in this regard. One of those worth considering is the European Criminal Bar Association's initiative "Agenda 2020: A new roadmap on minimum standards for certain procedural safeguards"[536].

---

534 G. Jansen, The Need for a New Roadmap of Procedural Safeguards: a Lawyer's Perspective, *ERA Forum*, 22 (2021), pp. 279–294.

535 J. Ouwerkerk et al. (eds.), *The Future of EU Criminal Justice Policy and Practice. Legal and Criminological Perspectives*, Brill Nijhoff, 2019, p. 261.

536 ECBA Initiative 2017/2018 "Agenda 2020: A new Roadmap on minimum standards of certain procedural safeguards", https://www.ecba.org/extdocserv/20180424_ECBA_Agenda2020_NewRoadMap.pdf.

In justifying the need for such a project, it was pointed out that "Apart from the right to be present in trials (Directive 2016/343/EU) the entire trial phase suffers from a lack of protection (including remedies) for defendants due to national differences without any legally binding and functional concrete minimum standards. Despite the general clauses in Art 6, 13 ECHR, in Art 14 ICCPR and in Art 47 ff CFEU and the corresponding jurisprudence the daily practices in certain Member States provides multiple violations of these rules which are applicable for the accused and/or the defence lawyer"[537].

Consequently, the ECBA proposed a Roadmap 2020 which should include research by studies, impact assessment(s) by the European Commission and finally legislation by means of directives or regulations (Art 82 TFEU) on the following measures:

- Measure A: (Pre-Trial) Detention and European Arrest Warrant
- Measure B: Certain Procedural Rights in Trials
- Measure C: Witnesses' Rights and Confiscatory Bans
- Measure D: Admissibility and Exclusion of Evidence and other Evidentiary Issues
- Measure E: Conflicts of Jurisdiction and ne bis in idem
- Measure F: Remedies and Appeal
- Measure G: Compensation

The need for Measure F is justified as follows: "In all phases of criminal proceedings it is necessary to grant effective legal remedies in order to improve the quality of criminal proceedings and judicial decisions including judgements. Procedural guarantees including the right to be heard are not sufficiently protected (i.e. practically and efficiently not only theoretically and illusory). One of the most crucial issues is the factual prevention of the defence from information (evidence, files) during the investigative stage of a criminal proceeding. (...) Prevention from access to information avoids justice and fairness of any proceeding[538]".

Of course, the draft put forward by ECBA should be read only a seed of the work that needs to be done in order to have legislation in place to regulate, among other things, remedies. What is important is that this signals the need for further

537 ECBA Initiative 2017/2018 "Agenda 2020: A new Roadmap on minimum standards of certain procedural safeguards", https://www.ecba.org/extdocserv/20180424_ECBA_Agenda2020_NewRoadMap.pdf.

538 ECBA Initiative 2017/2018 "Agenda 2020: A new Roadmap on minimum standards of certain procedural safeguards", https://www.ecba.org/extdocserv/20180424_ECBA_Agenda2020_NewRoadMap.pdf.

proceedings at EU level on this issue both when it comes to comprehensive regulation of remedies and taking them into account for various procedural issues. The Roadmap 2020 proposal opens up the field for discussion and builds awareness. This is borne out by the articles emerging on the subject[539], as well as by the working documents produced within the European Union. For example, the Communication from the Commission to the European Parliament, the Council, the European Economic and Social Committee and the Committee of the Regions "Digitising justice in the European Union: A set of possibilities"[540] clearly indicates that any action relating to the digitalisation of justice must be implemented in full compliance with fundamental rights, such as the rights to the protection of personal data, to a fair trial and to an effective remedy, and the principles of proportionality and subsidiarity. It remains to be hoped that the next few years will bring even more bold developments on this issue.

7. Summary

This chapter discusses instruments containing provisions on remedies available to the accused in the event of a violation of his procedural rights in criminal proceedings. These are contained in five directives: Directive 2012/13/EU, Directive 2013/48/EU, Directive 2016/343/EU, Directive 2016/800/EU and Directive 2016/1919/EU. In each of the above-mentioned directives, ultimately only a laconic provision requiring Member States to provide remedies in the event of a breach of the rights contained in the individual directives was included[541]. However it is clear from the working documents that this is a compromise agreed by the very conservative member states on this issue. They have thus gained almost unlimited flexibility in choosing how to implement the right to an effective remedy.

---

539 C. Riehle, A. Clozel, 10 Years after the Roadmap: Procedural Rights in Criminal Proceedings in the EU Today, *ERA Forum*, 20 (2020), pp. 321–325; G. Jansen, The Need for a New Roadmap of Procedural Safeguards: A Lawyer's Perspective, *ERA Forum*, 22 (2021), pp. 279–294.

540 Communication from the Commission to the European Parliament, the Council, the European Economic and Social Committee and the Committee of the Regions Digitalisation of Justice in the European Union: A toolbox of opportunities, COM/ 2020/710 final.

541 A. Soo, (Effective) Remedies for a Violation of the Right to Counsel during Criminal Proceedings in the European Union: An Empirical Study, *Utrecht Law Review*, 14 (2018), p. 19.

The directives resulting from the Roadmap to Strengthen Procedural Rights of Suspected or Accused Persons in Criminal Proceedings, adopted in 2009, have introduced many international standards into European criminal procedure[542]. They undoubtedly also represent a further step in popularising the right to an effective remedy. However, too little is known about how this right is to be implemented in practice. The laconic provisions have signalled the need to regulate this issue, but have left too much discretion to the Member States[543]. It is rightly noted that "The end of this legislative process should not be the end of the road and action should continue to be taken at European Union level to strengthen the rights of suspects or accused persons in criminal proceedings and thereby reinforce the principle of mutual recognition and mutual trust that underpins it[544]. Especially in these times, mutual trust is not at all self-evident, as can be seen in the increasing case law of the Court of Justice of the European Union".

Moreover, without setting specific requirements, it is clear that countries are seeking to implement the relevant rights provided for in the Directives at a minimum level. It is therefore difficult to speak of a European standard, mutual trust and consequently the operation of the mutual recognition principle[545]. On the contrary, other problems arise, such as the lack of a common understanding of the application of remedies (access, speed, procedure, costs, suspensive effect, exclusion)[546]. It is therefore important to develop a theoretical framework on the effectiveness of remedies in the European context. To succeed in strengthening procedural guarantees, we should start with awareness[547]. A good starting point

542 C. Riehle, A. Clozel, 10 Years after the Roadmap: Procedural Rights in Criminal Proceedings in the EU Today, *ERA Forum* 20, (2020), pp. 321–325.

543 S. Prechal, *Directives in EC Law*, New York 2005, pp. 7–8; K. Kiejnich, *Harmonization of EU Criminal Law – Issues of Implementing EU Directives*, in: A. Kłos, J. Misiuna, M. Pachocka, A. Szczerba-Zawada (eds.), *European Union and Its Values: Freedom, Solidarity, Democracy*, Warsaw, 2020, p. 37.

544 M. Kusak, *Mutual Admissibility of Evidence in Criminal Matters in the EU. A Study of Telephone Tapping and House Search*, Antwerpen, 2016, pp. 23 and 147.

545 A. Willems, *The Principle of Mutual Trust in EU Criminal Law*, Oxford et al., Hart, 2021.

546 V. C. Ramos, M. Luchtman, G. Munteanu, *Improving Defence Rights: Including Available Remedies in and (or as a Consequence of) Cross-Border Criminal Proceedings*, EUCRIM 3/2020, pp. 230–248.

547 P. Chmielnicki, J. Paśnik, Ochrona trwałości schematów działania za pomocą norm prawnych jako kryterium efektywności prawa, in: P. Chmielnicki (ed.), *Pochodzenie, tworzenie i efektywność prawa*, Warsaw, 2014, pp. 363–386.

seems to be the statement: "The rights of the individual include the right to an effective remedy, an essential aspect for improving the quality of criminal proceedings (...)[548]".

Bibliography

Literature

Chmielnicki P., Paśnik J, *Ochrona trwałości schematów działania za pomocą norm prawnych jako kryterium efektywności prawa*, in: Chmielnicki P. (ed.), *Pochodzenie, tworzenie i efektywność prawa*, Warsaw, 2014.

De Bondt W., Vermeulen G., The Procedural Debate. A Bridge Too Far or Still Not Far Enough?, *EUCRIM* 4, 2010.

Efrat A., Assessing Mutual Trust among EU Members: Evidence from European Arrest Warrant, *Journal of European Public Policy*, no. 26, 2019.

Jansen G., The Need for a New Roadmap of Procedural Safeguards: A Lawyer's Perspective, *ERA Forum* 22, 2021.

Kiejnich K., Harmonization of EU criminal law – issues of implementing EU directives, in: A. Kłos, J. Misiuna, M. Pachocka, A. Szczerba-Zawada eds., *European Union and Its Values: Freedom, Solidarity, Democracy*, Warsaw, 2020.

Kiejnich-Kruk K., *Prawo do skutecznego środka naprawczego w postępowaniu dowodowym*, Warsaw, 2023.

Kolendowska-Matejczuk M., Mrowicki M., *Prawo do informacji o własnych prawach w postępowaniu karnym jako jeden z wymiarów edukacji praw człowieka*, Krakowskie Studia Międzynarodowe, 4, 2019.

Kusak M., *Mutual Admissibility of Evidence in Criminal Matters in the EU. A Study of Telephone Tapping and House Search*, Antwerpen, 2016.

Loof R., Shooting from the Hip: Proposed Minimum Rights in Criminal Proceedings throughout the EU, *European Law Journal* 12, no. 3, 2006.

Marguery T., European Union Fundamental Rights and Member States Action in EU Criminal Law, *Maastricht Journal of European and Comparative Law*, no. 2, 2013.

Nowicki M. A., *Wokół Konwencji Europejskiej. Komentarz do Europejskiej Konwencji Praw Człowieka*, Warsaw, 2013.

548 E. Sellier, A. Weyembergh, *Criminal Procedural Laws across the European Union: A Comparative Analysis of Selected Main Differences and the Impact they Have over the Development of EU Legislation*, 2018, https://www.europarl.europa.eu/thinktank/en/document.html?reference=IPOL_STU%282018%29604977.

Ouwerkerk J. et al. (eds.), *The Future of EU criminal justice policy and practice. Legal and criminological perspectives*, Brill Nijhoff, 2019.

Pivaty A., Beazley A., Daly M. Y., de Vocht D., ter Vrugt P., Strengthening the Protection of the Right to Remain Silent at the Investigative Stage: What ROLE for the EU Legislator?, *New Journal of European Criminal Law* 12, no. 3, 2021.

Prechal S., *Directives in EC Law*, New York, 2005.

Radic I., Right of the Child to Information according to the Directive 2016/800/EU on Procedural Safeguards for Children Who Are Suspects or Accused Persons in Criminal Proceedings, *EU and Comparative Law Issues and Challenges Series*, no. 2, 2018.

Ramos V. C., Luchtman M., Munteanu G., Improving Defence Rights: Including Available Remedies in and (or as a Consequence of) Cross-Border Criminal Proceedings, *EUCRIM* 3, 2020.

Rap S. E., Zlotnik D., The Right to Legal and Other Appropriate Assistance for Child Suspects and Accused, *European Journal of Crime, Criminal Law and Criminal Justice*, 26, 2018.

Riehle C., Clozel A., 10 Years after the Roadmap: Procedural Rights in Criminal Proceedings in the EU Today, *ERA Forum* 20, 2020.

Sellier E., Weyembergh A., *Criminal Procedural Laws across the European Union: A Comparative Analysis of Selected Main Differences and the Impact they Have over the Development of EU legislation*, Bruxelles, 2018.

Sellier E. (ed.), *Criminal Procedures and Cross-Border Cooperation in the EU Area of Criminal Justice. Together But Apart?*, Bruxelles, 2020.

Soo A., (Effective) Remedies for a Violation of the Right to Counsel during Criminal Proceedings in the European Union: An Empirical Study, *Utrecht L, Rev* 14, 2018.

Spronken T., Vermeulen G., Vocht D., van Puyenbroeck L., *EU Procedural Rights in Criminal Proceedings*, Maastricht, 2009.

Starzyński P., 7.1.2.4. Akty wprowadzające i zalecenia Komisji Europejskiej, in: P. Hofmański, C. Kulesza (eds.), *System Prawa Karnego Procesowego Tom 6. Strony i inni uczestnicy postępowania karnego*, Warsaw, 2016.

Šadl U., The Role of Effet Utile in Preserving the Continuity and Authority of European Union Law: Evidence from the Citation Web of the Pre-accession Case Law of the Court of Justice of the EU, *European Journal of Legal Studies*, no. 1/8, 2015.

Van Dijk P., van Hoof F., van Rijn Arjen, Zwaak Leo (red.), *Theory and Practice of the European Convention of Human Rights*, Cambridge-Antwerp-Portland, Intersentia, 2018.

Van Puyenbroeck L., Vermeulen G., Towards Minimum Procedural Guarantees for the Defence in Criminal Proceedings in the EU, *International and Comparative Law Quarterly* 60, no. 4, 2011.

Willems A., *The Principle of Mutual Trust in EU Criminal Law*, Oxford et al., Hart, 2021.

Judgements

ECtHR judgment of 30.6.2005, 11931/03, Teteriny v. Russia, HUDOC

ECtHR judgment of 31.10.2006, 41183/02, Jeličić v. Bosnia and Herzegovina, HUDOC

ECtHR judgment of 17.7.2007, 52658/99, Mehmet and Suna Yigit v. Turkey, HUDOC

ECtHR judgment of 27.11.2008, 36391/02, Salduz v. Turkey, HUDOC

Legal Acts

Commission Green Paper of 26 April 2006 on the presumption of innocence COM/2006/174/final

Commission Recommendation of 27 November 2013 on procedural safeguards for vulnerable persons suspected or accused in criminal proceedings 2013/C 378/02, OJ C 378/8

Directive 2012/29/EU of the European Parliament and of the Council of 25 October 2012 establishing minimum standards on the rights, support and protection of victims of crime, and replacing Council Framework Decision 2001/220/JHA, L 315, 14.11.2012

Directive 2012/13/EU of the European Parliament and of the Council of 22 May 2012 on the right to information in criminal proceedings, L 142, 01.06.2012

Directive 2013/48/EU of the European Parliament and of the Council of 22 October 2013 on the right of access to a lawyer in criminal proceedings and in European arrest warrant proceedings, and on the right to have a third party informed upon deprivation of liberty and to communicate with third persons and with consular authorities while deprived of liberty, L 294, 06.11.2013

Directive 2014/41/EU of the European Parliament and of the Council of 3 April 2014 regarding the European Investigation Order in criminal matters, L 130, 01.05.2014

Directive 2014/42/EU of the European Parliament and of the Council of 3 April 2014 on the freezing and confiscation of instrumentalities and proceeds of crime in the European Union, L 127, 29.04.2014

Directive (EU) 2016/343 of the European Parliament and of the Council of 9 March 2016 on the strengthening of certain aspects of the presumption of innocence and of the right to be present at the trial in criminal proceedings, L 65, 11.03.2016

Directive (EU) 2016/680 of the European Parliament and of the Council of 27 April 2016 on the protection of natural persons with regard to the processing of personal data by competent authorities for the purposes of the prevention, investigation, detection or prosecution of criminal offences or the execution of criminal penalties, and on the free movement of such data, and repealing Council Framework Decision 2008/977/JHA, L 119, 04.05.2016

Directive (EU) 2016/800/EU of the European Parliament and of the Council of 11 May 2016 on procedural safeguards for children who are suspects or accused persons in criminal proceedings, L 132, 21.05.2016

Directive (EU) 2016/1919 of the European Parliament and of the Council of 26 October 2016 on legal aid for suspects and accused persons in criminal proceedings and for requested persons in European arrest warrant proceedings, L 297, 04.11.2016

Green Paper on pre-trial detention "Strengthening mutual trust in the European judicial area – A Green Paper on the application of EU criminal justice legislation in the field of detention", COM(2011) 327 final

Resolution of the Council of 30 November 2009 on a Roadmap for strengthening procedural rights of suspected or accused persons in criminal proceedings (Text with EEA relevance), C 295

Treaty on the Functioning of the European Union, C 326, 26.10.2012

Others

Commission Staff working document summary of the impact assessment accompanying the Proposal for a Directive of the European Parliament and of the Council on the right to information in criminal proceedings, COM 2010/ 392 final..

Commission Staff working document impact assessment accompanying the document Proposal for measures on the strengthening of certain aspects of the presumption of innocence and of the right to be present at trial in criminal proceedings, COM/2013/821/final.

Communication from the European Criminal Bar Association (ECBA) of 15 May 2013, http://ecba.org/extdocserv/20130515_ECBAonMeasureE.pdf (access: 06.03.2019)

Communication from the Commission to the European Parliament, the Council, the European Economic and Social Committee and the Committee of the Regions Digitalisation of Justice in the European Union: A toolbox of opportunities, COM/2020/710 final

Council Framework Decision 2003/577/JHA of 22 July 2003 on the execution in the European Union of orders freezing property or evidence, L 196, 02.08.2003, p. 45–55

Council Framework Decision 2006/783/JHA of 6 October 2006 on the application of the principle of mutual recognition to confiscation orders, L 328, 24.11.2006, p. 59

The EU Agency for Fundamental Rights (FRA), *Handbook on the European law relating to the rights of the child*, Luxemburg, 2015

European Criminal Bar Association, *Agenda 2020: A new Roadmap on minimum standards of certain procedural safeguard*, 2017

European Parliament legislative resolution of 9 March 2016 on the proposal for a directive of the European Parliament and of the Council on procedural safeguards for children suspected or accused in criminal proceedings, COM/ 2013/0822 – C7-0428/2013 – COD/2013/0408

European Commission press release of 28 May 2013, MEMO/13/468; speech by Viviane Reding, ice-President of the European Commission, at the press conference of 6 June 2013; European Commission press release of 19 June 2013, MEMO/13/589

Opinion of the Committee on Legal Affairs for the Committee on Civil Liberties, Justice and Home Affairs on the proposal for a directive of the European Parliament and of the Council on the right to information in criminal proceedings (COM(2010)0392 – C7 0189/2010 – 2010/0215(COD)), 27.01.2011

Opinion of the European Economic and Social Committee on the "Proposal for a Directive of the European Parliament and of the Council on the right of access to a lawyer in criminal proceedings and on the right to communicate upon arrest", COM/2011/326 final – COD/2011/0154

Opinion of the European Economic and Social Committee on the Proposal for a Directive of the European Parliament and of the Council on the strengthening of certain aspects of the presumption of innocence and of the right to be present at trial in criminal proceedings, COM/2013/821, final

Press Release 3034th Council meeting Justice and Home Affairs, Luxembourg, 7–8 October 2010, 14423/10

Press Release 3043rd Council meeting Justice and Home Affairs Brussels, 8 and 9 November 2010, 15848/10

Press Release 3051st Council meeting Justice and Home Affairs Brussels, 2–3 December 2010, 16918/10

Press release of the 3121st Council meeting Justice and Home Affairs, 27 and 28 October 2011, No 16042/11

Press release of the 3172st Council meeting Justice and Home Affairs, 7 and 8 June 2012, No 10760/12

Proposal for a Council Framework Decision on certain procedural rights in criminal proceedings throughout the European Union, SEC(2004) 491

Proposal for a Directive of the European Parliament and of the Council on the right of access to a lawyer in criminal proceedings and on the right to communicate upon arrest, COM/2011/0326 final - COD 2011/0154

Proposal for a Directive of the European Parliament and of the Council on the strengthening of certain aspects of the presumption of innocence and of the right to be present at trial in criminal proceedings, COM/2013/0821 final - COD/2013/0407

Proposal for a Directive of the European Parliament and of the Council on provisional legal aid for suspects or accused persons deprived of liberty and legal aid in European arrest warrant proceedings, 27 November 2013, COM/2013/824/final

Proposal for a Directive of the European Parliament and of the Council on the strengthening of certain aspects of the presumption of innocence and of the right to be present at trial in criminal proceedings – General approach, 4 December 2014, no. 16531/14

Proposal for a Directive of the European Parliament and of the Council on procedural safeguards for children suspected or accused in criminal proceedings, 27 November 2013, COM/2013/0822 final – COD/2013/0408

Report from the Council on the Proposal for a Directive of the European Parliament and of the Council on the right of access to a lawyer in criminal proceedings and on the right to communicate upon arrest, 6 December 2011, no. 18215/11

Report of 18 May 2015 on the Proposal for a Directive of the European Parliament and of the Council on provisional legal aid for suspects or accused persons deprived of liberty and legal aid in European arrest warrant proceedings, no. A8-0165/2015

Report on the proposal for a directive of the European Parliament and of the Council on the right to information in criminal proceedings, COM 2010/0392 – C7-0189/2010 – 2010/0215(COD), A7-0408/2011, 25.11.2011

Working version of Directive of the European Parliament and of the Council on procedural safeguards for children suspected or accused in criminal proceedings given by the Council representative by letter of 16 December 2015 to approve the position of the European Parliament, no. 15272/15

Piotr Karlik

Chapter 5 Concept of effective legal remedies in common law

1. Introduction

The issue of an effective remedy against abuses of power is discussed in both continental and common law. We can encounter various forms of abuse, transgression, or even violation of the law by representatives of state bodies. Some of them have far-reaching effects in the sphere of personal rights, others affect more the public, and still others are indifferent. Hence, it is crucial to properly distinguish between these cases and determine whether and to what extent remedies are available to prevent these incidents or allow for the repeal of their negative consequences. After all, the more individualized the violation of individual rights and guarantees, the more protective mechanisms should be in place to preserve the resulting rule of law. This is particularly true of the criminal process, where violations of individual rights can occur, which can even result in critical consequences. The lack of tools to remedy these consequences will make them irreversible, and thus such a legal system will reward lawlessness. Thus, it is evident that the issue of an effective remedy is one of the more pressing problems of the judiciary, also unfamiliar to countries in the common law area. At the same time, the process of the formation of this law over hundreds of years shows a large degree of variation in the approach to the issue itself. Therefore, it is worth looking at the origins and roots of this institution, to better understand its basic meaning.

2. Historical background and development of the right to a remedy

2.1. UK perspective

The right to an effective remedy is one of the oldest rights in the common law system and can be traced back to the enactment of the Magna Carta in 1215. The initial proposals made in the Great Charter on the field at Runnymede were finally confirmed in the final version of the Charter in 1225 in Chapter 29[549].

549 T. R. Phillips, The Constitutional Right to a Remedy, N.Y.U. School of law, pp. 1309–1345; It is worth noting here that the original version of Magna Carta placed due

Consequently, the guarantees of the provisions of this monument of the law resulted in the transfer of the right to declare a violation from local feudals to the organized system of royal courts.

The modern understanding of the right to an effective remedy, however, was not adopted until 1641, thanks to the interpretation of the provisions of the Magna Carta provided by Sir Edward Coke in his foundational work: Second Part of the Institutes of the Laws of England[550].

He stated that: "*Every subject of this realm, for injury done to him in goods, lands, or person, by any other subject, be he ecclesiastical, or temporall,… or any other without exception, may take his remedy by the course of the law, and have justice, and right for the injury done to him, freely without sale, fully without any deniall, and speedily without delay*". In the Magna Carta, therefore, researchers rightly see the origins of the British system of Petitionary and Remedial Rights[551]. As indicated earlier, the right to petition (Chapter 61 of the Magna Carta) was also a remedy but was eventually withdrawn due to its far-reaching provisions. However, it is worth looking at the proposed content at the time: "*If we…offend in any respect against any Man, or transgress any of the articles of the peace or of this security, and the offence is made known to four of the … twenty-five barons, they shall come to us… to declare it and claim immediate redress. If we …. make no redress within forty days… the four barons, who may distrain upon and assail us in every way possible, with the support of the whole community of the land, by seizing our castles, lands, possessions, or anything else saving only our own person and those of the queen and our children, until they have secured such redress as they have determined upon. Having secured the redress, they may then resume their normal obedience to us*"[552].

Nevertheless, over time, petitions addressed to the King began to function anyway, which necessitated the generation of a procedure for the recognition of these petitions, in which the development of the remedies system is also seen. Petitions addressed directly to the King were forwarded to the Chancellor, which

process rights in chap 39 and a right to a remedy in chapter 40, so the final version of 1225 combined these two guarantees into one under chapter 29. As a result of the work on the text, the originally planned guarantee of chapter 61, i.e., the right to petition, was also omitted.

550 Hastings Lyon & Herman Block, Edward Coke: Oracle of the Law 348.

551 S.M. Roesler, Comment, The Kansas Remedy by Due Course of Law Provision; Defining a Right to a Remedy, 47 *U. Kansas Law Review* pp. 657–58 (1999).

552 B.P. Cover, First amendment right to a remedy, *I.U. College of Law*; 50 UC Davis L. Rev. p. 1741 (2017).

were then recognized by the Chancery Court, which became independent from the King, which then evolved into courts of equity. It is up to them to develop the maxim according to which: "equity will not suffer a wrong without a remedy"[553]. This was later made clear in the now-famous Ashby v. White case, where the court held that the: "*If the plaintiff has a right, he must of necessity have a means to vindicate and maintain it, and a remedy if he is injured in the exercise or enjoyment of it; and indeed it is a vain thing to imagine a right without a remedy; for … want of right and want of remedy are reciprocal… Where a man has but one remedy to come at his right, if he loses that he loses his right*"[554]. Thus, it is evident that British culture has developed two types of guarantees for asserting violations of rights: a right to a remedy from the courts and a right to petition the King and Parliament.

The importance of the right to a remedy has grown significantly over the years, such that Sir William Blackstone described it as one of critical importance to preserving and securing the fundamental rights of the individual to life, liberty and property[555].

2.2. United States' perspective

Undoubtedly, American law, along with recycling the achievements of British jurisprudence, has also taken over the standards derived from the guarantee of the right to a remedy. This can be seen primarily at the level of state law, where in as many as forty state constitutions the right to a remedy is expressed either indirectly or directly. In most states that have adopted the direct expression of this guarantee, we can encounter the following version: "*That all courts shall be open, and every person, for an injury done him in his person, property or reputation, shall have remedy by the due course of law*"[556]. However, it is quite apparent that there is a significant disparity in the approach to this issue within the US. In the remaining states, which, although in the minority, nevertheless make up a significant number, the right to an effective remedy is treated as a historical

553 Ibidem, p. 1764.

554 Ashby v. White (1703) 92 Eng. Rep. pp. 126, 137.

555 W. Blackstone, Commentaries *124.

556 Constitutions of: Alabama, Arizona, Colorado, Connecticut, Delaware, Florida, Idaho, Indiana, Kentucky, Louisiana, Mississippi, Missouri, Montana, Nebraska, North Carolina, North Dakota, Ohio, Oklahoma, Oregon, Pennsylvania, South Dakota, Tennessee, Texas, Utah, Washington, West Virginia, and Wyoming.

legacy[557]. Such differentiation is mainly due to the lack of a comparable guarantee at the level of the national Constitution[558], and the Supreme Court's reluctance to interpret it from due process[559]. This was mainly explained by this, that adopting right to a remedy provision would have raised substantial federalism concerns, and that the right to remedy was already encompassed by the right to petition[560].

Looking historically, the development of the American doctrine of the right to an effective remedy developed based on a lack of confidence in the level of protection of individual rights by the institutions of British law. Hence, provisions appeared in individual state constitutions that introduced direct protection of guarantees, through the adoption of the right to a remedy. This happened as early as 1776 when Pennsylvania and Delaware adopted the right to a remedy in a written constitution.

In America, the right to an effective remedy has been used from the very beginning and has allowed the repeal of numerous laws restricting rights, among other things, an individual's access to pursue his or her rights in court. One of the first, if not the first, example of the invocation of this guarantee was the upholding a Massachusetts law that abolished the common-law right of landowners to sue mill owners for flooding and substituted a payments schedule instead[561]. In a similar vein stated The Supreme Court of Errors and Appeals of Tennessee while invalidating a statute providing a two-year moratorium on executing on a judgement for debt unless the creditor agreed to accept the notes of certain banks in satisfaction[562]. Right to a remedy has also become the basis for the repeal of restrictive court rules, such as the need to file any motion for a new trial only on the first Saturday after the end of the first[563]. Further examples of the use of right to a remedy have allowed the repeal of unnecessary fees on access to court[564]. More examples included the repeal of laws restricting access to the courts for Union supporters during the Civil War[565], or, above all, workers'

557 W.C. Koch Jr., Reopening Tennessee's Open Court Clause: A Historical Reconsideration of Article I, Section 17 of the Tennessee Constitution, 27 *U. Mem. L. Rev.* pp. 333, 341 (1997).
558 T. R. Phillips, The Constitutional..., p. 1317.
559 Silver v. Silver, 280 U.S. pp. 117, 122 (1929).
560 B.P. Cover, First amendment, p. 1783.
561 Stowell v. Flagg, 11 Mass. (9 Tyng) 364, 365 (1814).
562 Townsend v. Townsend, 7 Tenn. (Peck) 1 (1821).
563 Pawley v. McGimpsey, 15 Tenn. (7 Yer.) 502 (1835).
564 Harrison, Pepper & Co. v. Willis, 54 Tenn. (7 Heisk.) 35, pp. 45–47 (1871).
565 Davis v. Pierse, 7 Minn. 13, 20 (1862).

rights and the possibility of pursuing tort claims[566]. Subsequent rulings have only reaffirmed the role of the right to an effective remedy and allowed for the opening of the judicial path in many aspects of the functioning of individuals. One of the fundamental rulings of the time, which indicated the limits of the right to a remedy, is the ruling of Mattson v. Astoria[567], in which The Oregon Supreme Court held that: "*the constitutional provision guarantying to every person a remedy by due course of law for injury done him in person or property... was intended to preserve the common-law right of action for injury to person or property, and while the legislature may change the remedy or form of procedure, attach conditions precedent to its exercise, and perhaps abolish old and substitute new remedies, it cannot deny a remedy entirely*".

Today, the development of remedy clause has been observed primarily in the fight against laws limiting the ability to sue against medical malpractice, the rights of architects, builders and constructors[568].

3. Basic forms of abusing the law in common law systems

3.1. Abusing the law in UK

British law recognise at least several types of forms of abuse of the law. These include such cases as breach of the law, misuse of power, overuse of law and abuse of law, abuse of process. What comes to the fore is that the issue of violation of the law or the powers granted is of a graded nature. Consequently, British law distinguishes such violations of law that do not result in a violation of the sphere of individual rights. It can also be noted that the concept of a broad abuse of rights extends to a great many spheres of public life.

3.1.1. Breach of law

As already mentioned, the construction of abuse of rights is gradable in British law. Consequently, a distinction is made between such cases of non-compliance with the letter of the law that do not lead to a violation of individual rights. It therefore does not take a qualified form and can be considered in principle

566 Kirby v. Pa R.R. Co., 76 Pa. 506, 508 (1875); Eastman v. County of Clackamas, 32 F. 24 (D. Or. 1887).

567 65 P. 1066 (Or. 1901).

568 Austin v. Litvak, 682 P.2d 41 (Colo. 1984); Shessel v. Stroup, 316 S.E.2d 155 (Ga. 1984); Carson v. Maurer, 424 A.2d 825 (N.H. 1980).

only at the level of moral judgment or professional responsibility[569]. These types of cases occur commonly and are subjected to scrutiny by, among others, the Supreme Court, which may ultimately qualify a case as significant. In other respects, these cases from the point of view of individual rights are irrelevant.

3.1.2. Abuse of law (power)

Only when it is recognized that a particular case of breach of law has led to significant interference and thus worsening of the situation of the individual, it is possible to recognize it as an abuse of law. Thus, it can be concluded that abuse of law is a qualified form of breach of law and must be considered at a completely different level of involvement of state bodies. As it seems, only such violations of law must also result in the actualization of corrective mechanisms that will allow for an effective legal response. At the same time, this is not about tools of a political nature, but about the legal options available to the individual to act within the framework of a specific case of violation of his rights and guarantees. What is important is that the recognition of a violation as a qualified form – especially within the executive branch – is carried out based on a detailed procedure, where the final vote belongs to the Supreme Court[570].

3.1.3. Misuse of power

Another cited example of abuse of law (misuse of power) is the so-called King's consent rule. This is the King's authority to approve laws regulating the scope of so-called royal prerogatives. This is not regulated by law in any way, nevertheless the requirement to obtain the King's consent is regulated by numerous laws[571]. However, it is pointed out that in a situation where the queen vetoes laws unfavourable to herself or members of the royal family, a kind of abuse of the law occurs. Consequently, it is possible to conclude that the queen's consent is not necessary in each case. Is not needed where the impact on the Crown is too indirect or too remote, or where there is unlikely to be an impact, or the impact is likely to be too insignificant. This is referred to as *a de minimis* test, and its implementation makes it possible to determine the cases that require King's consent.

---

569 Walumba Lumba (Congo)v Secretary of State for the Home Department [2011] UKSC 12.

570 www.files.justice.org.uk

571 (See. Bradley, Ewing and Knight, Constitutional and Administrative Law, Pearson, 17th Ed. (2018) p. 258; G. Bartlett, M. Everett, The Royal Prerogative, No. 03861, London 2017, p. 9.

3.1.4. *Abuse of process*

In turn, about the criminal proceedings themselves in the context of potential abuse, the concept of abuse of process (abuse of process) is very often used. This is a concept that regulates exceptional situations in which there is a risk that the prosecution has abused its powers in the context of ongoing proceedings and there is a need to suspend them (**stay proceedings**). However, this is an exceptional measure, and its application depends on the demonstration by the accused and his counsel that indeed the continuation of the proceedings will result in a violation of the proceedings. This issue is only hinted at here and will be addressed further in the discussion of remedies.

3.2. Abusing the law in United States

In the legal system of the United States, we can encounter a multiplicity of terms referring to the abuse of rights in a broad sense. This is a consequence of the fact that abuse of a right per se can be spoken of at many levels. US law is by no means unique in this regard. The jurisprudence of the Supreme Court, as well as the federal courts, indicates that irregularities resulting from abuse of the law can occur at the level of the executive branch, which includes the US president himself, legislation, but also, and perhaps above all, the application of the law. It is precisely the cases of individual violations or abuses of the applicable law in the context of individual cases of an individual that seem to be the most momentous from the perspective of shaping the system of remedies. This is because the actions taken in this field are a clear indicator of the level of protection of the participants in the proceedings.

3.2.1. *Institutional abuse*

This is a situation in which there is improper treatment of a person or groups of people because of violations of their rights, guarantees or standards by institutions or broader state bodies. This is most often the result of the lack of appropriate internal regulations, the qualifications of individuals, as well as the abuse of power by representatives of these entities.

In this case, one of the remedies available is the possibility to ask for a judicial review of such action (Judicial review). Depending on the type of case, it will be possible to turn to the state courts and, as a last resort, even to the Supreme Court. The criterion for evaluation here will primarily be acting within the framework of the Constitution and respecting the rights and guarantees expressed therein. Key in this regard was the enactment of the 14th Amendment to the US Constitution, which first and foremost extended so-called fundamental rights (bill of rights), to all states. According to its content: "*All persons born or naturalized in the United States, and subject to the jurisdiction thereof, are citizens of the United States and of the State wherein they reside. No State shall make or enforce any law which shall abridge the privileges or immunities of citizens of the United States; nor shall any State deprive any person of life, liberty, or property, without due process of law; nor deny to any person within its jurisdiction the equal protection of the laws*".

3.2.2. Legal abuse

These are cases of "abuse of the law", which may involve the actions of any of the participants in the broader proceedings, including criminal proceedings. Consequently, we can speak of abuse of the law by representatives of law enforcement agencies, representatives of the judiciary, but also by the parties and their representatives. This is a consequence of the adoption of the adversarial model of criminal proceedings, which grants far-reaching rights to the parties, among other things, in the shaping of evidence. The discovery of these abuses during the proceedings can have various consequences for the proceedings – from the inadmissibility of evidence to the nullification of the trial (depending on the procedure) and can also result in the initiation of disciplinary proceedings against the person who committed such a violation.

A special role within this concept of "abuse of the law" is played by abuses committed by the public prosecutor. Cases of behaviour when such situations occur are referred to as "prosecutorial misconduct" and can be fraught with far-reaching consequences. The above construction is most like the concept of abuse of rights as understood on continental grounds and derived from the current standards of the European Convention on Human Rights and Fundamental Freedoms. Although in this respect the two legal systems are separate from each other, one can see quite a lot of similarities in defining the key areas of violation. This makes it possible to identify both corrective mechanisms and prevent the occurrence of such phenomena in the future.

4. Due process of law as a background for effective legal remedies in US legal system

4.1. Mistrial, reversal, or dismissal of the case as legal remedies

In the case of abuse of the law in the context of ongoing criminal proceedings, we can basically speak of two types of applicable remedies. The first will refer to the consequences within the proceedings themselves, i.e., the impact of the violation on the course of the trial, while the second type will focus on the broader issue of compensation. In the case of the first type of remedy, three types of possible consequences of revealing the abuse are basically indicated: a mistrial, a reversal of the judgment (reversal) or a dismissal of the case (dismissal). The differences that exist between these remedies are significant and largely depend on the timing of the abuse allegation. Ultimately, however, all these measures derive their source from the 5th Amendment to the US Constitution. According to this guarantee:

> *No person shall be prosecuted for a capital crime or other heinous offense without an indictment passed by a grand jury on its own initiative or at the request of a prosecutor, unless it be a case involving the land or naval forces or the militia in active service during time of war or public danger. Nor may anyone be punished twice for the same offense on life or limb. No one may be compelled to testify in a criminal case against himself, or be deprived of life, liberty or property without proper justice. Private property may be seized for public use only with just compensation.*

From this provision, and in fact from the case law based on it, the "due process of law" standard (a model of due process) is unambiguous, which provides the basis for taking corrective action when an abuse of the law is found. This standard was reiterated and upheld in the 14th Amendment to the US Constitution. It is this standard that has become the starting point for recognizing and identifying further types of abuse. Courts, as well as parties seeking legal protection, primarily refer to the guarantees of the due process for law standard. This is, among other things, a consequence of the characteristics of common law, particularly US federal law, which is based on the principle of stare decisis and, as such, lacks an elaborate state law that could serve as a point of reference or a self-contained source of individual guarantees. Hence the great importance of the rules described in the Constitution, which not only set minimum standards in the descriptive layer, but also, and perhaps most importantly, provide an unlimited source for seeking rights and freedoms rooted in that standard.

Situations falling within the general construction of abuse of rights, may also be caused by circumstances beyond the control of any of the participants in the proceedings, or be the result of the action of the judge or judges themselves. These are, of course, exceptional situations, but nevertheless, given their significance and importance, they involve far-reaching consequences from the point of view of the proceedings themselves. Among the above are, first, the "Manifest Necessity Doctrine" (Manifest Necessity Doctrine); deadlock in the attitude of the jury (Deadlock jury); or prejudice against a party (prejudice). The occurrence of any of these circumstances can result in a mistrial.

The doctrine of manifest necessity is most often used in situations beyond the control of the parties (e.g., weather conditions), however, in certain exceptional circumstances they can be a consequence of the prosecution or defense representatives (e.g., a prosecution witness slandered the defendant's attorneys for committing the same crime that is the subject of the trial). In such cases, the presiding judge (trial judge) is authorized to declare a mistrial[572].

An impasse in the jury's vote can also be grounds for a mistrial if it is established beyond a reasonable doubt that the jury is unable to reach a unanimous decision. Such a situation can also be caused by a deliberate act by the jurors to bring about a mistrial and thus relieve them of their duty.

However, the most momentous and at the same time the most serious violations are situations in which any bias against the case or the person of the suspect or the state itself will be revealed. It is therefore about any violation of the principle of objectivity and impartiality[573]. Another example of a situation where there will be a mistrial is, for example, the failure of the judge to follow the judge's instructions on how the jury should proceed.

4.2. Harmless error doctrine as limitation for legal remedies in US system

However, as practice shows, the courts very rarely reach for tools to repeal abuses committed during proceedings[574]. This happens because of the need to incur additional costs of the proceedings, or the release of a suspect due to a procedural error. As if in return, the courts use the concept of "harmless error" ("harmless error doctrine"). This means that the abuse committed does not necessarily automatically trigger the need to set aside the judgment, annul it or dismiss the case, in a situation where the abuse did not cause harm to the proceedings, or was irrelevant to the case. This approach to the issue at hand has become quite common, since as early as 2001, in more than 87 % of cases with a finding of abuse, the courts invoked the concept of "harmless error".

5. Catalogue of legal remedies available in UK legal system

In general, there are two grounds for suspending proceedings. This was strongly emphasized by the Court of Appeal Queen's Bench Division Case in its judgment

---

572 State v. Grays, 276 N.C. App. 21(2021).

573 State v. Wilson, 314 N.C. 653 (1985).

574 W.M. Landes & R.A. Posner, Harmless Error, 30 J Legal studs. pp. 161, 182–92 (2001).

of May 12, 2014. (*No: 2014 02162-02166 B5*) ("*As is clear from decisions such as Attorney General's Reference (No 2 of 2001) [2004] 2 AC 72, there are two categories of case in which the court has the power to stay proceedings for abuse of process. These are, first, where the court concludes that the accused can no longer receive a fair hearing; and, second, where it would otherwise be unfair to try the accused or, put another way, where a stay is necessary to protect the integrity of the criminal justice system. The first limb focuses on the trial process and where the court concludes that the accused would not receive a fair hearing it will stay the proceedings; no balancing exercise is required. The second limb concerns the integrity of the criminal justice system and applies where the Court considers that the accused should not be standing trial at all, irrespective of the potential fairness of the trial itself*").

The first, of a procedural nature, allows for the suspension of proceedings in a situation where the court comes to believe that the defendant will not be guaranteed a fair trial – in procedural terms. However, it is pointed out that the invocation of this premise – although an exclusive prerogative of the court – should be exceptional. "*The crown is usually responsible for bringing prosecutions, and prima facie, it is the duty of the court to try persons who are charged before it with offences which it has power to try. Nonetheless the courts retain an inherent jurisdiction to restrain what they perceive to be an abuse of their process. This power is of great constitutional importance and should be … preserved. It is the policy of the courts, however, to ensure that the criminal proceedings are not subject to unnecessary delays through collateral challenges, and in most cases any alleged unfairness can be cured in the trial process itself. We must therefore stress from the outset that this is residual (and discretionary) power of any court to stay criminal proceedings as an abuse of its process is one which ought only to be employed in exceptional circumstances, whatever the reasons submitted for invoking*"[575].

Among the reasons that allow for the suspension of proceedings due to the inability to guarantee a fair trial, the following are pointed out first and foremost:

- significant delay in the hearing of the case – in this regard, it has been repeatedly pointed out that there is a direct connection between the speed, or more efficiently, of the proceedings and a party's right to a fair trial. To demonstrate the existence of this connection in a particular proceeding, it is necessary to conduct a test of whether such delay resulted in the inability to conduct a fair trial.

575 *R (Ebrahim) v Feltham Magistrates' Court [2001] 1 All ER 831.*

"The Divisional Court held, at p 169D-E, that the test at common law was whether delay had given rise to such prejudice that no fair trial could be held: Tan v Cameron [1992] 2 AC 205, 222–224, per Lord Mustill. In its judgment no such prejudice was shown, and in the Court of Appeal Schiemann LJ was of the same opinion: [2000] 2 WLR 1420, 1459A-B. The respondents say that the approach taken by these courts was wrong in law, as there was no requirement to show actual prejudice. The nature of the common law right which they asserted in your Lordships' House appeared to me to be virtually indistinguishable in this respect from the right under article 6(1), so I do not need to dwell on this part of their argument. I shall deal with the issue of delay on the assumption that the test which they must satisfy is that which requires to be satisfied to demonstrate that there was a breach of the Convention right and that prejudice, while relevant if it exists, does not require to be demonstrated"[576];

- evidentiary problems – the destruction or loss of evidence in proceedings – in a fundamental ruling, the Higher Court of England and Wales, in refusing to find a violation of the law, pointed out that the evaluation of the conduct of law enforcement agencies in collecting and recording evidence must always be individual in nature. It is crucial to determine whether the omissions, if any, that led to the destruction or loss of evidence constituted a flagrant violation of the applicable regulations, or whether they were of an innocent nature. At the same time, the court noted that not every loss or destruction of evidence must lead to a finding of abuse of law[577];
- excessive publicity of the case – in the case of the participation of jurors in the proceedings, who, through access to public information presented in the media, could lose objectivity to the case, which would cause risks to procedural guarantees, as well as the stability of the verdict itself ("*Applications for a stay of proceedings of the ground of abuse of process, founded on prejudicial media publicity, are a growth area in our criminal process. In R v McCann (1991) 92 Cr App R 239 the Court of Appeal held that such an application should have succeeded in quite extraordinary circumstance. During closing speeches in a terrorist trial where the defendants had exercised their right to silence the Secretary for Northern Ireland and Lord Denning took part in radio or television broadcast, which might have been heard by the jury, in which they equated the exercise of the right of silence with guilt. Equally, in R. Michelle and Lisa*

576 Porter v. Magill; Weeks v. Magill [2002] 2 A.C. 357, HL.
577 *R (Ebrahim) v Feltham Magistrates' Court [2001] 1 All ER 831.*

Taylor (1994) 98 Cr App R page 361 this court held that unremitting, extensive, sensational, inaccurate and misleading press coverage of the trial was one reason why the guilty verdict was unsafe")[578];

- the prosecutor's failure to disclose information, which consequently prevented the defendant from exercising his right to counsel. Thus, there was undeniably a violation of the right to a fair trial ("*The proceedings could be stayed not only where a fair trial was impossible but also where it would be contrary to the public interests in the integrity of the criminal justice system that a trial should take place. There were an infinity variety of cases, but a judge must weigh in the balance public interest in ensuring that those that were charged with grave crimes should be tried and the competing public interest in not conveying the impression that the court would adopt the approach that the end justifies the means.*

  There can be no doubt that the piecemeal disclosure made during the trial was disruptive, made the task of defence counsel impossible")[579].

5.1. Additional reasons to justify the existence of injustice within the process

However, in the jurisprudence of British courts, one can also encounter other grounds indicating the existence of injustice in the ongoing trial, and thus the inability to guarantee a fair trial[580]. Foremost among these are:

- bias of the judge;
- unreasonable delay in approving the decision;
- imbalance of parties in the proceedings;
- violation of the presumption of innocence.

> *The Court of Appeal four matters were identified under the broad heading of unfairness: [2000] 2 WLR 1420, per Schiemann LJ, at p 1453H. These were (a) apparent bias on the part of the auditor, (b) unreasonable delay on the part both of the auditor and on the part of the Divisional Court in confirming the decision by the auditor, (c) failure on the part of the Divisional Court to hold a fair balance between the auditor and Dame Shirley Porter and (d) breach by the Divisional Court of the presumption of innocence. The Court of Appeal was not persuaded that there had been any unfairness which would justify allowing the appeal.*

---

578 R. v. Abu Hamza [2007] 1 Cr.App.R. 27.
579 R. v. Salt *[2015] 1 WLR 4905.*
580 Magill v. Porter [2001] UKHL 67 (2001).

5.2. The interests of justice as a rationale for suspending proceedings

The second relates to issues unrelated to the process as such, as it is possible to suspend the proceedings for the sake of the administration of justice The case law primarily points to violations of the rules of the process of the court (Violation of the Process of the Court), the violation of which may cause consequences in the form of suspension of proceedings. However, as has been repeatedly emphasized, the creation of a closed catalogue of such situations is impossible in practice, due to the diversity of potential behaviour. The key point here is that the courts should assess each violation individually and decide on its ultimate impact on the process. („*Elaborating upon the law in relation to this head of abuse, it has been described as arising "where it offends the court's sense of justice and propriety to be asked to try the accused in the particular circumstances of the case. The categories of cases in which it may be unfair to try the accused will include, but are not confined to, those cases where there has been bad faith, unlawfulness or executive misconduct. Cases where the courts have considered this type of abuse of process to arise have tended to involve very serious examples of malpractice and unlawfulness*")[581].

A classic example of such a situation would be the breaking of a promise not to prosecute an offender for specific acts. In such a case, however, it is necessary to provide a statement from the authority on the assurance that the person will not be prosecuted. Another example justifying the suspension of proceedings is the deliberate manipulation of the procedure by the prosecutor[582].

6. Influence of The Charter of Fundamental Rights of the European Union on common law system from UK perspective

6.1. Human Rights Act 1998

Guarantees under the European Convention on Human Rights and Fundamental Freedoms apply in the UK legal system. An individual in the UK is equally subject to the protection of the European Court of Human Rights. However, it is worth noting that most of the provisions contained in the ECHR were incorporated into the domestic legal order because of the Human Rights Act 1998, which came into force in 2000 (an act known as the Convention Rights Act). The primary

---

581 R. v. Crawley [2014] EWCA Crim. 1028.

582 R v. Rotherham Justices ex parte Brough [1991] C.O.D. 89.

purpose of such an action was to shorten the legal route for UK citizens. This is because it became possible to directly invoke the Convention's guarantees at the level of national law, without having to initiate a lengthy procedure before the ECHR. Nevertheless, it should be noted, there is no regulation in this law equivalent to Article 13 of the ECHR – the right to an effective remedy. However, this does not mean that such a remedy is not provided for in British law.

6.2. Criminal Justice Act 2003 and Criminal Justice and Court Act 2015

Certain issues in the area of the possibility, for example, of appealing certain decisions when a party to the proceedings disagrees with them, are provided for by such acts as the Criminal Justice Act 2003 and the Criminal Justice and Court Act 2015, which regulate the course of criminal proceedings in the UK. However, as it turned out in practice, the above regulations proved to be insufficient, especially in terms of guaranteeing the so-called effective remedy. This was particularly highlighted in the case of Hammerton vs. United Kingdom (Application No. 6287/10), where a detainee was deprived of his right to representation. As a result, the ECHR found a violation of the right to a fair trial and awarded appropriate compensation ("As regards its finding of a violation of Article 13, the Court accepts that the lack of a fully "effective" domestic remedy, which prompted the applicant to lodge an application under the Convention to obtain adequate redress, was liable to have caused him some frustration.").

6.3. Human Rights Act Remedy Order 2018

As a result of the above situation, a discussion has begun in the UK on the need to change the existing legislation and amend the Human Rights Act. Recently, the Human Rights Act Remedy Order 2018 was being processed, which provides for the right to compensation for damages caused by a judge's decision. Eventually, the new regulations went into effect in October 2020. The key wording is Section 9 (3) In proceedings under this Act in respect of a judicial act done in good faith, damages may not be awarded otherwise than-(a)to compensate a person to the extent required by Article 5(5) of the Convention, or (b)to compensate a person for a judicial act that is incompatible with Article 6 of the Convention in circumstances where the person is detained and, but for the incompatibility, the person would not have been detained or would not have been detained for so long. In the aforementioned provisions, direct reference can be made to specific provisions of the ECHR.

7. Summary

The above analysis clearly shows that there is a rich tradition in common law regarding the right to an effective remedy. It is one of the cornerstones of the due protection of individual rights, regardless of where one sees the source of it. On the other hand, however, there is a growing need to regulate this right to increase the standard of protection of individual guarantees against their unauthorized violation. This is particularly evident at the level of the criminal process, where the consequences of the lack of adequate protection, or even the inability to exercise the right to a due remedy, are by far the most far-reaching. Discussion of this issue has been going on in both the UK and the US for quite some time, and different paradigms of approach to this issue are evident. A paradigm shift in the standards for protecting the right to an effective remedy in the common law system is therefore to be expected, and this should be viewed positively.

Bibliography

Literature

Bartlett G., Everett M., *The Royal Prerogative*, No. 03861, London, 2017.

Bradley A. W., Ewing K. D., Knight C., *Constitutional and Administrative Law*, Pearson, 17th ed., 2018.

Coke E. *Oracle of the Law*, Houghton Mifflin, 1929.

Cover B. P., First Amendment Right to a Remedy, I.U. College of Law, *50 UC Davis Law Review*, 2017.

DeBoer M. J. The Right to Remedy by Due Course of Law – A Historical Exploration and an Appeal for Reconsideration, *Faulkner Law Review* 6, 2014.

Koch Jr. W.C., Reopening Tennessee's Open Court Clause: A Historical Reconsideration of Article I, Section 17 of the Tennessee Constitution, *27 U. Memphis. Law Review* 333, no. 341, 1997.

Phillips T. R., The Constitutional Right to a Remedy, *N.Y.U. Law Review* 78, 2003.

Posner R. A., Landes W. M., "Harmless Error," *30 Journal of Legal Studies*, 161, 2001.

Roesler S. M., Comment, The Kansas Remedy by Due Course of Law Provision; Defining a Right to a Remedy, 47 U. *Kansas Law Review*, 1999.

Judgements

Ashby v. White (1703) 92 Eng. Rep. 126, 137

Austin v. Litvak, 682 P.2d 41 (Colo. 1984);

Carson v. Maurer, 424 A.2d 825 (N.H. 1980).
Davis v. Pierse, 7 Minn. 13, 20 (1862).
Eastman v. County of Clackamas, 32 F. 24 (D. Or. 1887).
Harrison, Pepper & Co. v. Willis, 54 Tenn. (7 Heisk.) 35, 45–47 (1871).
Kirby v. Pa R.R. Co., 76 Pa. 506, 508 (1875);
Magill v. Porter [2001] UKHL 67 (2001).
Pawley v. McGimpsey, 15 Tenn. (7 Yer.) 502 (1835).
Porter v. Magill; Weeks v. Magill [2002] 2 A.C. 357, HL.
R (Ebrahim) v Feltham Magistrates' Court [2001] 1 All ER 831.
R. v. Abu Hamza [2007] 1 Cr.App.R. 27.
R. v Salt *[2015] 1 WLR 4905.*
R v. Rotherham Justices ex parte Brough [1991] C.O.D. 89.
Shessel v. Stroup, 316 S.E.2d 155 (Ga. 1984);
State v. Grays, 276 N.C. App. 21(2021).
State v. Wilson, 314 N.C. 653 (1985).
Silver v. Silver, 280 U.S. 117, 122 (1929).
Stowell v. Flagg, 11 Mass. (9 Tyng) 364, 365 (1814).
Townsend v. Townsend, 7 Tenn. (Peck) 1 (1821).

Legal Acts

Human Rights Act 1998 (c. 42).
Criminal Justice Act 2003 (c. 44)
Criminal Justice and Court Act 2015 (c. 2)
Constitution of the United States
Magna Carta 1297

Paweł Wiliński

Chapter 6 Discussing effective legal remedies

1. Identification of ELR

The ongoing crisis of confidence of European states in each other's value system and understanding of the essence of the rule of law is of crucial importance for the integration of EU law in the sphere of criminal law[583]. This crisis hinders the cooperation of national procedural authorities.[584] However, it does not slow down the pace of legal transactions or reduce the need to protect the rights and freedoms of individuals.[585]

A closer analysis of ELR concept presented in earlier chapters leads to a number of thoughts and observations.[586] The effectiveness of protection mechanisms is of particular importance for the protection of the legal order.[587]

---

583 See Auke Willem: *The Principle of Mutual Trust in EU Criminal Law*, Oxford et al., Hart 2021, 312–320, also Jannemieke Ouwerkerk et al. (eds.), *The Future of EU Criminal Justice Policy and Practice. Legal and Criminological Perspectives*, Brill Nijhoff, 2019, p. 261. See also E. Wieczorek, *The Legitimacy of EU Criminal Law*, Hart 2020, pp. 16–20, 141–167; P. de Gert, Division of Competences beetwen National and European Levels with Regard to Justice and Home Affairs, in: *Police and Justice Cooperation in the New European Boarder*, Kluwer Law International 2002.

584 See Sellier Elodie (ed.), *Criminal Procedures and Cross-Border Cooperation in the EU Area of Criminal Justice. Together But Apart?*, Bruxelles 2020, p. 459; D. Flore, The Issue of Mutual Trust and the Needed Balace Between Diversity and Inuty, in: C. Briere, A. Weyembergh (eds.), *The New Balances in EU Criminal Law. Past, Present, Future*, Hart 2020, pp. 157–164. See also A.Klip, *European Criminal Law, an Integrative Approach*, Intersentia 2016; G. Vermeulen, Mutual Recognition, Harmonisation and Fundamental (procedural) Rights Protection, in: M. Martin (ed.), *Crime, Rights and the EU: the Future of Police and Juditial Cooperation*, London 2008.

585 Efrat A., Assessing mutual trust among EU members: Evidence from European Arrest Warrant, *Journal of European Public Policy*, no. 26 (2019), p. 656 an next.

586 See K. Kiejnich, Harmonization of EU Criminal Law – Issues of Implementing EU Directives, in: A. Kłos, J. Misiuna, M. Pachocka, A. Szczerba-Zawada eds., *European Union and Its Values: Freedom, Solidarity, Democracy*, Warsaw, 2020, pp. 37–39.

587 See Gora A., de Vilde P., The Essence of Democratic Backsliding in the European Union: Deliberation and Rule of Law, *Journal of European Public Policy*, no. 29 (2022), 342 an next; G. Davies, Democracy and Legitimacy in the Shadow of Purposive Competences, *European Law Journal*, no. 21 (2015).

It is not only a matter of knowing but also understanding the essence of the guarantees granted to the individual in international law and knowing how to use them.[588] Among the many of these rules, the guarantee of an effective legal remedy contained in Article 13 of the European Convention on Human Rights (ECHR)[589] and Article 47 of the Charter of Fundamental Rights of European Union (CFR)[590], from which the right of the individual to an effective remedy derives, deserves special attention.

The essence of a remedy within the meaning of Article 13 of the ECHR [591] and Article 47 of the CFR boils down to providing an individual with an opportunity to remedy a violation of his or her freedom or rights, "so far as is possible in the particular case". The ELR concept specifically provides a bulwark against defective action by the State and its organs. It also serves to protect against the conduct of the procedural authorities in criminal proceedings, including that which is in the nature of an abuse of sovereign power.

From the perspective of the legal system ELR is a measure which enables the competent State authority to confront with an alleged violation of any individual protected rights and, if it considers that a violation has occurred, to award appropriate compensation (ECHR). From procedural perspective ELR can be understand also as an access to a tribunal in a properly constituted procedure whenever there is an alleged violation of rights and freedoms guaranteed by the law of the UnionCJEU.[592] In this respect, it should be borne in mind that

588 T. Marguery, European Union Fundamental Rights and Member States Action in EU Criminal Law, *Maastricht Journal of European and Comparative Law*, no 2 (2013), 283 and next.

589 See P. Hofmański, A. Wróbel, w: *Konwencja o Ochronie Praw Człowieka i Podstawowych Wolności. Tom I. Komentarz do art. 1–18*, red. A. Barcz, C. H. Beck 2010, pp. 723–754.

590 See A. Wróbel (red.), *Karta Praw Podstawowych Unii Europejskiej. Komentarz* (*Charter of Fundamental Rights of European Union. Commentary*), C.H. Beck 2020, pp. 1103–1206.

591 See See Guide on *Article 13 of the European Convention on Human Rights. Right to Effective Legal Remedy*, Council of Europe 2022, https://www.echr.coe.int/documents/d/echr/guide_art_13_eng.

592 This is the same with the right to a fair trial since both systems guarantee enforcement at national level also application of instruments meeting respected standards from ECHR and CFR. See more on the concept i.a. T. Brooks (ed.), *The Right to a Fair Trial*, Routledge 2009; P. Leanza, O. Pridal, *The Right to a Fair Trial. Article 6 of the European Convention on Human Rights*, Kluwer International 2014. In broader concept A. Clooney, P. Webb, The Right to a Fair Trial in International Law, Oxford Univ. Press 2021; D. Weissbrodt, *Declaration of Human Rights and the International*

art 47 CFR is of paramount importance for EU Member States since offering more extensive protection coming from explicitly guaranteed access to a remedy before a "tribunal". If the EU Charter of Fundamental Rights does not apply, the ECHR may apply, as EU Member States are also States Parties to the ECHR.

The scope of the right to effective legal remedy covers both horizontal[593] and vertical relationships, meaning that it is intended to protect individuals against any unlawful actions, irrespective of the responsible entity's status. The judicial protection therefore extends to violations by private persons, EU institutions as well as national authorities, not excluding legislative bodies and supreme courts.[594] In this sense, it constitutes an integral component of the rule of law. At the same time, the principle of effective judicial protection upholds the entire system of European Union law, which could not function if national courts did not adhere to the related principles of equivalence and effectiveness.

This right has not always been appreciated or sufficiently recognised until now. However, it is universal. It is defined in terms of its effect and not in terms of its form (see Chapters 2–3). It serves to protect the individual against violation of his or her fundamental freedoms guaranteed by the European Convention on Human Rights and the Charter of Fundamental Rights.[595]

The remedy is to be "effective" and vested "in the competent state authority". These concepts are vague in nature. We can find no legal or any other definition. There are multiple attempts for clarification based on the meaning of "effectiveness". Guidance for their precise understanding should be sought in the jurisprudence of the ECtHR and the Court of Justice of European Union (CJEU,Chapters 2–3). From that we can say that effective:

- is defined most often by a desire result.
- must lead in each case to the annulment of the challenged decision.
- must be heard before a tribunal that meats standards of independence, established by law, applying rules of law and independent.

Covenant on Civil and Political Rights. Articles 8, 10 and 11 of the Universal Declaration of Human Rights, Brill 2021.

593 See E. Frantziou, The Horizontal Effect of the Charter of Fundamental Rights of the EU: Rediscovering the Reasons for Horizontality, *European Law Journal* 21, no. 5 (September 2015), pp. 659–661.

594 See opinion of Advocate General Leger in Case C-224/01, Kobler v. Republik Osterreich, 8 April 2003, pp. 25–52, Case C-224/01, pp. 31–36 and Case C-46/93 and C-48/93, p. 36.

595 W. Piątek, The Right to an Effective Remedy in European Law: Significance, Content and Interaction, *China-EU Law Journal,* 6 (2019).

- implies an exhaustive examination of the relevant legal and factual circumstances of the case.

and means:

- to consider all the questions of fact and law that are relevant to the case.
- to exercise of rights conferred by the law of the EU (the principle of effectiveness)[596]
- to achieve the aim of the legal instruments adopted by the EU institutions.
- to ensure that the rights conferred upon individuals may be effectively pursued before the courts.
- to ensure direct and immediate protection of the interests of those persons who may be affected by any possible infringement of their rights.
- that effectiveness of compensatory measures is also manifested in the amount of awarded redress.
- also, that the procedure for recognizing the measure itself must be structured in such a way as to fulfill the standards of fair trial.

It must be stressed that the ELR primarily refers to systemic deficiencies, not to irregularities in the procedure carried out in a particular case. Thus, it obliges to introduce instruments that serve to combat certain fixed, repetitive and defective actions of state bodies. They must therefore be by their nature flexible and at the same time universal. An effective remedy should therefore be available in the case of a justifiable (not necessarily well-founded) allegation of a violation of any Convention right, hence its universality.

A distinction should be made between two different situations requiring a measure, where the criterion is the violator. One is different when the violation of Convention rights is committed by organs or officials of the State, and the other when the violation is committed by an individual, a third party. Obviously, each state party to the Convention is obliged to effectively protect the individual in both systems. However, the extent of the resulting obligations may differ substantially. However, if there is a violation of the individual's Convention rights on the part of the state authorities, the state of violation may be cumulative. Indeed, there may be a double violation of the same provision of the Convention – first in material terms and then in procedural terms.

596 Case C-326/96, Levez v. T. H. Jennings (Harlow Pools) Ltd, 1 December 1998, p. 18 and Case C-120/97, Upjohn Ltd v. The Licensing Authority established by the Medicines Act 1968 and ot., 21 January 1999, p. 32.

The domestic legal system is the point of reference for seeking a remedy of an effective nature.[597] For this reason, States Parties attempt to meet their treaty obligations in a variety of ways.[598] In the first instance, they make use of the existing instruments in a given legal system, either by suddenly discovering their remedial character, or by giving it a new scope or meaning, or, finally, by making it appear effective, by pointing to a specific legal instrument and, as a last resort, by introducing new legal institutions. In doing so, states cannot justify the ineffectiveness of national measures by invoking organisational problems or procedural specificities. Procedural autonomy does not exempt States from the obligation to provide minimum guarantees.[599]

A remedy must be provided to anyone who makes a substantiated allegation of a violation of his or her Convention rights.[600] It is to ensure that the allegation is investigated, and where possible, lead to the remedying of the violation.[601]

The requirement to provide a remedy is assessed in relation to the specific situation, in relation to the rights of the individual concerned. Despite its systemic nature, it encompasses the imperative of a correct individual response to the violation and the need for remedy. For this reason, however, it does not at the same time imply a general and universal obligation on the part of the State to introduce in every such situation a new and universal remedy, a kind of complaint to challenge a right incompatible with the Convention.[602]

The effectiveness of a remedy relates to the existence of a legal instrument and not to its effect. Indeed, it only expresses the right of access to an appropriate procedure within the national system, but no guarantee of a favorable outcome

597 See Z. Mataga, *Effectivness of Domestic Remedies under the ECHR (Article 13)*, Budapest 2002.

598 See W. Piątek, The Right to an Effective Remedy in European Law: Significance, Content and Interaction, *China-EU Law Journal* (2019), 6.

599 See D. Flore, The Issue of Mutual Trust and the Needed Balace Between Diversity and Inuty, in: C. Briere, A. Weyembergh (eds.), *The New Balances in EU Criminal Law. Past, Present, Future*, Hart 2020, pp. 157–164.

600 ECtHR judgment of 25.03.1983, 5947/72, 6205/73, 7052/75, 7061/75, 7107/75, 7113/75, 7136/75, Silver and Others v. The United Kingdom, HUDOC.

601 ECtHR judgment of 21.02.1986, 8793/79, James and Others v. The United Kingdom, § 81, HUDOC; ECtHR judgement of 21.6.1986 *Lithgow and Others v. The United Kingdom*, 9006/80; 9262/81; 9263/81; 9265/81; 9266/81; 9313/81; 9405/81, § 205, HUDOC.

602 S. Miettinen, The Evolution of Competence Distribution Between the European Union and the meber States in the Criminal Field, in: C. Briere, A. Weyembergh (eds.), *The Needed Balances in EU Criminal Law. Past, Present, Future*, Hart 2020, 35–64.

in every case can be derived from it. The authority dealing with the complaint is not obliged to take it into account without any further conditions. It is sufficient for the measure to be available and to enable the individual's allegations to be dealt with.[603]

The effective nature of the measure is expressed either in its ability to prevent the alleged violation or its continuation, or to provide an adequate remedy for any violation that has already occurred.[604] Such a measure, in order to be effective, should first and foremost prevent the infringement or its continuation. However, if preventive action is not possible or has not had the desired effect, the aim should be to restore the desired state of affairs or to provide adequate compensation.[605]

2. Key features of ELR

Remedies should be remedial in nature, and thus their purpose should be to restore the lawful situation. For the actual remedying of the infringement, it is necessary to select measures that respond to the needs of the specific case. This can be seen from an analysis of the case law of the European courts. The characteristics of an effective remedy are not easy to specify, but they can be reconstructed. The analysis presented in e previous chapters makes it possible to identify the basic features of an ELR. By making a certain, although not exhaustive, summary of them, we can indicate that a remedy:

(a) should be available to the party[606]. The possibility of a remedy must not depend on an arbitrary decision by the state authorities. Everyone has a right to a remedy and personal status must not preclude an effective remedy. No national procedure constitutes effective protection of the rights of the

---

603 ECtHR Judgement of 4.2.2003, *Lorsé And Others v. The Netherlands*, 52750/99, § 96, HUDOC *"the word "remedy" within the meaning of Article 13 does not mean a remedy bound to succeed, but simply an accessible remedy before an authority competent to examine the merits of a complaint".*

604 ECtHR judgment of 26.10.2000, 30210/96, Kudła v. Poland, HUDOC judgment of 26.10.2000, 30210/96, Kudła v. Poland, § 158, HUDOC.

605 *At the same time, the remedy required under Article 13 must be "effective" (...) in such a way that it either prevents the alleged infringement or its continuation or provides adequate redress for an infringement that has already occurred.* (ECtHR Judgement of 15.1.2009, 33509/04, § 97, HUDOC).

606 *The term "effective" means that the remedy must be adequate and accessible* (ECtHR judgment of 10.09.2010, 31333/06, McFarlane v. Ireland, HUDOC, § 108).

individual if the persons concerned cannot use it or can do so only to a limited extent. The initiative to initiate the procedure should therefore in principle belong to the party and not to the State authority.

(b) The remedy must be genuinely and not merely formally available to the complainant, and for that reason the costs of access to the ELR are also relevant – the costs associated with filing a complaint about violation, the fear of incurring high costs if the infringement is not established, the taxes charged on the compensation obtained, make the measures inaccessible and consequently ineffective.

(c) It should be tailored to the alleged violation – and therefore be adequate. The nature and rank of the right infringed determines the extent of the States' obligations. This means that the remedy should enable an adequate response to the allegations made.[607]

(d) It should be proportionate to the violation it seeks to respond to – the nature of the potential violation determines the shape of the measure in question. This implies that there is no obligation to over-react to violations of a minor degree or nature and prevents a measure from being considered effective if there is too great a disproportion between the nature of the violation and the nature of the measure and its ability to restore or compensate;

(e) It should be effective in concrete terms and capable of securing either restitution or compensation and should therefore offer a reasonable prospect of a favourable outcome. It attaches great importance to this and indicates that the remedy must be "effective", both in practice and in law[608]. The above term clarifies the requirement for a remedy to be effective[609].

(f) It should be provided in a timely manner – as the appropriateness of a remedy may be compromised by taking too long to process it[610]. The procrastination of procedures designed to identify and remedy violations of Convention rights can undermine the effectiveness of remedies. Of course, speeding up procedures must not be at the expense of accessibility and efficiency.

(g) It does not presuppose the effect of a positive outcome – the remedy need not therefore be successful in every case, but care must be taken to ensure that there is a sufficient chance of a violation being established when the grounds for it exist.

607 ECtHR judgment of of 5.2.2002, Čonka v. Belgium, nr 51564/99, HUDOC, § 79.

608 McFarlane v. Irland, § 114.

609 ECtHR judgment of 24.4.2014 A.C. and Others v. Hiszpania, 6528/11, HUDOC, § 87.

610 ECtHR judgment of 13.12.2012, De Souza Ribeiro v. France, 22689/07, HUDOC, § 81.

(h) It should be practical rather than theoretical – and thus should have a real and not a declared character. This means much less emphasis on its design, its consistency with the existing procedural system, its setting in the historical context, but on its concrete – here and now – application to a specific situation and the result it allows to be obtained.
(i) The effectiveness of the State's obligations in ensuring ELR depends on the gravity of the guarantees breached. In terms of the highest-ranking rights, the state's obligation is to ensure that the authorities respond to the complaint with sufficient speed and efficiency. In the case of a risk of irreparable harm, this usually means suspending the implementation of the challenged action. For example, in the case of the risk of torture, the mere prospect of being able to seek redress after the fact would not constitute sufficient protection of human rights. Similarly, in the field of expulsion from the territory, a remedy devoid of automatic suspensive effect does not meet the conditions of effectiveness required under Article 13 of the Convention.[611]

An effective remedy, in this view, is any measure that can be freely chosen, but nevertheless one that will best lead to the expected result – the remedying of what has been violated.

3. ELR for prevention, restoration, and compensation

As a survey of the jurisprudence of the two European courts shows the concept of legal remedies is in practice usually based on dual – either preventive either compensatory nature. However, we can conclude that in a broad sense there are three types of remedies: preventive, restorative and compensatory. Together they serve for preventing the alleged violation or its continuation, restoring the original condition or of providing adequate redress for any violation that has already occurred. We should also welcome solutions that combine these three types of measures, ensuring the cessation of the infringements and the prevention of future infringements, as well as compensation for the damage suffered.

From Court of Justice and ECHR jurisprudence we draw conclusion that in general application of a specific measure or type of remedy alone (preventive, restorative and compensatory) does not imply that the system of measures is considered effective or ineffective, but in situation can be recognised as such. In the newest jurisprudence of ECHR a lot of attention is given to the protection

611 ECtHR judgment of 24.4.2014 A.C. and Others v. Hiszpania, 6528/11, HUDOC, § 88.

of the impartiality of the court and proper remedies bringing back fairness of the trial.[612]

Compensatory measures should apply primarily in cases where the violation has occurred in the past and is not continuing at the time of the remedy. Preventive measures are applicable in the situation of a diagnosed systemic violation of freedoms and rights. The are preferable for some violations as measures conducive to further violations (f.e. art. 8 ECHR). Restorative instruments are appropriate only if restoring the original condition means the actual and sufficient reversal of negative effects.

Pecuniary compensation is always considered to be a proper, yet not always complete remedy. Of course, in such situations the amount of compensation has its own meaning. Discretion of national courts must be provided as national courts are better able to relate the amount of compensation to the realities of the case and the practice of national courts in this regard. It is therefore acceptable even if it will be lower than that awarded by other courts in similar cases. Monetary compensation is yet not always proper and expected.

From this perspective many forms of restoration or non-pecuniary compensation must be regarded. Very often we see mixed character of such a measure: leniency of the judgment; right of family members to actively participate in compensation proceedings for the deprivation of life, as a form of compensation for their loss; investigation and criminal or disciplinary liability, also judicial review for the rectification of infringements committed at previous stages of the proceedings. It is not excluded that more firm instruments may be introduce, like to exclude evidence in serious violation of right (f.e. evidence obtained as a result of police incitement, recording of a private "interrogation", confession received during tortures; also Salduz, Adamkiewicz, but contrary Ibrahim and Others, Beuze, Simeonovi, see more Chapter 2). Discontinuance of proceedings may be considered an effective remedy in response to protracted proceedings. In some situations, an effective remedy is understood as special procedural action, f.e. judicial control, while in some situations as a result to be received, f.e. exclusion of a judge. In case of violation of the right to counsel the possibility to challenge evidence, repetition of actions with participation of defence counsel, appeal proceedings or challenging the legality of the search must be regarded. An adequate measure in exceptional situations may be decision of inadmissibility of the prosecution and the discontinuance of the proceedings, or modification of sentence. We can also allow the possibility of exclusion of

612 See K. Lenaerts, I. Maselis, K. Gutman, *EU Procedural law*, Oxford Univ. Press 2014.

a judge as effective remedy for an allegation of impartiality. Among existing effective instruments, we must remember about possibility of raising a complaint about the length of the proceedings – with its strong preventive character and mitigation of the sentence as an effective remedy for lengthy proceedings.

4. Elements of ELR system

The group of ELR is made up of legal instruments of a heterogeneous nature. ELR may be used: (a) to declare the interests of the individual to protect rights and freedoms, (b) to prevent a harm or its recurrence, (c) to undo a harm, (d) to compensate for damage. This diversity corresponds to the different needs and to the different factual and legal situations faced by a person whose freedoms and rights have been violated or have been unjustly restricted. Sometimes they are designed to ensure that certain actions are repeated. Sometimes they will be for the purpose of the restoration of the original situation. At other times they will make it possible to compensate for the damage that has already been done. Sometimes it will be possible and necessary to respond by eliminating malfunctioning legal mechanisms. For these reasons in view of the nature of the measure we can also indicate that remedial effect should be concentrated on one or more of the following purposes: (a) cessation, (b) assurance, (c) reparations, (d) restitution, (e) compensation, (f) satisfaction.[613]

In previous Chapters 2–4 we outlined how most of these elements work in practice. But, to structure in some practical way a list of instruments creating the system, it can be said that the ELR system consists of at least following elements used by national systems to remedy violations of rights and freedoms[614]:

1. Appealing instruments (*apellatio*) – i.e. means of reviewing judgments and other decisions rendered, appeals, complaints;[615]

---

613 See also G. Boars, *Public International Law. Contemporary Principles*, Elgar Publishing 2023, pp. 306–311.

614 See P. Wiliński, *Nadużycie uprawnienia przez prokuratora i sędziego w procesie karnym*, Warsaw 2023, pp. 195-230.

615 Interesting to notice that institutions like appeals are not always classified as ELR. European approach is more focused on concrete situation or scope of action (f.e. redress) than on the essence of the institution. Only if we start discussing concept of ELR we suddenly notice that those well-known institutions are in fact or can be core elements of ELS system. This is partially also answer for a question why so many EU Member States accepts so easily obligation to introduce ELR in particular legal instruments of European cooperation. See more point 5 of this Chapter.

2. Measures of renovation (*renovatio*) – for the reversal of final decisions and the repetition of defective proceedings – extraordinary measures such as cassation or reopening of proceedings;
3. Restorative measures (*restitutio*) – aimed at restoring the original situation (restitutio in integrum), such as orders for the restitution of property taken away, the release of property securities, the restitution of the object of a guarantee.
4. Compensatory measures (*compensatio*) – measures aimed at compensating for damage that cannot be reversed, such as lost liberty, material damage suffered:

   (a) material compensation – where the losses are pecuniary or personal and it is possible to compensate them by financial means – these are different forms of compensation and reparation.
   (b) non-pecuniary compensation – where a possible means of compensation is a specific act, such as an apology.
   (c) procedural reparation – where direct restitution is not possible, but a permissible means will be the granting and obtaining of additional procedural benefits, e.g. additional time to make a declaration of intent, to file an appeal, to recognise the effectiveness of an earlier action;
   (d) compensatory reduction of criminal liability – where the legal system provides for the possibility of compensating for mistakes of the procedural authorities, violations of individual freedoms and rights by a reduction of the penalty, penal measures, the amount of the fine or other criminal measure imposed.

In addition to the above-mentioned – undoubtedly necessary – measures of precise response as direct and ad hoc instruments, applied to a specific case, there is often a need for measures with a long-term effect.

5. Disciplinary measures – the need for disciplinary measures against procedural bodies – police, prosecutors, judges – should not be excluded when it is their unlawful behaviour that needs correction.
6. Systemic measures – that is, systemic solutions designed and implemented to address structural deficiencies in the legal system – for example, a complaint about the length of criminal proceedings.[616]

616 See Morawska E., The Principles of Subsidiarity and Effectiveness: Two Pillars of an Effective Remedy for Excessive Length of Proceedings within the Meaning of Article 13 ECHR, *Polish Yearbook of International Law* 39 (2021).

5. Strong and week points of ELR

The fundamental difficulty in understanding and applying the ELR concept stems from the very essence of this construct. Its central point is the effect to be achieved and not the tool to be used.[617] It is very clear and comprehensible under the common law system[618], while at the same time, until recently, it seemed alien to the states of the civil law system.[619] This is because it stems from the development of the former system and the way of thinking about the application of law present in it. It is based, as we have already emphasised many times, on the criterion of the effect achieved – effective remedy. The primary importance is therefore not the means used, but the effect it leads to. Under various branches of law, whether civil, criminal, or administrative, what matters is not the formal remedy, but the effect of the remedy. This approach is, of course, also very attractive for Europe and the European common legal area. It allows for the effective construction of a system of effective remedies in a new legal environment, such precisely despite several decades of development as international law (ECHR) or the much younger European Union law.[620]

An important advantage of this construction is therefore consequently its practical nature. It represents an ideal way of combining everything according to the criterion of the value to be achieved, disregarding the differences contained in the elements to be combined (national systems). It must be stated that this construction, although it was not clear to everyone from the outset, was not used by chance.

---

617 Complex method of accessing remedies M. Eliantonio, Ch.W. Backes, C. H. van Rhee, T. Sproken, A. Berlee, *Standing Up for Your Right(s) in Europe. A Comparative Study on Legal Standing (Locus Standi) before EU and Memer States' Courts*, Intersentia 2012, pp. 24–27.

618 On meaning of the effect of legal instruments see i.a. G. Davies, Democracy and Legitimacy in the Shadow of Purposive Competences, *European Law Journal*, no. 21 (2015).

619 Interesting discussion see i.a. L. Carter, F. Pocar (eds.), *International Criminal Procedure. The Interface of Civil Law and Common Law Legal Systems*, Elgar Publishing 2013, on common law approach G. J. Chin, W. M. Oliver, *Experiencing Criminal Law*, West Academic Publishing 2015.

620 On that see A. Klip, *European Criminal Law, an Integrative Approach*, Intersentia 2016. G. Vermeulen, *Mutual Recognition, Harmonisation and Fundamental (procedural) Rights Protection*, in. M. Martin (ed.) *Crime, Rights and the EU: the Future of Police and Juditial Cooperation*, London 2008.

Under the law applied for centuries in civil law countries (e.g. Poland, France, Germany, the Netherlands, Italy or Spain)[621], the LR concept is familiar and understood only to a certain extent. Most often, it is identified with already existing national system of control, redress and compensation measures. Indeed, an extensive system of remedies, control and compensation exists in each of these countries. System is largely concerned not with the outcome but with the existence of instruments within the system. It is therefore extremely easy to limit one's thinking about ELR to the familiar catalogue of remedies. However, it was not built with the same premise as in the common law system. The formalism of legal constructions meant that each construction, its formal correctness, and its functioning were important. They became an integral part of the system and grew into the system. They became intrinsic features of the system, not always ensuring their effectiveness, but in each area of law evolving in a different direction, in each country regulating certain issues slightly differently. Its existence allowed the system to be identified as an appellate, revision, two-instance, three-instance system. These were primary issues. On the other hand, the issue of fairness, the restoration of balance, the reversal of irregular proceedings – that is, the results – received relatively less attention. This seems to have been due to several reasons, of which two obvious ones can easily be pointed out. Firstly, it was somehow assumed as self-evident that a system built correctly and logically, and therefore also effective from this point of view, ensures justice. Such a result seemed obvious. Secondly, in a system of concrete and very elaborate legal institutions, it is much easier to discuss the logic and efficiency of the system and more difficult to discuss the essence of justice itself. For a number of reasons, it is true to say that it is more a system based on form rather than result, although we cannot say that the result does not matter. On the contrary, steal remains the stated goal of all actions. Different, not to say polar opposite, is the perspective of building a legal system based on a sense of justice and from an understanding of what is the essence of law shaping a procedural system (common law system). In it, the ELR construction is innate at its core. However, to be sure, the challenge to real efficiency is the structuring of such a system, i.e. the introduction of legal rules of a universal nature.

621 See: M. Reimann, R. Zimmermann (eds.), *The Oxford Handbook of Comparative Law*, Oxford Univ. Press 2021; P. Wiliński, Criminal Procedure, in: W. Dajczak, T. Nieborak, P. Wiliński (eds.), *Foundations of Law. Polish Perspective*, Wolters Kluwer 2021; M. Bohlander, *Principles of German criminal procedure*, Hart 2004; V. Krey, *German Criminal Procedure Law*, Kohlhammer 2009; C. Elliott, *French Criminal Law*, Routledge 2001.

The reflection of this dualism of legal order-building in European states had to be properly recognised also in the implementation of the ELR concept.[622] It is evident, albeit only on closer inspection, in both ECHR and CJEU jurisprudence. In both cases, attempts to incorporate an elaborate system of formal procedural constructions into a kind of "outcome concept" are evident. Existing institutions and remedies are not assessed as to their consistency with the European or EU system. The judgments do not provide enough assessments as to the rationality of the existence, the correctness of the functioning of these, and not others, very specific legal institutions. The tribunals formulate "outcome assessments" – i.e. mostly only whether the national restitutive and compensatory instruments lead to the expected result – the stopping of the infringement and the compensation of losses.

Much of the jurisprudence of both courts (ECHR, CJUE) on ELR is still not fully understood or perhaps underestimated (especially, it seems, in states based on *civil law*). The most common approach is to evaluate individual judgements concerning ELRs, rather than to see the general conclusions of their review. Member States often tend to analyse in detail mainly those judgments that relate directly to their legal system. In contrast, they are often superficial in assessing those that relate to other national systems. States assess the judgments made in their cases to what extent a particular institution has been positively or negatively reviewed in a particular set of circumstances, to what extent its existing form is salvageable. If it needs to be modified, it should certainly be modified as little as possible. As a consequence, however, the ELR concept is not looked at in general, holistic or comprehensive terms.

For essentially the same reasons, there is no full analysis of the system of national measures in terms of the implementation of the standards under Article 13 ECHR and Article 47 CFR. Deeper, comprehensive reflections and analyses are postponed as far as possible. It should be noticed that the vague (also deliberately) jurisprudence of both Courts favours in some way this approach.

At the same time, still in many states, orders to bring national measures into line with the requirements of the LR cause a certain distance.[623] This does not degenerate into apparent reluctance, since it is not appropriate to express it, but

---

622 See also E. Wieczorek, *The Legitimacy of EU Criminal Law*, Hart 2020, 16–20, 141–167; A. Estelle, *The Principle of Subsidiarity and Its Critique*, Oxford Univ. Press, 2002; C. Peristeridou, *The Principle of Legality in EU Criminal Law*, Intersentia 2015.

623 See i.a. K. H. Brodersen, V. Glerum, A. Klip, *The European Arrest Warrant and In Absentia Judgements*, Eleven Int Publishing 2020, pp. 140, 150–153, 164.

into a certain reserve and a passive attitude of waiting for further rulings by both courts. These will bring either a more welcome confirmation that the existing measure in the national system meets the ELR criteria, or a message forcing a change. However, the change will only be as big as necessary, usually not bigger. Thus, the strength of the ELR concept is also its weakness. It has great potential to integrate national systems, but the chosen integration model is time-consuming and its effectiveness depends on the will of European countries.

Ultimately, however, changes, although not seen quickly enough or in a wide enough perspective, are nevertheless still taking place. They lead not to the exchange of legal instruments but to their adaptation. What is taking place is an agreement on the way in which measures capable of ensuring ELR are to function, and thus an outcome is being achieved. The natural next step in the considerations and conclusions presented here should therefore be an in-depth analysis of national legal systems in this broad perspective.

We must not forget that a certain threat, and at the same time an advantage of ELRs, is the possibility of limiting the scope of the ELR obligation. In particular, as the ECtHR jurisprudence shows, the Court does not imply an obligation on the State to provide a remedy for every alleged violation of Convention rights (Chapter 2). The obligation is limited by the Court to so-called "arguable claims", i.e. justified complaints. Thus, the application of the measure can be limited to serious situations which require a response. However, care must be taken in selecting these situations so as not to exclude from the scope of the measure situations which are seemingly unimportant, but which significantly undermine the rights of individuals and the guarantees to which they are entitled. The rationale for limiting the right to a remedy is also the need to protect other rights and freedoms. The protection of the good administration of justice or the protection of public health may constitute limitations on the right to a remedy. The limitation of the right to a remedy must not violate its essence. Limitation should be examined in each case in terms of desirability, adequacy, and proportionality[624].

Assessing the ELR from yet another point of view, we can say that it is a construction strongly linked to legal concepts much more recognisable. Effective legal remedies are often linked to the principle of effective judicial protection (EU perspective), is reflected in the broader concept of the right to a fair trial

624 On that more N. Emiliou, *The Principle of Proportionality in European Law: A Comparative Study*, Kluwer 1996.

(Conventions' perspective), or to the rule of law (common law perspective)[625]. On the one hand, the inclusion of the ELR in much more widespread and well-known legal concepts popularises and makes credible this instrument. This allows the ELR to be considered part of an established legal tradition in the European space. On the other hand, however, it makes it more difficult to obtain an independent position and an individual approach to this particular guarantee. It is not difficult to see this from the example of the Convention on Human Rights that the right to an effective remedy has for a very long time, in fact until recently, been considered a subsidiary part of the right to a fair trial (see Articles 13 and art. 6 of the Convention, Chapter 2). Same time it can obviously bring some concreate consequences as to popularity of the ELR themself, the development of their standards but also risk of remaining not fully independent.

6. ELR and integration of criminal law in EU

The obligation to ensure the effectiveness of the direct and independent introduction of European instruments is, in some way, a relict of the international law principles derived from the concept of state independence.[626] Member States fulfil their obligations through the proper implementation of European instruments[627] in such a way as preserves the integrity of their internal legal systems.[628] However, from this perspective the quality of implementation

---

625 L. Pech, A Union Founded on the Rule of Law: Meaning and Reality of the Rule of Law as a Constitutional Principle of EU Law, *European Constitutional Law Review* 6, no. 3 (2010), p. 372.

626 See H-W Micklitz, B. de Witte (eds.), *The European Court of Justice and the Authonomy of the Member States*, Intersentia 2012; P. Craig, G. de Burca (eds.), *The Evolution of EU Law*, Oxford Univ Press 2011, pp. 465–71. More on essence of independence of states G. Boars, *Public International Law. Contemporary Principles*, Elgar Publishing 2023; M. N. Shaw, *International Law*, Cambridge Univ Press 2008; J. Crawford, *Brownlie's Principles of Public International Law*, Oxford Univ Press 2008.

627 See P. de Gert, Division of Competences beetwen National and European Levels with Regard to Justice and Home Affairs, in: *Police and Justice Cooperation in the New European Boarder*, Kluwer Law International 2002; T. Gadkowski, *Introdution: International Law and Domestic Law (General Issues)*, in: A. Gerecka-Żołyńska (ed.), *International Legal Sources of Implementation of the Humanitarian Principle in the Process of Imprisonment*, Poznań 2021, pp. 1–28.

628 See Perez C. S.: What about Fundamental Rights? Security and Fundamental Rights in the Midst of a Rule of Law Breakdown, *New Journal of European Criminal Law* 13, no. 4 (2022), 526–545. See Montaldo Stefano, Intersections among EU Judicial Cooperation Instruments and the Quest for an Advanced and Consistent European

becomes key to the integrity of the common European system[629], and the foundation and condition for achieving a common standard.[630] For all these reasons, it is of particular importance for the European Union and all its Member States that this commitment carries real content – all common instruments must be implemented in full and not purely for the sake of appearances.[631]

Until two decades ago, guarantees derived mainly from the European Convention for the Protection of Human Rights and Fundamental Freedoms (ECHR) protected the rights of participants in criminal proceedings in the European Union.[632] The simultaneous membership of EU Member States in the Council of Europe made this arrangement possible.[633] Over time, it proved inadequate, partly because it was too general in formulating the principles to be implemented and enforced in States Parties.[634] Problems arose, inter alia, because of differing interpretations of the general provisions.[635] Therefore, there was a real lack of uniform standards of protection and instruments to approximate legal solutions in the EU Member States in the future.[636]

Judicial Space: The Case of the Transfer and Surrender of Convicts in the EU, *New Journal of European Criminal Law* 13, no. 3 (2022), pp. 252–269.

629 See A. Efrat, Assessing Mutual Trust among EU Members: Evidence from European Arrest Warrant, *Journal of European Public Policy*, no. 26 (2019), pp. 656–675.

630 See De Bondt W., Vermeulen G., The Procedural Debate. A Bridge Too Far or Still Not Far Enough?, *EUCRIM*, no 4 (2010), 163–167; Loof R., Shooting from the Hip: Proposed Minimum Rights in Criminal Proceedings throughout the EU, *European Law Journal*, 12, no. 3 (2006), pp. 421–430.

631 See also van Puyenbroeck L., Vermeulen G., Towards Minimum Procedural Guarantees for the Defence in Criminal Proceedings in the EU, *International and Comparative Law Quarterly* 60, no. 4 (2011), pp. 1017–1038.

632 See A. Williams, *EU Human Rights Polices: A Study of Irony*, Oxfor Univ Press 2004, pp. 139–169.

633 See principal policy documents and multilateral legal instruments on international and European criminal law G. Vermeulen (ed.), Essential Texts on International and European Criminal Law, Maklu 2015.

634 On this issue see also E. Cape, Z. Namoradze, R. Smith, T. Sproken (ed.), *Effective Criminal Defence in Europe*, Intersentia 2010.

635 Even 'mutual trust' instrument appeared to be not enough effective, see i.a. D. Flore, The Issue of Mutual Trust and the Needed Balace Between Diversity and Inuty, in: C. Briere, A. Weyembergh (eds.), *The New Balances in EU Criminal Law. Past, Present, Future*, Hart 2020, pp. 157–164.

636 See also Wieczorek Irene: *The Legitimacy of EU Criminal Law*, Oxford et al., Hart, 2020, 243 and next S. Steinborn, The EU as a Role Model? – Innovative Maximum Standards for Suspects and Defence Rights v. International Minimum Standards,

Despite the difficulty of defining the concept of the ELR precisely and of defining it in relation to all specific guarantees, where it has been possible to establish a European standard (resulting from the content of the ECHR and the jurisprudence of the ECtHR and the CJEU) there has generally been a corresponding regulation in the Directive.[637] This meant the introduction of an ELR for the protection of a particular guarantee. Also when in practice it proved impossible to enforce this obligation on Member States (cf. Directive 2013/48/EU).

ELR concept influence the autonomy of national legal systems. Despite the freedom of choice of procedure and remedy, both jurisprudence of CJEU and ECtHR underlines obligation of states ant their respected legal systems when exercising their competence to proper organization of the judiciary to comply with the obligations arising for them under European standards and union law (Chapters 2–3). It is the role of national legal systems to ensure the effectiveness of law, including the effective legal remedies for protection of fundamental rights.[638] In recent years there is a visible deficit of some states to fill their obligations to ensure protection of judicial independence (as an integral part of the judiciary) and falls within the essence of the right to effective judicial protection and the fundamental right to a fair trial (see Poland, Hungary in recent period 2015–2023).

The mere commitment of an EU Member State and its assurance of the implementation of these guarantees does not mean that the guarantees will always be implemented in the right way.[639] There is no clarification of the definition of a legal remedy and no description of its characteristics in any of EU Directives implementing ELR (see f.e. Directive 2012/13/EU or Directive

---

European Criminal Law Review, 4 (2014); M. Kusak, *Mutual Admissibility of Evidence in Criminal Matters in the EU. A Study of Telephone Tapping and House Search,* Antwerpen 2016, pp. 23–35.

637 See P. Wiliński, K. Kiejnich-Kruk, Right to an Effective Legal Remedy in Criminal Proceedings in the EU. Implementation and Need for Standards, *Review of European and Comparative Law,* 54, no. 3 (2023), pp. 147–167.

638 Also A. Williams, *EU Human Rights Polices: A Study of Irony*, Oxfor Univ Press 2004, pp. 139–169.

639 See: De Bondt W., Vermeulen G., *The Procedural Debate. A Bridge Too Far or Still Not Far Enough?*, EUCRIM 2010, no. 4, pp. 163–167; Loof R., Shooting from the Hip: Proposed Minimum Rights in Criminal Proceedings throughout the EU, *European Law Journal* 12, no. 3 (2006), pp. 421–430; van Puyenbroeck L., Vermeulen G., Towards Minimum Procedural Guarantees for the Defence in Criminal Proceedings in the EU, *International and Comparative Law Quarterly* 60, no. 4 (2011), pp. 1017–1038.

2013/48/EU). Instead, the reluctance of Member States to describe remedies in more detail became apparent during the discussion phase. Sometimes a Member State does not intend to implement new dedicated solutions but instead tries to demonstrate that the guarantees are already provided by the existing procedural institutions, even when these are insufficient, or changes are in fact necessary (f.e. access to a lawyer during first interrogation). At other times, the regulations that seem to exist do not provide real procedural protection. As a result, the practice of criminal proceedings deviates from the expected standard. Often countries' declarations and explanations of their assessment of the implementation could not be easily verified because of the lack of clear standards. This may hinder the proper implementation of the Directives and, consequently, the real harmonisation of laws between Member States. This is one of the silent reasons why, in fact, Member States do not implement Directives or implement them incorrectly.[640]

We may still observe how ineffective EU legislation becomes especially when confronted with national systems and rules of admissibility of evidence.[641] As discussed in details in Chapter 4 on the basis of implementation of Directive 2013/48/EU a specific remedy was indicated: evidence obtained in breach of the right to a lawyer or in situations where a derogation from this right was allowed should become inadmissible unless its use would not infringe the right of the defense. During the legislative procedure, the obligation of Member States to implement regulations to exclude evidence from a criminal procedure was abandoned. It was made clear that the requirement for an effective remedy does not interfere with the national system for the admissibility of evidence.[642] The Directive grants the accused the right to an effective remedy, but it is impossible to understand from the content of the Directive what such a remedy might be,

---

640 S. Prechal, *Directives in EC Law*, New York 2005, pp. 7–8.

641 On that i.a. Ch. Claverie-Rousset, The Admissibility of Evidence in Criminal Proceedings between European Union Member States, *European Journal on Criminal Law* 2013, n 2; M. Kusak, *Mutual Admissibility of Evidence in Criminal Matters in the EU. A Study of Telephone Tapping and House Research*, Maklu 2016; M. Kusak, *Mutual Admissibility of Evidence and the European Investigation Order: Aspiration Lost in Reality*, ERA Forum 2019, vol. 19.

642 From different perspective see M. Wąsek-Wiaderek, Admissibility of Statements Obtained as a Result of "Private Torture" or "Private" Inhuman Treatment as Evidence in Criminal Proceedings: Emergence of a New European Standard? *Revista Brasileira de Direito Processual Penal* 7, no. 1 (2021), pp. 343–374.

and what would be its functions, objectives, and results. We must assess this solution negatively.[643]

In some situations, the ELR doctrine may mandate Member States to introduce more direct and strong measures if other indirect measures are not sufficient, e.g. in the case of confessions made by suspects or defendants in violation of the right to remain silent or the right not to incriminate oneself. In this context, account should be taken of the jurisprudence of the European Court of Human Rights, according to which the admission of confessions obtained under torture or other ill-treatment in violation of Article 3 ECHR as evidence for the purpose of establishing the relevant facts in criminal proceedings would render the proceedings as a whole unfair. Courts and judges should respect the rights of the defence and the fairness of the proceedings, as it seems obvious that any inferences drawn from the fact that suspects or defendants enjoy the right to remain silent or the right not to incriminate themselves should be excluded. Without this, the right would only be illusory if suspects or accused persons had to fear that their non-cooperation or silence would be used against them in subsequent criminal proceedings. This is the only way to ensure that suspects or accused persons can effectively exercise these rights without fearing that such exercise may be used against them at a later stage. In this regard, the Directive also provides a specific and immediate remedy that any use of evidence obtained in breach of these rights is not permitted, except in very exceptional cases where the use of such evidence will not prejudice the overall fairness of the proceedings.

The drafters of the Directives unequivocally endorse the acquis of the European Court of Human Rights, but at the same time often set lower standards for Member States – see Directive 2016/343/EU in terms of protecting the rights of defendants and suspects. Some solutions seem to be easier for Member States to implement – e.g. a remedy for infringement of the right to legal aid ex officio – where a party should be able to lodge a complaint with the competent procedural authority, which will examine whether his or her right has in fact been infringed. In some situations the remedy is specified only in broad and general manner, mainly by its nature of: as in Directive 2016/800/EU remedies for violations of the right to be assisted by counsel should be remedial in nature and remedies for violations of the right to be appointed counsel should be controlling in

643 On that more in Polish Kiejnich-Kruk K., *Prawo do skutecznego środka naprawczego w postępowaniu dowodowym* (The right to an effective remedy in evidence proceedings), Wolters Kluwer 2022.

nature. The right to an individual assessment has not yet been the subject of EU regulation.

Another issue is that still the development of clear and uniform rules in EU is hampered by divergent interpretations of the same or similar guarantees of individual rights. This is from the very beginning an obstacle to the full approximation of the legal systems of the Member States especially in the field of criminal law (but not only). Not all attempts to introduce ELR have been successful. Some remedies were proposed but were not introduced – as it was in Directive 2016/343/EU – a specific remedy for violations of the right to silence – a prohibition on the use of the accused's statements as evidence[644].

The development of standards for the protection of individual rights, sustained by the case law of the ECtHR and the Court of Justice in Luxembourg includes the concept of ELR. It has been reflected in current criminal law instruments of the Member States of the European Union. In this context we can argue that ELRs remain an attractive instrument for the European integration of legal systems[645]. ELR strength is expressed i.a. in the creation of more uniform law and interpretative guidelines in respect of specific rights and freedoms.

Certainly, an opportunity to increase the importance of the ELR concept in the integration of legal systems is the global approach that has prevailed in recent times. Indeed, it is aptly recognised in recent case law of the European Courts (see Chapters 2 and 3) that even if a single measure does not meet the conditions expressed in the Convention or the Charter, the totality of the measures available to the applicant and their effectiveness must be assessed.

Bibliography

Boars G., *Public International Law. Contemporary Principles*, Elgar Publishing, 2023.

Bohlander M., *Principles of German Criminal Procedure*, Hart, 2004.

Brodersen K. H., Glerum V., Klip A., *The European Arrest Warrant and In Absentia Judgements*, Eleven Int Publishing, 2020.

644 See Opinion of the European Economic and Social Committee on the Proposal for a Directive of the European Parliament and of the Council on the strengthening of certain aspects of the presumption of innocence and of the right to be present at trial in criminal proceedings, COM/2013/821, final.

645 See P. Wiliński, K. Kiejnich-Kruk, *Right to Effective Legal Remedy in Criminal Proceedings in the EU. Implementation and Need for Standards, Review of European and Comparative Law*, 54, no. 3 (2023),.

Brooks T. (ed.), *The Right to a Fair Trial*, Routledge, 2009.

Cape E., Namoradze Z., Smith R., Sproken T. (ed.), *Effective Criminal Defence in Europe*, Intersentia, 2010.

Carter L., Pocar F. (eds.), *International Criminal Procedure. The Interface of Civil Law and Common Law Legal Systems*, Elgar Publishing, 2013.

Chin G. J., Oliver W. M., *Experiencing Criminal Law*, West Academic Publishing, 2015.

Claverie-Rousset Ch., The admissibility of evidence in criminal proceedings between European Union Member States, *European Journal on Criminal Law* no. 2, 2013.

Clooney A., Webb P., *The Right to a Fair Trial in International Law*, Oxford Univ. Press, 2021.

Craig P., de Burca, G. (eds.), *The Evolution of EU Law*, Oxford Univ. Press, 2011, pp. 465–71.

Crawford J., *Brownlie's Principles of Public International Law*, Oxford Univ. Press, 2008.

Davies G., Democracy and Legitimacy in the Shadow of Purposive Competences, *European Law Journal* no. 21, 2015.

De Bondt W., Vermeulen G., The Procedural Debate. A Bridge Too Far or Still Not Far Enough?, *EUCRIM*, no. 4, 2010.

de Gert P., *Division of Competences beetwen National and European Levels with Regard to Justice and Home Affairs*, in: *Police and Justice Cooperation in the New European Boarder*, Kluwer, 2002.

Efrat A., Assessing Mutual Trust among EU Members: Evidence from European Arrest Warrant, *Journal of European Public Policy*, no. 26, 2019.

Eliantonio M., Backes Ch.W., van Rhee C. H., Sproken T., Berlee A., Standing up for Your Right(s) in Europe. A Comparative Study on Legal Standing (Locus Standi) before EU and Memer States' Courts, *Intersentia* , 2012, 24–27.

Elliott C., *French Criminal Law*, Routledge, 2001.

Elodie S. (ed.), *Criminal Procedures and Cross-Border Cooperation in the EU Area of Criminal Justice. Together But Apart?*, Bruxelles, 2020.

Emiliou N., *The Principle of Proportionality in European Law: A Comparative Study*, Kluwer 1996.

Estelle A., *The Principle of Subsidiarity and Its Critique*, Oxford Univ. Press, 2002.

Flore D., The Issue of Mutual Trust and the Needed Balace Between Diversity and Inuty, in: C. Briere, A. Weyembergh (eds.), *The New Balances in EU Criminal Law. Past, Present, Future*, Hart, 2020.

Frantziou E., *The Horizontal Effect of the Charter of Fundamental Rights of the EU: Rediscovering the*

Gadkowski T., Introdution: International Law and Domestic Law (General Issues), in: A. Gerecka-Żołyńska (ed.), *International Legal Sources of Implementation of the Humanitarian Principle in the Process of Imprisonment*, Poznań, 2021.

Gora A., de Vilde P., The Essence of Democratic Backsliding in the European Union: Deliberation and Rule of Law, *Journal of European Public Policy*, no. 29, 2022.

Guide on *Article 13 of the European Convention on Human Rights. Right to Effective Legal Remedy*, Council of Europe, 2022, https://www.echr.coe.int/documents/d/echr/guide_art_13_eng.

Hofmański P., Wróbel A., w: *Konwencja o Ochronie Praw Człowieka i Podstawowych Wolności. Tom I. Komentarz do art. 1–18*, A. Barcz, C. H. Beck, red. 2010.

Kiejnich K., Harmonisation of EU Criminal Law – Issues of Implementing EU Directives, in: A. Kłos (ed.), *European Union and Its Values: Freedom, Solidarity, Democracy*, CeDeWu, 2020.

Kiejnich-Kruk K., *Prawo do skutecznego środka naprawczego w postępowaniu dowodowym* (The right to an effective remedy in evidence proceedings), Wolters Kluwer, 2022.

Klip A., *European Criminal Law, an Integrative Approach*, Intersentia, 2016.

Krey V., *German Criminal Procedure Law*, Kohlhammer, 2009.

Kusak M., *Mutual Admissibility of Evidence in Criminal Matters in the EU. A Study of Telephone Tapping and House Search*, Antwerpen, 2016.

Kusak M., Mutual Admissibility of Evidence and the European Investigation Order: Aspiration Lost in Reality, *ERA Forum* 19, 2019.

Leanza P., Pridal O., *The Right to a Fair Trial. Article 6 of the European Convention on Human Rights*, Kluwer International, 2014.

Lenaerts K., Maselis I., Gutman K., *EU Procedural Law*, Oxford Univ. Press, 2014.

Loof R., Shooting from the Hip: Proposed Minimum Rights in Criminal Proceedings throughout the EU, *European Law Journal* 12, no. 3, 2006.

Marguery T., European Union Fundamental Rights and Member States Action in EU Criminal Law, *Maastricht Journal of European and Comparative Law*, no. 2, 2013.

Mataga Z., *Effectivness of Domestic Remedies under the ECHR (Article 13)*, Budapest, 2002.

Micklitz H.-W., de Witte B. (eds.), *The European Court of Justice and the Authonomy of the Member States*, Intersentia, 2012.

Miettinen S., The Evolution of Competence Distribution Between the European Union and the meber States in the Criminal Field, in: C. Briere, A. Weyembergh (eds.), *The Needed Balances in EU Criminal Law. Past, Present, Future*, Hart, 2020.

Montaldo S., Intersections among EU Judicial Cooperation Instruments and the Quest for an Advanced and Consistent European Judicial Space: The Case of the Transfer and Surrender of Convicts in the EU, *New Journal of European Criminal Law* 13, no. 3, 2022.

Morawska E., The Principles of Subsidiarity and Effectiveness: Two Pillars of an Effective Remedy for Excessive Length of Proceedings within the Meaning of Article 13 ECHR, *Polish Yearbook of International Law* 39, 2021.

Opinion of the European Economic and Social Committee on the Proposal for a Directive of the European Parliament and of the Council on the strengthening of certain aspects of the presumption of innocence and of the right to be present at trial in criminal proceedings, COM/2013/821, final.

Ouwerkerk J. et al. (eds.), *The Future of EU Criminal Justice Policy and Practice. Legal and Criminological Perspectives*, Brill Nijhoff, 2019.

Pech L., A Union Founded on the Rule of Law: Meaning and Reality of the Rule of Law as a Constitutional Principle of EU Law, *European Constitutional Law Review* 6, no. 3, 2010.

Perez C. S., What about Fundamental Rights? Security and Fundamental Rights in the Midst of a Rule of Law Breakdown, *New Journal of European Criminal Law* 13, no. 4, 2022.

Peristeridou C., *The Principle of Legality in EU Criminal Law*, Intersentia, 2015.

Piątek W., The Right to an Effective Remedy in European Law: Significance, Content and Interaction, *China-EU Law Journal* 6, 2019.

Prechal S., *Directives in EC Law*, New York, 2005,.

Reimann M., Zimmermann R. (eds.), *The Oxford Handbook of Comparative Law*, Oxford Univ. Press, 2021.

Shaw M. N., *International Law*, Cambridge Univ. Press, 2008.

Steinborn S., The EU as a Role Model? – Innovative Maximum Standards for Suspects and Defence Rights v. International Minimum Standards, *European Criminal Law Review* 4, 2014.

van Puyenbroeck L., Vermeulen G., Towards Minimum Procedural Guarantees for the Defence in Criminal Proceedings in the EU, *International and Comparative Law Quarterly* 60, no 4, 2011.

Vermeulen G., Mutual Recognition, Harmonisation and Fundamental (Procedural) Rights Protection, in: M. Martin (ed.) *Crime, Rights and the EU: the Future of Police and Juditial Cooperation*, London, 2008.

Vermeulen G. (ed.), *Essential Texts on International and European Criminal Law*, Maklu, 2015.

Wąsek-Wiaderek M., Admissibility of Statements Obtained as a Result of "Private Torture" or "Private" Inhuman Treatment as Evidence in Criminal Proceedings: Emergence of a New European Standard? *Revista Brasileira de Direito Processual Penal* 7, no. 1, 2021.

Weissbrodt D., *Declaration of Human Rights and the International Covenant on Civil and Political Rights. Articles 8, 10 and 11 of the Universal Declaration of Human Rights*, Brill, 2021.

Wieczorek E., *The Legitimacy of EU Criminal Law*, Hart, 2020.

Wiliński P., Criminal Procedure, in: W. Dajczak, T. Nieborak, P. Wiliński (eds.), *Foundations of Law. Polish Perspective*, Wolters Kluwer, 2021.

Wiliński P., *Nadużycie uprawnienia przez prokuratora i sędziego w procesie karnym*, Warsaw, 2023.

Wiliński P., Kiejnich-Kruk K., Right to an Effective Legal Remedy in Criminal Proceedings in the EU. Implementation and Need for Standards, *Review of European and Comparative Law* 54, no. 3, 2023.

Willem A. *The Principle of Mutual Trust in EU Criminal Law*, Oxford et al., Hart, 2021.

Williams A., *EU Human Rights Polices: A Study of Irony*, Oxfor Univ. Press, 2004, 139–169.

Wróbel A. (red.), *Karta Praw Podstawowych Unii Europejskiej. Komentarz* (*Charter of Fundamental Rights of European Union. Commentary*), C.H. Beck, 2020.

Paweł Wiliński

Closing remarks

The right to an effective legal remedy as an entitlement to protection of individual rights under European law (including procedural rights in criminal proceedings) is guaranteed by Article 13 ECHR and Article 47 CoFEU. As this book's research shows neither of these concepts (under Council of Europe law system or EU law) requires any particular form of remedy to be offered. The only common requirement is that the remedy is "effective in practice as well as in law". The type of remedy required depends on the circumstances of each case.

According to research close connection between concept of effective remedies under Art 47 CoFEU and under Art. 13 ECHR has its direct consequences. Systems are separate but most of rights in the Charter are described similarly to rights in the Convention. Although right to ELR under Art. 47 CoFEU applies only when Member States are implementing EU law and Art. 13 ECHR has broader scope of application in practice both standards merge and create a common space for the protection of the rights of individuals. Creates strong binding relation difficult to tear and separate.

The right to an effective remedy can be considered a still under-appreciated yet crucial right of the individual guaranteed in the European legal system. It allows individuals to seek redress for violations of their rights. In turn, national legal systems impose an obligation to provide remedies that sufficient to ensure the effective judicial protection of rights in fields covered by Union law.

From the research we can observe that ELR received independent position as an instrument. The evolution of the ELR suggests that the right to an effective remedy will play an increasingly important role. It will also gradually become more important, still coexisting with the broad concept of a fair criminal trial, but no longer as a mere part of it, but as an essential complement to it. What they have in common is among many the importance of the right to access to independent judicial authorities. This is an essential component of internal access to justice. The right to a remedy should be "determined by competent judicial, administrative or legislative authorities, or by any other competent authority provided for by the legal system of the State".

The research carried out in this book gives an answer for the question on current standard of European concept of effective legal remedies. Leads us to the general conclusion that the modern concept of ELR is much more than a retribution for a violation of the law or a remedy. It is more than a simple construct of legal remedies in relevant procedures but a broader concept of a result that should be sometimes achieved even by not identified instrument bringing remedy to the situation. It is a concept for the creation of legal environment for the restoration of the individual's rightful position in the legal system. Thus, in essence, the genesis of the ELR concept understood and developed in this way is to be sought in the development of thinking about the effectiveness of remedial instruments inherent in the common law system. In it, a descriptive formulation of the result to be pursued, rather than the means to get there, was formulated in a contemporary manner. For this evolutionary approach we can assume that its importance will grow successively.

From the research carried in the book we can conclude also that the concept of ELR can be an useful instrument for integration of national criminal law systems in Europe. We need ELR concept to support human rights protection, share and develop common standards recognition – how can be properly and legally promoted and fostered before the domestic systems and courts. We also see that the mechanism of the ELR has the effect of strengthening the protection of individual rights within the European legal system. The right to an effective remedy must be primarily enforced at national level. The analysis carried out in the previous chapters allows a positive verification of this thesis.

Effective legal remedies is not the same that effective legal reform. But what European justice system demands most – effective execution of existing laws or correction of laws for better protection? Here we touch the long-standing universal question of how to fix a deficient justice system and achieve implementation of common standards? By a new law or reinterpretation of law or practice? Legislation seems to be for many still the best answer for wrong practice or unclear law. We observe different approaches to that dilemma in European criminal law, in national systems and in cooperation between countries. But we shall rather see all groups of instruments (effective legislation and effective remedies) not as opposing options but as elements of the same evolution of criminal justice system in Europe. In that perspective ELR should serve protection of rights and freedoms in action. Should be first option for personal protection from violation and form of redress. While law reform should only take place when a proper analysis reveals significant structural dysfunctions in binding law.

However, the relationship between ELR and legislation is not so straightforward. Indeed, sometimes it is the very consequence of the existence of an ELR right that changes to existing law are required. This research gives also materials and analysis for further study on national legislation on how to implement ELR properly. Under EU law, Member States are legally bound to establish systems of legal remedies and procedures to ensure respect for the right to effective judicial protection guaranteed by EU law. After all, this is often the case when implementing Council Directives. Although Member States are reluctant to do so, it is sometimes unavoilable and necessary. In the absence of national implementing measures, for example, a national court may be powerless to entertain a challenge, leaving the applicant without a forum for remedial redress.

Further consequences, assessed also by the criterion of the obligation to introduce an ELR, appear where Member States have failed to amend existing national legislation or have incorrectly implemented a directive. The failure to implement a directive may also give rise to state liability for damages. To open the perspective of State liability following conditions are to be met: the EU directive must have conferred right on individual; the right must be clearly defined; and most important there must be a "causal link" between the Member States' failure to implement the directive and the loss suffered.

The analysis of the European ELR standards presented in this book should serve for further research. One of their main directions should certainly be to analyse national remedy systems and the level of implementation of ELR concepts into national law. The discussion on the features of ELRs should then continue. The European Courts have a duty to further develop their standards. There is much to be said about what it means that the legal remedy must be available, adequate, proportionate, practical and effective. Most importantly, however, in this discourse, the essence of the remedy should not be forgotten. First and foremost to be effective legal remedy should be good enough to have the effect of restoring the right or to allow for compensation for the infringement.

Rights without remedies have no value. Without the possibility of their effective execution they become mostly theoretical declarations of belief in certain values. Thus, rights always need both protection from violations and efficient reactions for their violations. The European concept of ELR should be evaluated from this perspective.

Ius, Lex et Res Publica
Studies in Law, Philosophy and Political Cultures

Edited by
Anna Jaron

Vol. 1 Anna Jaron: Socio-Economic Constitutional Rights in Democratisation Processes. An Account of the Constitutional Dialogue Theory. 2012.

Vol. 2 Stanisław Filipowicz: Democracy – The Power of Illusion. 2013.

Vol. 3 Teresa Dukiet-Nagórska (ed.): The Postulates of Restorative Justice and the Continental Model of Criminal Law. As Illustrated by Polish Criminal Law 2014.

Vol. 4 Agnieszka Kupzok: Enforcement of Patents on Geographically Divisible Inventions. An Inquiry into the Standard of Substantive Patent Law Infringement in Cross-Border Constellations. 2015.

Vol. 5 Alicja Jagielska-Burduk / Wojciech Szafrański: Legal Issues in Cultural Heritage Management. A Polish Perspective. 2016.

Vol. 6 Maciej Mataczyński (ed.): The Takeover of Public Companies as a Mode of Exercising EU Treaty Freedoms. 2017.

Vol. 7 Maciej Barczewski (ed.): Value of Information. Intellectual Property, Privacy and Big Data. 2018.

Vol. 8 Pawel Smoleń, Marcin Burzec: Introduction to Polish Tax Law. 2018.

Vol. 9 Łukasz Pohl, Konrad Burdziak: Judicial Interpretation of the 1997 Criminal Code Provisions on Self-Defence. 2019.

Vol. 10 Adam Szot: Judicial Review of Administrative Discretion. The Influence of Court Decisions on Administrative Actions. 2019.

Vol. 11 Michał Peno / Konrad Burdziak (eds.): The Concept of Modern Law. Polish and Central European Tradition. 2019.

Vol. 12 Leszek Leszczyński / Bartosz Liżewski / Adam Szot (eds.): Potential of Precedent in the Statutory Legal Order. 2019.

Vol. 13 Łukasz Bolesta: In Search of a Model for the Legal Protection of a Whistleblower in the Workplace in Poland. A legal and comparative study. 2020.

Vol. 14 Paweł Chmielnicki / Adam Sulikowski (eds.): New Perspectives on Legislation. A Comparative Approach. 2020.

Vol. 15 Marcin Burzec / Beata Kucia-Guściora / Paweł Smoleń: Agricultural Activity in Poland: A Fiscal and Legal Study. 2020.

Vol. 16 Magdalena Półtorak / Ilona Topa (eds.): Women, Children and (Other) Vulnerable Groups. Standards of Protection and Challenges for International Law. 2021.

Vol. 17 Josef Albert Fox: Die polnische Verfassung vom 3. Mai 1791. Hintergründe der Entstehung und der Außerkraftsetzung. Stellung Polens im Zeitalter der Aufklärung. 2021.

Vol. 18 Barbara Janusz-Pohl (ed.): Juvenile Justice Systems: Poland-Brazil-Portugal. 2021.

Vol. 19 Leszek Leszczyński: General Reference Clauses in the Judicial Process. Context of Legislative Intentions Interpretative Discretion. 2021.

Vol. 20 Francisco J. Campos Zamora: Das Problem der Begründung richterlicher Entscheidungen. Eine Analyse auf der Grundlage der Theorie der juristischen Argumentation. 2021.

Vol. 21 Aneta Skorupa-Wulczyńska: Language Rights of the Citizen of the European Union. 2022.

Vol. 22 Mateusz Osiecki: International Legal Aspects of Aerial Terrorism. Methods of Law Enforcement in Avia-tion. 2022.

Vol. 23 Vladimír Sharp / Gabriela Blahoudková / Jakub Handrlica (eds.): Law, Pandemics and Ownership Restrictions. 2022.

Vol. 24 Piotr Kasprzyk / Anna Konert: Drones – Future of Aviation Law? Interference of Public Law in Private Law. 2023.

Vol. 25 Szymon Pawelec (ed.): Consensual Procedures in Criminal Law – Comparative Perspective. 2023.

Vol. 26 Dorota Pudzianowska: The Statelessness in Public Law. 2023.

Vol. 27 Bogusław Przywora / Aleksander Wróbel: Formalised Access to Pre-jurisdictional Free Legal Aid. Analysis based on Example of Ukraine, Poland, Great Britain and Sweden. 2023.

Vol. 28 Ewa Dawidziuk / Patricia Panero / Anna Tarwacka (eds.): Family, Law, and Society: from Roman Law to the Present Day. 2023.

Vol. 29 Marian Grzybowski / Bogusław Przywora / Aleksandra Syryt (eds.): Free Legal Aid, Theory, Legal Basis and Practice. European Standards. 2023.

Vol. 30 Karolina Gmerek: Trial as a Social Communication Occurrence. Interactions Between Professional and Non-professional Participants of a Trial. 2023.

Vol. 31 Paweł Wiliński (ed.): Effective Legal Remedies in Criminal Justice System. European Perspective. 2024.

www.peterlang.com

www.ingramcontent.com/pod-product-compliance
Ingram Content Group UK Ltd.
Pitfield, Milton Keynes, MK11 3LW, UK
UKHW041826031026
15587UKWH00002B/586

9 783631 913260